15.⁰⁰

Literature and Negation

Literature and Negation

Maire Jaanus Kurrik

New York   Columbia University Press

Library of Congress Cataloging in Publication Data

Kurrik, Maire Jaanus.
    Literature and negation.

    Includes bibliographical references and index.
    1. Fiction—History and criticism.   2. Litera-
ture—Philosophy.   3. Negation (Logic) in litera-
ture.   4. Negation (Logic)   I. Title.
PN3347.K8   809.3′3   79-15949
ISBN 0-231-04342-2
ISBN 0-231-04343-0

Columbia University Press
New York   Guildford, Surrey
Copyright © 1979 Columbia University Press
Printed in the United States of America

Vanaemale

CONTENTS

PREFACE

I became interested in the distinction between conscious and unconscious negation, essentially the distinction between Hegel's and Freud's definition of negation. My idea was to seek a connection between the activity of negation and the development of tragic character in the novel. In 1973–74, a grant from the NEH for such a project gave me the freedom to explore my interest in a variety of disciplines: philosophy, logic, theology, psychology, linguistics, and literary theory.

I began by asking myself the simplest questions. What happens when I say or hear no? Is human negation separable from affirmation? What are the primal yes and no for modern imaginative-speculative thought? How does negation function in different dialectical models? What is the orthodox Western experience and tradition of negation? Are there significant, dramatic variations or turning points in this tradition? And if these do not yield a traditional genealogical order—one in which the present is derived from the past in orderly succession and in which the old is causally entwined with the new—do they suggest any kind of order? How did the discovery of historical perspective modify our conception of negation? At what moment did we become aware of a need to create a philosophy, aesthetic, and criticism of negation?

It appeared to me possible to write a genealogy of negation, although not an ideal history, for a number of reasons having to do both with the elusive nature of negation and the double (traditional and modern) definition of genealogy. First, negation is itself a principle of division and difference. It is the rupture without which thought cannot begin. Hegel defined negation as a synchronic splitting, and negativity as its diachronic consequence. Negation demands some kind of mediation and this mediation in turn introduces the necessity of some kind of leveling or ordering. Negation is a pivotal moment, a moment suggesting the possibility of a return, a return to what may have been excluded, lost, dominated, or suppressed in the mediation or a return to what was as yet undifferentiated, nonelaborated, whole, or unified before the act of negation. For Hegel, negation and negativity are at the core of any system (being) or any process (becoming). Hegel's own stress on the importance of both helped to make possible the critical and destructive use of negation by his followers.

What Hegel called only the past's incompleteness, Feuerbach and Marx called its falsification and mystification, and Nietzsche its suppressions and lies. By aggravating its disjunction, these thinkers brought to a close the unity of dialectical thought with the idea of totality, and its long hegemony. With this rupture and demise much else was changed: the conception of the unknown, of subjectivity, and novelistic form. Within the novel, major transformations occurred in the interrelation of its ironic, dialogic, and tragic components. Conscious rational negation gave way to a more perplexed and random vision of unconscious negation, to a vision of the repressed instincts and their vissicitudes. In retrospect it would appear that Hegel's elaboration of negation and negativity is the new event which made possible the modern criticism of negation and, ultimately, the modern genealogist's special concern with history as a series of accidents, errors, deviations, reversals, and chance dominations.

By the criticism of negation I mean the necessity of studying a text outside of itself, from the perspective of what it excludes and in the cultural context that illuminates the exclusion. Thus, superficially, the criticism of negation appears to be the exact opposite of both New Criticism and Structuralism; yet, its goal is also a more complete understanding of the text, an understanding completed in and by the knowledge of what the text is not, its principle of selection, of inclusion and exclusion. It tries to apprehend and confront these exclusions in a nontragic way. I hope that this work might provide a background and make some contribution to such an approach and such a criticism.

I would like to thank the National Endowment for the Humanities for their grant of time without which this study would not have come into being. I would like to thank several colleagues and friends for their interest and encouragement along the way: Ruth M. Kivette, Barry Ulanov, Eleanor Tilton, Morton W. Bloomfield, Mardi Valgemäe, M. C. Bradbrook, Robert Boyers, Philip West, Tom Lewis, and John Stadler. I feel indebted to Natalie A. Sonevytsky for her skillful and cheerful help with references in the library. I feel especially indebted to Melanie Du Bois Custer for her penetrating critical comments which influenced me decisively, and also to George Stade and Angus Fletcher for their comments and their happy, extraordinary way of being generous. My deepest thanks go to Remington Patterson for a trust quite beyond encouragement that enabled me to start writing and to continue. I would like to thank Helena Morell for her friendship, my husband for his love, and Mrs. Hanna Kaik, Hedda, and Vello for playing with Ilomai when I couldn't.

An earlier version of chapter 4, "Negation and the Tragic," appeared in *The Centennial Review* (Spring 1976) and is used with permission of the editors.

I am indebted to Hughes Massie Ltd. and Grosset & Dunlap for permission to quote lines from *The Poems of St. John of the Cross*, translated by John Campbell, copyright © Hughes Massie; to E. P. Dutton for permission to quote lines from *Phèdre* by Jean Racine, translated by Margaret Rawlings, copyright © 1961 Margaret Rawlings; to the University of Toronto Press to quote lines from Goethe's *Faust*, translated by Barker Fairley, copyright © 1972 University of Toronto Press; to Merlin Press for permission to quote from Georg Lukács' *The Theory of the Novel*, translated by Anna Bostock, copyright 1971 © Merlin Press; to Orion Press and Viking Penguin for permission to quote from Gaston Bachelard, *The Philosophy of No: A Philosophy of the New Scientific Mind*, translated by G. C. Waterston, copyright © 1968 Orion Press; to the Seabury Press for permission to quote from Theodor W. Adorno's *Negative Dialectics*, translated by E. B. Ashton, English translation copyright © 1973 The Seabury Press; to Samuel Beckett and Prentice-Hall to quote from *Samuel Beckett: A Collection of Critical Essays*, copyright © 1965 Prentice-Hall; to Samuel Beckett and Grove Press for permission to quote from *The Unnamable*, copyright © 1965 Grove Press; and to Grove Press for permission to quote from Alain Robbe-Grillet, *For a New Novel: Essays on Fiction*, translated by Richard Howard, copyright © 1965 Grove Press.

CHAPTER 1

The Genealogy
of Negation

Negation and affirmation appear to be inexorably linked. Consciousness, in so far as we know it, appears to be a rhythm of affirmation and negation, a power of asserting and denying, of constituting and deleting. Language, also, is a relation between affirmation and negation. The word (or sign) is a presence based on absences, having meaning only because it distinguishes, contrasts, and excludes. It seems impossible, therefore, to speak of a genealogical order of negation alone, to derive negation from a past or ancestor of its own outside of this perpetual polarity of negation and affirmation.

Theologically, in fact, the West has made the very concept of genesis almost synonymous with affirmation, forcing any discussion of negation to begin with affirmation. Historically, furthermore, the West has long made affirmation primary, associating it with a whole series of positive, originating forces: God, being, life, presence, reality, actuality, unity, totality, oneness, stasis. Anyone can extend the list. Affirmation, it is felt, "draws together" or makes the symbol. It is integration, coherence, accord. The power to draw together has had a special supreme value for us. By contrast, therefore, negation comes, unavoidably, to be associated with the remaining negative polarities, with the devil, with death, nothingness, nonbeing, annihilation, with the nongodly or the merely human. Negation, taken as the antonym of symbolic, is diabolic, a "tearing apart," a sundering, separating, dividing, alienating, dissociating. It is linked to the dispersed, the dismembered, the disparate, to the idea of the many, to becoming. These clusters of associations with affirmation and negation are some of the most basic and recurrent ones. They provide the kind of affective basis from which we may judge a desire for death or nonbeing as abnormal or ·deviant. However, exchanges and reversals between the positives to be affirmed and the negatives to be denied can and have taken place. It is with the closer examination of the history of these moments of reversal and exchange that I am concerned.

Genesis

God only affirms. The Creation is God's affirmation and our origin. Each of the days of Creation ends in an affirmation, in "and it was so" or in "*it was* good." "*It was* good" is repeated six times, and finally climaxes in a seventh, "*it was* very good" (Gen. 1). Being, "to be," "it is," is a good. The perfect Yes, the Yes of God, is all positive being, form, order, substance, light. Yes is comprehensive, creative power, and addition. Yes is oneness, identity, sameness, a feeling of perfect accord, satisfaction, recognition. What is basic in our reading of Genesis is the fundamental effect of the depth and inclusiveness of this powerful and awesome affirmation.

The question whether God could also negate, whether he could not also annihilate the Creation, was posed in various ways, insistently, in the Middle Ages. Early scholastic interpreters were also bothered by the obvious fact that chaos and darkness precede Creation, that it is a creation *ex nihilo*. Did nothingness, therefore, precede God, or was God both nothing and something, Yes and No? These were questions that repeatedly arose. The history of the answers is fascinating, but for the purposes of this study all that needs to be said is that the questions were stilled or that the anxiety underlying them was dispelled by strong figures like Anselm, Aquinas, Saint Augustine, and Nicholas of Cusa, figures who succeeded not so much by replying as by proving that the questions were all too simple and human an approach to the mystery of the divine, that they were inadequate, irrelevant, or unequal to a discussion of the deity.[1] Cusanus, for example, removed God from the order of the human intellect and from the humanly comprehensible by defining him as the nonother, as nothing other than himself and as nothing other than the world. God's very nature is to be nonother, and the nonother by its definition admits of no difference, no otherness whatsoever. Cusanus veiled God in a positive, affirmative mystery, a transcendental antitheticality, by creating a negative theology, and it is interpretations similar to his that dominated the West.

Genesis begins with acts of creation, naming, and affirmation that are also acts of division and separation. But the act of division here ("and God divided the light from the darkness") has no negative associations. The division is a separation without or free of alienation. It is purely positive, identical to the power of creation and making. The principle of sundering, of "tearing apart," is one with the act of "drawing together." Form is both separating and making coherent. Genesis establishes that God has or is form, substance, and light. Thus, implicitly, the formless, the void, non-being, darkness, and by extension negation, are the absence of the good or God. Here are the basic polarities, and a reason for the primacy the West has given to being and form. Sequence, the first day, begins together with the establishment of these basic antitheses.

The first use of negation in Genesis occurs in the context of the prohibition. God negates when he issues the negative commandment, "thou shalt not eat" of the tree of the knowledge of good and evil (Gen. 2). But this negative commandment is preceded by a positive gesture: "Of every tree of the garden thou mayest freely eat." The negative applies only to a small area of exclusion. And the excluded area has itself to do with the power of division, of differentiation, of excluding and including. It would seem that God is reserving this very power of differentiation for himself, giving Adam only an awareness of division without the right to exercise it. God appears to be implicitly asking Adam only to affirm the creation while explicitly forbidding him the power of choosing between affirmation and negation, hence denying him the power of negation.

The conditions are set in such a way that should Adam ever acquire the power to differentiate, to say both yes and no, he would be appropriating it from another, from God. It is from the beginning God's. Thus it is, in our sense of the word, a superego power, derived from the other, and not an ego activity. By division, God created forms from chaos. In Adam's hands the power becomes ethical, breeding judgments of good and evil, and alienating separations. It is also interesting that this area of the negative and the negated which God creates as an excluded or an outside can only be expropriated, brought inside, by an act of eating. This is reminiscent of Freud's idea of the bodily origin of negation. We affirm what we take in and negate that which we do not wish to take into the body. The body is the barrier between the inside and the outside.[2]

In Genesis we ingest the original negation, the excluded area; we eat the prohibition of the other. The immediate consequence of this act is a sense of differentiation and opposition, a sense of hidden versus revealed, of dressed versus naked, of God versus man. The spontaneous consequence is a sense of separation, alienation, and fear. Adam suddenly fears God and hides. He is also suddenly capable of indirection and lying; he argues that he did not take and eat the apple from the tree, but that he received it from Eve, whom he received from God: "The woman whom thou gavest *to be* with me (Gen. 3)." Thus, it is as if he received the apple from God. He is defensive in a new, passive-aggressive way, saying in fact to God: it's really your fault not mine; I did not do it—you did. It is a refusal to accept responsibility that is characteristic of a self caught in the morality of the other. And in a sense, the negation and refusal of responsibility within such a code is defensible exactly because the code *is* to begin with that of the other and not strictly that of the self. The self has ingested the notions of the other.

The woman likewise refuses responsibility, laying the blame on the serpent, who had denied that the apple connoted death: "Ye shall not surely die." For the serpent, the apple is divinity, and partly rightly so, for the exclusion from the garden and the prefigurations of pain, strife, sorrow, and death that follow have to do with God's recognition of man's new power, a power which may also put in his reach the tree of life. Man is excluded not only to be punished, but in order to be excluded from something else, something supremely positive. In this moment in Genesis we see the rise of a series of negations—God's, the devil's, Adam's, Eve's—and the source of our traditional association of negation with the devil (who speaks and negates), with evil, guilt, death, pain, separation, differentiation, and punishment. The notions of division, separation, and polarity, which had no negative associations earlier, come into an alliance with pain and death. By contrast, affirmation is lack of differentiation, Eden, oneness, and identity. Here is ample reason for dreading negation and favoring affirmation.

Perhaps the most interesting use of the negative in Genesis occurs right after the prohibition when God says: "*It is* not good that the man should be alone." The "it is not good" echoes the formulation "it is good," repeated earlier. The creation of woman is as if based upon a negative judgment of man's adequacy alone, or a negative evaluation of human solitude, whereas all the other acts of creation were unpremeditated. What prompts her creation is, in the final instance, the preceding perception of a need, a lack, an absence. This act of creation differs from the others by including negation and absence, by not being purely affirmative. Here the perception of absence clearly precedes presence and initiates the latter. Here God shows an awareness of the negative, associating it forever with solitude, absence, and need. This is more clearly a paradigm of human creation, where presence presupposes absence, and where the perception of absence institutes the creative act. For man, the primal lack is the absent other subject. Man stands in an emptiness which provokes the creation of Eve. In this instance, negation is the masculine, affirmation the feminine, *"das Ewig-Weibliche."* Just as any concept is complex because it is the product of two acts of the mind, affirmation and negation, so will the creation of any future human body be complex, the product of two parents of different sex.

The Medieval and Renaissance worlds elaborated these Biblical valorizations of affirmation and negation, and it is to the history of the rearrangement and systematization of these valorizations, commencing in the Renaissance, that this chapter addresses itself in order to study the ever-new dialectical plays of negation and affirmation.

I asked myself to what use have negation and affirmation been put in different systems? What was the function of negation and affirmation in various dialectical methods and models? In each case, what was subsumed under negation and what under affirmation? When, furthermore, were negation and affirmation considered equal forces, and where and when was primacy given to one or the other? What was at issue in this drama of an alterating and shifting foregrounding or backgrounding of our powers of negation and affirmation?

Ficino

A beautiful example of the primacy of affirmation is found in the Neo-Platonism of Ficino. In his *Five Questions Concerning the Mind* Ficino assumes an identity between the inner form of our mind and God. The mind is but a miniature version of the One. The mind strives, but only in order to return to rest and its divine origin. The end of the mind is to know God, or Oneness, or in a sense itself. In this formal tautological fantasy, what was within the One was positive and to be affirmed; what was outside was negative and a source of torment. For Ficino, everything was within except the body and the senses. These were outside the eternal, golden circle which is the beautiful synonymity of the human soul and God. All our Promethean torment issued from an outside, nondivine source.

Here we see in its clearest form yet another primary association with affirmation, that it is something inside, something inner, something deep within subjectivity. Yet the perfect affirmation is an accordance between an inside and an outside. Both something deep within the self and something outside can be affirmed as divine. The ambivalence here is whether the self is affirmed for itself or for being the other. Is the self God or a self? Are they the same or distinct? Who is who? The question of the self's fundamental uniqueness, otherness, or autonomy does not arise for Ficino because of his overwhelming sense of satisfaction in being a self in otherness. What is important to him is to affirm his sense of being included in perfection.

The basic schema which can derive from Ficino is as follows:

the One	the many
Form	formlessness/strife
inside	outside
included	excluded
affirmed	negated
the mind	the body

What belongs to the subject but is excluded is the body. Somehow Ficino does not know what to make of it, except to make it the source of the experience of strife and antitheticality.

The fundamental dialectical model underlying Ficino's argument is that of the One and the many.[3] The One is defined as the Logos, or, theologically, as God. The many is the phenomenal, real, unworthy, a negativity—in brief, that which has to be negated in order for the Logos or One to appear. In Neo-Platonism and Platonism a systematic and logical denial is practiced for the sake of a final affirmation of the One, the eidos. Complete affirmation is postponed or delayed in the dialectic and reserved for the ultimate goal. In a sense, dialecticism is practiced only up to the point where the Logos is glimpsed, and then dialecticism turns into pure affirmation. The ultimate affirmation has the characteristics of pure abstraction, distillation, totality. The ultimate weight is thrown on the affirmation, the One.

Saint John of the Cross

Within this dialectical model of the One and the many, the boldest
adventure in negation was made by the mystics. They dared to renounce
all of the self, trusting in nothing worldly, not even in the divine part of
the self, to reach pure being or the very heart of affirmation. The mystics refrained from all determinations in the hope that by making the
mind wholly a structure of negations, the nonworldly other would break
in, filling up the empty, receptive self. Here, the only thing worthy of
being affirmed is the outside, the other, the objective, but it can only be
affirmed when it is experienced within.

The goal of mysticism, as of Platonism and Neo-Platonism, is affirmation. The act of affirmation is valued above the act of negation. But what
is important for us is the new way in which the mystics associated
human power with the power of negation, and the new consciousness
that they had of negation. They realized that for us negation is, in a
sense, of greater practical importance than affirmation. Or perhaps we
can say that they realized that we can only reach perfect affirmation
through negation. Since human reason cannot deal with infinite values,
it can only make negative determinations and say what God is not—not
finite, temporal, deceptive, and so on. Our real constitutive and determining power is a negative one; we can only define, at least the absolute, by exclusion, by saying what it is not. Similarly, we can turn this
power of negation upon ourselves and say that we are not, until we
become a part of the Other.

Mystical negation, because of its radical abolition of the subjective,
was psychologically an eminently complex and fearful experience and
entailed the repression or sublimation of all distrust, doubt, and fear.
"My *me* is God," said Saint Catherine of Genoa, "nor do I know my
selfhood save in Him."[4] The self or subjective is entirely displaced by
the objective or other. The radicality lies in the total negation of the
subjective, whereas in Neo-Platonism, the denial of the self is only partial. In the latter, the affirmation applies to an inmixture of the subjective and the objective. In mysticism, the affirmation applies only to
another, albeit experienced within. The power of negation is felt more
completely in the mystical act and allowed to make nought the soul. The
climax of the negation comes in "the dark night of the soul," a recreation

in the subjective realm of the state of chaos in Genesis. It is a state of total privation, spiritual aridity, and lovelessness in which the certitude of God's absence mounts to a terrified sense of self-annihilation, proving that the self exists only with God. According to Saint John of the Cross:

> That which this anguished soul feels most deeply is the conviction that God has abandoned it, *of which it has no doubt;* that He has cast it away into darkness as an abominable thing . . . the shadow of death and the pains and torments of hell are most acutely felt, and this comes from the sense of being abandoned by God, being chastised and cast out by His wrath and heavy displeasure. All this and even more the soul feels now, for a terrible apprehension has come upon it that thus it will be with it for ever. It has also the same sense of abandonment with respect to all creatures, and that it is an object of contempt to all, especially to its friends.[5]

The self alone is radical unpleasure. The degree of the mind's emptiness is absolute and the emptiness is purely negative: the self has been abandoned because it is loathsome. The modality of mystical negation is that of a radical trust and mistrust, of presence–absence. There is no doubt, at one extreme, of total absence or abandonment, or, at the other, of total presence and union.

Paradoxically, the aim of mystical negation is once again perfect affirmation or a state of "no-lessness." It is this state of distinctionless identity with the divine, of trusting communion, of total presence which Saint John of the Cross describes at the end of one of his most beautiful poems, "Upon a gloomy night." It is a song "of the soul in rapture at having arrived at the height of perfection, which is the union with God by the road of spiritual negation."

> Within my flowering breast
> Which only for himself entire I save
> He sank into his rest
> And all my gifts I gave
> Lulled by the air with which the cedars wave.

> Over the ramparts fanned
> While the fresh wind was fluttering his tresses,
> With his serenest hand
> My neck he wounded, and
> Suspended every sense with its caresses.

Lost to myself I stayed
My face upon my lover having laid
From all endeavour ceasing:
And all my cares releasing
Threw them amongst the lilies there to fade.[6]

The last line, "Entre las azucenas olvidado," literally means "amongst the lilies already forgotten." The *unio mystica* is a beatific nothingness where all that the soul was is "forgotten."

To possess a soul resolved in Christ means that one's deepest interiority gets to rest. "In the beginning of all things/ The Word lived in the Lord at rest."[7] The Word rests in God. Christ is the Word; to be with Christ means simultaneously to be with the Word at rest in God, in the beginning. This is the rest, the dream that is everything. Here is what Saint John calls his "blessed," "lucky" night, a radiant darkness. This night is "lovelier than the dawn," giving birth to the body of his soul even as it "kills" his earthly body and senses with "caresses." The disembodied soul acquires a new body. Within his "flowering breast" Christ comes to sleep: "Allí quedó dormido" means "there, on my breast, my love fell asleep." It is an idyllic scene of unending tenderness recollecting simultaneously the primordial scene of bliss, the garden of paradise, and the image of the favorite and envied apostle John resting his head on the bosom of Christ. What could be more beautiful than the condensation of these two images of greatest bliss? The rhythm of the images (and it is sound and rhythm that convey the unconscious aspect of language as grammar reflects the conscious aspects) breathes love and satisfaction. "Lost to myself I stayed/ My face upon my lover having laid." This is not self-negation, although the earthly body has been lost or exchanged for a spiritualized body, but the involuntary desire to throw away all that is human at the moment of divine invasion: "Threw them amongst the lilies there to fade." The mystery—what of the human is left here? what is still human in the transfigured soul?—cannot be answered. The climax is an oblivion of the human that is bliss.

Saint John of the Cross's poem reverses the Platonic procedure, the movement from the body to the spirit; here we move from the mind to the body and beyond it by an act of abandonment. All the sweetness, ineffability, and freedom that we think belongs to the spirit is attributed to a new body, which becomes the basis of a new experience. In Platonism, the vision of the eidos of beauty, which is, as Diotima says, "the final cause of all our former toils" is a state of alert, awake, hyper-perceptive revelation, a state of intense seeing.[8] In Saint John of the Cross we are led not to seeing or revelation, but to feeling, to sleep, and to forgetfulness, or not even to that, because all the mechanisms by which we feel or see are "thrown away." Thus, the mystics can indeed say that what is felt is not felt by the self or as the self, but what is felt is the other, the divine. The self is nothing but the ability to contain, to hold fast that Presence which makes all else in the world appear as absence.

What Saint John attains may be called a state of radiant, "no-less" unconsciousness. There is no "No" in the unconscious, said Freud.[9] Dreams, despite their "demonic" ability to deceive or disguise by displacement or condensation, by strange amalgamations, distortions, or trivializations, cannot negate the way consciousness does by making use of the rules of grammar and logic. Dreams, like myths, induce or deter by changes of intensity. They transform but they do not truly repress or delete. The mystic's negation transforms the subjective completely, giving all that is positive to the other or opposite, while moving from the word to the dream, from consciousness to unconsciousness. If God is apprehended by anything that can still be called subject, it is by some unknown unconsciousness.

Mysticism is an experiment in negation that avoids the problem of becoming or temporality, and finally also that of subjectivity. In mysticism there is no autonomous subjectivity since the self *is* the other. It takes place within a dialectical model of the One and the many, within which negation and affirmation oscillate between degrees of presence and absence, of absolute existence or nonexistence. The dark night of the soul is an experience of annihilation and death, but the model itself guarantees that the annihilation is only of one pole of the supreme opposition; the subjective is annihilated in favor of the objective in which it is then recovered. What is common to Neo-Platonism and mysticism is the association of affirmation with presence, oneness, or the other, the objective. Negation is associated with absence, all or part of subjectivity, and the many. The distant is paradoxically defined as the necessary presence—necessary also for the subjective, if it wants to experience affirmation.

A very different experience of presence (affirmation) and absence (negation) results from the introduction of the notion of movement or becoming, or temporality. The basic dialectical model of movement sees affirmation and negation in terms of a simultaneous "here," "now," present, and a "not here," "not now," absent. Thus, becoming is an inmixture of being and nothingness, or "between" absence and presence. What is striking about the dialectical model based on movement is that it makes impossible or problematic the idea of perfect affirmation or negation by making impossible the idea of repetition or identity. When absence produces change in what was present, the absent can no longer return to presence or be recaptured. Mutability is a constant flow of absence. It is a repetition of the experience of absence without a return to the presence that had been.

Another striking fact about the dialectical model of movement is that within it negation becomes a constant, ineluctable, and far more equal partner with affirmation. Whereas the dialectical model of the One and the many induces illusions of perfect affirmation or of negation for the sake of affirmation, and whereas this model seems to provoke special efforts at total affirmation or negation, the dialectical model of movement seems not to allow such special efforts. However it does allow totalizing interpretations; in the flow of mutability one can accent the constant destruction or the constant creation of the new. It is fairly evident, moreover, given the long philosophical and theological association of unity, stasis, and affirmation, that when the ancient dialectical model of movement did come to predominate in the Renaissance, the first responses to it were rather negative and sceptical. Mutability was experienced as a loss and as an absence, and therefore attempts were made to oppose it. Yet, in the long run, it was mutability which broke the association of God with stasis and rest.

Milton's *Paradise Regained*

One of the greatest statements of opposition came from Milton in *Paradise Regained*. One can read it as a text which attempts to rescue and to assert the priority of affirmation—as a defense of the perfect Yes. Milton refuses to renounce the possibility of global negations and affirmations. He refuses to accede to a fate that resigns us only to perpetual and partial negations and affirmations, a temporal fate of constant antithetical experiences of presence and absence.

Within the perpetual antithetical reality of negation and affirmation there are various intensities of these values. What the dialectical model of the One and the many allowed, both within Neo-Platonism and Christianity, was a kind of global negation and affirmation that is mere nostalgia for us today. For one factor which controls or contributes to the intensity of a negation or an affirmation is the dimension to which it refers. The more total or global the object or reference the greater the force or impact of the negation or affirmation. One reason, no doubt, for the special grandeur of the allegorical figures and characters produced by the Renaissance is that they were in fact representations of such global, albeit intensely felt and subjective, affirmations and negations.

Milton's Christ is, par excellence, a figure who exemplifies affirmation. And affirmation here signifies the power to hold on to a vision of the One, of being, stasis, God. Christ begins his manhood in ignorance and trust. Satan attempts to instill in him anxiety and distrust. As Christ answers his temptations, "temperately (2.378)," "calmly (3.43)," "patiently (2.432)," his trust deepens together with his knowledge of providential history until his discourse seems to embrace more and more, reaching to the beginning and the end.[10] Satan is ignorant that this growing interior vision has fostered Christ's trust to the point where he is no longer at all capable of being moved psychologically by Satan's challenges. Every offer of Satan refused by Christ removes Christ further from particulars and the many, opening him up to generality and the idea of the One. Christ, in that vision opened up and made possible by his denials, has as if ceased to hear Satan. At the end Milton only uses the epithet "unmov'd" for Christ (3.386, 4.109). "Unmoved" summarizes the deepest intentionality of this stark and magnificent denial of the world. Christ trusts in God's time, rejecting the anxiety of mutability and also interiority, because the inside should be God, even in man. This godhood within man can, however, only be achieved if the self remains contentless. The same contentless, de-empirized, ambiguous God-man self is prized in Milton as in Neo-Platonism and mysticism.

The special heroism of Christ derives from his opponent Satan who is given all the vital, positive human energies that we have valued as our virtues—a desire for action, change, movement, self-development, self-sufficiency, autonomy, self-knowledge, justice—together with a dose of rebellion, mistrust, impatience, disobedience. Christ by contrast stands upon his one sole, negative certitude that man is not God, but God is. Christ is obedient to the man in himself, to becoming man. As he comes into his identity he comes to know what man needs above all—God. And thus he becomes simultaneously more God and man.

Christ, as the "Word" of God, knows the meaning of all words. He knows the answer to the riddle of man, what man is and what he needs, as no man knows it. This is why Satan is compared to the Sphinx in its fall, the monster which threw itself from the acropolis of Thebes into the river Ismenus when Oedipus found the answer, which was "man," to its riddle. And what is man, then? Man is not wisdom, or knowledge, or actualization. Because man is not these things, he has to trust that God is. The riddle is simple, but only a God-man, that hybrid category that alone bridges the gap between the two irreconcilable worlds of the finite and the infinite, could solve it, and furthermore, understand and believe it "without distrust or doubt (3.193)." Christ is lifted up by the angels in a vision, but Milton ends the poem simply: "hee unobserv'd/ Home to his Mother's house private return'd (4.639)." Christ's self-realization involves becoming more godlike because he insists upon being more like a man. It is godlike to be a God and yet to strive to be a man. Satan is merely a man with an unrestrainable urge to actualize his possibilities. But Christ rejects man's precipitous urge to actualize every possibility and potential. There is also the need to develop the potential of submission, obedience, temperance, patience, trust, humility, and passivity. One can know without using one's knowledge; one can be able to do without doing, and one can be God and yet remain man. God is he who can as a man exhibit indifference to historical and temporal possibility.

Paradise Regained is Milton's negation of the world of becoming or mutability, that incessant flow of absence, which seems to have created an inordinate desire for presence, for stasis, for stability, for an unchanging One that can be affirmed. Christ is a truly superhuman figure because he can in this world of mutability maintain his hold on the One "without distrust or doubt." Paradoxically, to be open to the vision of the timeless is to see oneself as constrained by the conditions of time. Time is the opportunity to see the timeless.

Spenser, Marlowe

In Spenser's *Mutability Cantos* there is a desire similar to Milton's to evaluate man's relation to the objective, the other, the static One. The demonic Titaness Mutability appears in order to claim her divinity and sovereignty. She is scornful, restless, ambitious, and above all violently anxious to be recognized in her supremacy. She is silenced by the mysterious figure of Nature who calls her "daughter" and tells her that she aspires to death. The cantos end with Spenser's prayer, an inward cry for certitude and purposiveness because the objective conditions have become paradoxical and impenetrable. Subjectivity, inwardness is the only frail force upon which a faith in stasis and eternity can still be based.

The insistent fact of mutability, heightened by the increased availability of historical knowledge, exacerbated the need to create powerful images and figures of affirmation and to reassert the actuality of a spatial world of stasis, presence, and unity. But, inevitably, the Renaissance world also created new and bold allegorical figures of negation, figures able to experiment with the powers of negation and to assess its consequences. These figures come also to be associated with time.

Marlowe's Doctor Faustus is one such figure who refuses to aspire to the objective, the stasis, and the One. Faustus wishes to affirm only the self, to appropriate it radically and to know it. "My me is me," he would answer to the mystic. Faustus' problem is to find himself in the world divided between God and the devil. His agonizing central question concerns the autonomy of his soul. Is his soul his own or not? And what is his nature? He appears to be a confused mixture of positive aspirations and denials. He denies God, and yet he wants to be godlike, to dominate the course of the world and to be free of all ambiguity. He denies the existence of hell, and yet he makes a pact with the devil. What he feels at the end is his desire to persist under any conditions, his temporal nature. The self refuses to be the other, and thus Faustus comes inevitably to be destroyed in the very coils of his own yearning, incomplete nature. That he is temporal is all he comes to know and all he finally seeks to evade in his final cries when he pleads for dismemberment, disintegration, or dispersal rather than total destruction. To be dispersed or formless, is better than not to be. But not to be is the price

Faustus pays for his refusal to apply negation to his subjectivity or any part of it. Faustus wants to appropriate the power of affirmation only for himself. His self and God are no longer identical.

We can see a new set of alliances between affirmation and negation being formed in the Renaissance largely because of a new independent sense of subjectivity and of time. In a work like *Doctor Faustus* the special ambiguity in a definition of self such as that propounded by Neo-Platonism is finally addressed. If the self is no longer the other, or divine, it is possibly devilish; nonetheless, it has still to be affirmed even if it is devilish. This is the new paradoxical alliance in Faustus; Faustus is clearly not Lucifer, yet since he refuses to acknowledge God, he must be closer to Lucifer than he is as yet to himself. Subjectivity here is appealingly positive and negative in a new way; it is violently torn, seeking a seemingly, inaccessible separateness and autonomy. God and the self can no longer be affirmed at the same time. Without God, Faustus gains some as yet very indefinite conception of his powers and possibilities but he loses eternity. The ultimate image of time here is utterly negative. Time is but a flow of destruction.

Shakespeare's *Timon of Athens*

If the self is not ambiguously semidivine, it may be subject to destruction not only by time but by the very powers of negation in the self. The greatest figure of pure negation produced in the Renaissance is no doubt Shakespeare's Timon of Athens. Timon experiences the lack of divinity (symbolized here by charity) in others, and refuses increasingly to have anything to do with the human enterprise. He expresses his immense disappointment by absolute negation.

Timon is Misanthropos. Misanthropy is the relationship to the other by hate, but it is still a relationship. Timon, however, must purify himself of all relationships if he is truly to undo creation, to undo being, to tear up the root of life itself and recreate nothingness. The way to his final purification becomes clearer to him after his last discussion with Apemantus, also a man-hater. "What wouldst thou do with the world, Apemantus, if it lay in thy power?" Timon asks. "Give it the beasts," replies Apemantus. "Wouldst thou . . . remain a beast with the beasts?" Timon asks, and to Apemantus's "aye" Timon replies that it is "a beastly ambition, which the gods grant thee t'attain to!" (4.3.321–28).[11] The options are clear: one can relate to man or to the beasts or, if to neither, then one must die. Suicide becomes the next logical step. Apemantus's misanthropy chooses the beastly over the human; Timon's misanthropy grows into a more radical hatred of life which can only culminate in self-negation and in the preference of nothingness over any form of being.

Timon negates not only the other but also himself. The necessary conclusion to the denial of the other is the denial and negation of the self. Man is not man without the other, without the other's recognition. Man becomes man when he is recognized by a man, by another. The self-sufficient man is either a god or monster, said Aristotle. Shakespeare adds that man alone is nothing. Suicide is the perfection of misanthropy; it is the consummation that Apemantus avoids. Suicide is also the way to be rid of language, of "sour words," for language is the way we relate to others:

> Thither come,
> And let my gravestone be your oracle.
> Lips, let sour words go by and *language end.*
> [5.1.221–23; italics mine]

Timon's suicide is a recommendation for universal suicide. In him "death . . . at others' lives may laugh" (4.3.381). His gravestone lies by the shore, beaten into oblivion by the waves, and no one may even stay to look at it. Let there be no relationships, no language, no looking at each other. True misanthropy has to come to a confrontation with self alone and has to end in a hatred of self. The essence of misanthropy is nihilism.

Nietzsche defined nihilism as the state in which "the sight of man makes us despond," that state in which the love, will, fear, and reverence for man is turned into a will not to be a man.[12] This is Timon's state when he meets his good servant Flavius, hence Flavius can do nothing for him. Flavius is merely *one*, senseless redemptive thing. "Thou redeem'st *thyself*," says Timon (4.3.507; italics mine). Shakespeare understood the radical meaning of the Biblical text: there is love or nothing. In the human community of fellowship the opposite of nothing is not faith, but love: "if I have faith great enough to move mountains, but have not love, I am nothing. If I give everything I have to feed the poor . . . but have not love, I gain nothing" (1 Cor. 13:2–3).[13]

The origin of Timon's negation appears to be the Biblical "*it is* not good that the man should be alone"; he discovers the fundamental and irreparable absence of the other. Timon is not destroyed by time as is Faustus, but by his discovery of human solitude, the lack of the other, his absence. Nothingness has become a goal, a telos for Timon. It has become "all things," the end, completion, an enticing purposive nothingness.

> My long sickness
> Of health and living now begins to mend,
> And nothing brings me all things.
> [5.1. 189–91]

In Timon's "will not to be a man," nothingness appears as a form of perfection.

The play is ultimately not about Timon but the world. "How goes the world?" we hear at the very beginning (1.1.3). The question is constantly what to do for the "world," what to recommend for the "world" as such:

> . . . the world is but a word.
> Were it all yours to give it in a breath,
> How quickly were it gone!
> [2.2.161–63]

In a sense the play is saying that Genesis is but a myth, a dazzling, beguiling, happy myth, a gift of mere words like the gifts of bankrupt Timon himself. In contradistinction to this affirmative, creative myth, Shakespeare presents us with another possibility. The play asks what would you do if you had the chance to say the "Word" that made the world? Timon answers that he would undo Genesis. Timon shifts from total affirmation to absolute negation at the moment when he realizes that no one but he has been deceived by the beauteous first myth; everyone else knew all along that the only true God is Gold.

In Shakespeare, Christianity is already a myth. Tragedy was reborn in the West the moment Christianity was perceived as a myth, as a mere background, as a forceless, powerless presence unable, in the final instance, to compel man.

The play is in substance godless; it is the dramatization of the perception of Christianity as a myth rather than as a functioning reality. In his anger and despair over the absence of grace in the world, Timon wishes an apocalyptic ending upon the entire enterprise. He rejects mankind, himself, and all of procreative nature. Timon's initial boundless love turns to boundless negation. But his initial giving was not direct but mediated by gold; also, it was a giving without receiving. Thus Timon's "yes" too, the play seems to say, was grounded upon his nothingness, his own privation of love and his inability, therefore, to love others. Timon does not know that love is both a giving and a receiving. Thus, the Timon who passes out gifts to his friends and refuses all returns and the Timon who passes out gold to the army in hate-sowing munificence are not strictly identical, but are yet causally linked and related figures. The play turns into a nightmare Last Supper:

> O you gods, what a number of men eat Timon, and he sees 'em not! It grieves me to see so many dip their meat in one man's blood.
>
> [1.2.39–42]

Gold is the only "visible god," as the imagery of the play relentlessly tells us (4.3.387).

The play's energy comes from its abbreviated, symbolic, childlike character, from its primitive use of "yes" or "no," and its ignorance of any kind of discrimination or reality testing. It presents a world of drastic moods: expectation-disappointment, presence-absence, acceptance-rejection, love-hate, being-nothing. It is a rarely unambivalent play. There is minimal control over the instinct to negate or to affirm. Disappointment exteriorized passes quickly from word or fantasy to deed, from curses, litanies of hatred, to the wish to kill, to be killed, and to die. Negation becomes absolute destruction. This is what is childish about it: the simplest wish of all is "I wish you were dead or I wish I were dead." Timon fulfills the former wish by bribing Alcibiades's army and the latter in his suicide. Destruction is unmediated, unreflected negation; it is negation's desire for immediate, complete realization.

Thus the West has its first taste of willed, subjective nothingness in the tragic theater of Shakespeare. Timon is not punished or destroyed by time as Faustus is; rather he is destroyed by the lack of fellowship between men. He is destroyed by the absence of love, and so are nearly all of Shakespeare's characters. He is autonomous both in life and in death. Thus Timon is the first monument to human negation, unrelieved by any affirmations or positives. Negation is represented here in its pure form as leading to separation, exclusion, destruction, death, and nothing, but it is a power man suddenly dares to exercise. The dangers of caring only for affirmation, which are that subjectivity and its constant experiences of partial or total negation and disappointment are ignored or repressed, are here avoided. The negativity is made to stand even at the cost of self-destruction. What is certain is that the self has powers; even if it has not the strength to affirm itself, it has the power to negate itself.

Shakespeare managed to establish a true subjective sense of nothingness because he understood that nothingness becomes a reality with the sense of solitude, and that in solitude and nothingness death has no meaning. For it is the significance of death that makes life serious and worthy. Death is the great indispensable contrast to life. When death means nothing life means nothing and vice versa. Life means nothing when it is unleavened by love. Shakespearean tragedy, in that it gives birth to a sense of subjective nothingness, to lifelessness and feelinglessness, makes an end of classical tragedy which depended on the significance of life and death. Now tragedy is a struggle with absence—the absence of death, life, feeling, the significant other or objective. In Macbeth's final soliloquy the accent falls on "nothing." Words are nothing, time is nothing, and man is nothing. Death is nothing because there are no feelings left. Desire has abandoned time because there are no significant others to make the self come into being and desire. If the self is left unsupported and solitary to affirm itself, it will turn to self-negation. Affirmation seems as if to presuppose something more than the mere self; it seems to demand or require some other, either deep within or without, something valuable, positive, desirable, trustworthy, and known. The self in solitude seems to turn to pure negation. The self by itself does not appear large, global, or valuable enough for an act of affirmation.

Tourneur's *The Revenger's Tragedy*

Doctor Faustus does not achieve complete autonomy because he does not succeed in his denials. Timon succeeds, but only at the moment of self-annihilation. Timon's and Doctor Faustus' negations have a grandeur because there is a heaven and hell to be defied. Their negations take place in a context of transcendence. In *The Revenger's Tragedy* the characters are locked into a purely secular world of human disorder, a world without transcendental resonance and meaning, where everything—even their acts of negation and self-destruction—become pointless, meaningless, and insane. In this world, death is no longer sacred, a divine or natural intervention in life, but something that in the hands of men turns to mere murder. Vendice is no Old Testament revenger, seeking vengeance as a way to restore a state of balance in a world of wild and arbitrary lawlessness. Vendice's revenge, which begins as a purpose, turns into excess, sadism, and lust. He is caught in the madness and obsession of punishment rather than in the good of order, correction, and transformation. In this world, ethical ideals appear as formal, lifeless, and fireless as does Castiza's chastity. To live by any ethical code is absurd, since "to be honest is not to be i' the world."[14]

Here the human is something so valueless and centerless that it can be trampled on or discarded without guilt or regret. Fundamentally, it is a skeleton fitted out with a kind of cerebral lust and instinct for calculation. To each other the characters are real only as objects of this calculated lust. When, in a climactic scene, the king is offered the stuffed skull of Vendice's former bethrothed in lieu of a live wench, he is unable to tell the difference. He kisses the poisoned lips of the skull, and dies, deceived in the satisfaction of his own lust, but made to watch the satisfaction of that of his wife in an act of adultery. This is the highest vengeance that Vendice can invent for a purely instinctual world. Only then, he must physically trample on the king as well. Alive we are instinct—the instinct of lust, revenge, greed; and dead we are the skull. In fact, since our lust can be so easily deceived by "false" flesh, by the mere pretense of flesh, the only truth is the skull, is death. All else is appearance, surface, falsehood, mask. We could not tell the difference between dead and live flesh if the former did not ultimately refuse our passions. The human and nonhuman are almost synonymous.

A world without transcendent resources or meaning is one without catharsis, loss, or the sense of wasted possibility, which we still feel in *Macbeth* or *Timon*. The world is so void, empty, and nonpurposive that there is nothing to lament when all die. There is almost no disappointment because there is from the beginning no hope or expectation. What substitutes for life is an endless, rational plotting and counterplotting. If it were not for this energy of plotting, tricking, testing, and scheming, we would already be in the voided world of a Flaubert or a Baudelaire. But all of man's wit and intelligence is engaged in superimposing a negative order upon the world. It seems that if there is no perfection and no ethical order, man will make his own order by using the powers of death and negation. Unable to achieve a positive order derived from culture, man imposes upon the world a negative order derived from nature. Death, the negation of existence, is used in a mad endeavor to survive. Man attempts to form the disorder into a negative order, since any order is apparently better than disorder.

No one in this play knows or trusts another; this is why even the son and daughter and mother have to test each other. In a world of trust there can be no such mutual testing. But the activity of testing and plotting, which substitutes for content and knowledge, matches the fundamental contentlessness of these characters. Finally, when the characters become trapped in their own interacting vengeance plots, they do so without regret because there is nothing positive that has been affirmed and that could now be regretted.

What we can perhaps say is that these plays appear to be the issue of an interim cultural period in which old values have lost their significance and new values are not yet born. Transcendence, the idea of a society based on Christ, and the Ten Commandments no longer have any reality. Man feels disoriented, and those things of which he is certain—time, his instincts, his lusts and aggressions—serve no guiding purpose and cannot be brought under the control of the ego or the superego. We do not know how cultural systems shift or mutate but we do know that these interim periods are periods of disorientation, disorder, decreation, and negation. Here there is nothing to be affirmed but mortality. The instincts reign uncontrolled. The attitude toward man is negative, condemnatory. Man is valueless, disgusting, merely lustful and instinctual, unsteadfast, unreliable, and rationally merely clever or tricky. He is a trapper of other men, a layer of nets, their destroyer. No positive value can be found in the other or hence in the self; the other appears as some kind of partial object, as does the self itself. And hence no meaningful relationship, outside of murder or lust, can be established with the other.

From the opening it is clear that everyone is just a skeleton, "apparelled" in flesh (p. 306). There are no tensions or dilemmas in the play, because there is only the semblance of purposiveness given by revenge. This is also why Vendice feels that: "My life's unnaturally to me, e'en compelled;/As if I lived now, when I should be dead" (p. 308). Life as a whole, robbed of all polarities, is from the beginning nothing but hell. What is missing is the other, the objectivity of some kind of witness to one's deeds and thoughts. Only the other can provide a vision of one's self and one's own guilt. But here the others are just like the self, which is made evident moreover by the rapid shift of identities and errors in identifying others. The only care one must take to avoid punishment is to evade being seen by these meaningless others. A few times the witness of God is evoked ("Is there no thunder left: Or is't kept up/ In stock for heavier vengeance?") only in order to point to the utter godlessness of this narrow, confined world, which we ultimately feel to be a place of madness for the exercise of madness between deaths (p. 363). And this madness has no divine dimensions; it is not eschatological, but strictly within men and their illusions and their imaginary relationship to themselves and others. Perhaps Vendice in his revenge is the maddest of all because he allows himself to be deceived into believing that the instinct of revenge is a goal. But certainly he cannot win our sympathy, not being as yet human, anymore than the other characters can who, all left to themselves in the world, seem unredeemable and worthy or capable only of destruction.

The Revenger's Tragedy is a more perfect example of the activity of negation detached from affirmation than was *Timon*. The world is defined as sheer negativity and absence. The subject is discovered in its autonomy but it finds nothing in itself to value or affirm. The subject is not able to be affirmed because it seems to be characterized by negations and destructive powers. Man seeks to be an orderer and creator but his devices are death. The effort to take death into one's own hands, away from God, leads merely and inexorably to quicker self-annihilation and decreation.

In *The Revenger's Tragedy* the associations with negation that are being exploited and elaborated issue out of negation's role in the context of the prohibition. By taking the right to differentiate between good and evil into his own hands, man confounds himself, becoming entangled in death and time. And here, as in *Doctor Faustus*, man destroys himself in a time that is mere death.

What we can perhaps say tentatively in the light of the Jacobean presentation is that if there is a radical disorder or imbalance between affirmation and negation, there is also a disorder between the subject and his very sense of being alive.

Interim Summary; Pico, Erasmus

In Ficino, Saint John of the Cross, and Milton, we saw instances where affirmation is foregrounded. These instances put negation in the service of affirmation. The content of the affirmation is essentially God and the timeless, a totality in which the self may participate to the degree that it is able to displace or transform all in the self that is not divine. What is important, however, about these affirmations is that they do involve negations and exclusions—in the case of the mystics, of nearly all that makes the human self truly different from God. Unlike Kierkegaard's Knight of Faith, the mystic does not win back the finite after his adventure in the infinite, rather he is given something completely new and much of what is human is simply abandoned.

By contrast, in Marlowe, Shakespeare, and Tourneur, we have instances where negation is foregrounded. But in these early attempts to negate transcendence, the negation turns back upon man as his own self-destruction. These heroes lose their unity with God and the timeless—as Mother Nature warned Mutability she would if she persisted—and become allied with time and death. In their experiments with negations, these heroes elaborate and reinforce what I earlier called our Biblical and common association with the power of human negation—the association, namely, with death, destruction, evil, disorder, and the bodily. Yet a new factor comes clearly into being with a hero like Faustus—man's desire for himself. Faustus does not achieve it, but his case begins to suggest that if autonomous subjectivity is born at all, it will have to be born out of a confrontation with death and time that surmounts them. Only after such a surmounting could any of these heroes emerge from their fundamental experience of displacement into nonbeing.

These somewhat extreme and unusual instances, hopefully, make clearer what was typically subsumed under affirmation and negation, and how one interrelated with being, the other with nonbeing. However, the Renaissance as a whole, or particularly the early Renaissance, is a period we associate predominantly with affirmation, syncretism, and reintegration. It is a period that tried to include, reabsorb, and reintegrate classical and Christian culture, rather than to select, exclude, or reject a part of that culture. Perhaps we can even say that it is a period that practiced inclusion and affirmation systematically. Exemplary here is the moment of Pico's defense of his ninety-nine theses, his heroic syncretism which attempted to reconcile the positive aspect of all conflicting and contradictory schools of thought. Perhaps Pico's is one of the finest moments in the history of affirmation, but it is made possible by his faith in the ultimate unity of truth or the Logos. The fundamental dialectical model underpinning Pico's vision is that of the unity of appearance and reality. In all phenomena there is something abiding, identical, and true, but this "is" appears only in the change and transformation of appearances. The many in Pico do not have to be denied, because the One is in a sense in all of them. Pico can more readily accept this world of emanations, appearances, and diversity because he affirms the ultimate unity of all truths.

The most characteristic works of the Renaissance achieve a unity of being and nonbeing beyond the extremes of negation and affirmation. The immortal example is Erasmus' *The Praise of Folly*, where all contradictions are stilled in parodoxy. Erasmus' vision of our incomprehensible duality makes all other visions of purification by way either of complete negation or affirmation seem simply impossible.

Erasmus' work functions as the dream does, according to the principle of "and"; it is propelled by an amalgamating, composite power equivalent to the power of condensation in dreams. Erasmus' irony rests upon a philosophy of the "and" for which the ultimate paradigm and guarantee is the figure of Christ. Christ is an "and," the ultimate oxymoron, the paradox compressed into two words, the God-Man, the incomprehensible hybrid or mixed category that guarantees the salvation of that other hybrid, Stultitia. Man is a wise fool, an inexorably linked conjunction of positive and negative, being and nothingness, a perfect example himself of the *serio ludere*. He is a limited being who has no limits, who must see double, think double, and feel double, because he is double. He should say both/and, but he is always saying either/or.

Erasmus' comic irony and the structure of his paradoxes are, as Rosalie Colie saw, a mirror image of the Renaissance world of being; they reflect its ontology and cosmology.

> In paradox, form and content, subject and object are collapsed into one, in an ultimate insistence upon the unity of being. Thinking in terms of paradox, or thinking about paradox, one cannot rely upon conventional categories; one must not accept, in Parmenides' formulation, the separate existences of the Many; or, in the scholastic formulation, the ineffability of each individual thing. One is forced to fuse categories, since paradox manifestly manages at once to be creative and critical, at once its own subject and its own object, turning endlessly in and upon itself.[15]

In other words, Erasmus' tautological world is underpinned by a philosophy that gives priority to the all, the One, to unity. Such a philosophy calls every determination a negation, every specific thing a negation of the all. It is a philosophy not yet critically conscious of division or separation. The very paradox of Renaissance thought reveals it as premodern thought. According to Colie:

> Paradox is not evolutionary, nor yet logically sequential. Paradox envelops rather than develops, folding all its parts into one unbroken, if asymmetrical, whole. In this sense, paradox is self-regarding, self-contained, and self-confirming; it attempts to give the appearance of ontological wholeness. The paradox of paradoxy persists even here, however, since paradoxes are, in fact, of all the rhetorical and literary forms the least self-contained. Paradox relies utterly upon its action in audience or beholder or reader. Paradox requires a beholder willing to share in its action and by thus sharing in it to prolong that action. Always "about" being, the paradox is not fully ontological, since by drawing attention to its own form and technique it demands a "wondrer," a reader to admire it and to wonder about it. Paradox must, in short, generate thought and even understanding. In yet another sense, paradox is paradoxical: each paradox begins an infinite activity, which, from Zeno on, has forced new minds to consider afresh the irresolute problems of the human understanding. Because of their almost imperceptible reaching out to involve their beholders and readers, paradoxes fit particularly that style called "baroque," in which a slanted perspective, a hand extended from a picture toward the beholder, or an actor turning directly to the audience were common devices appealing across conventional limits between "art" and "reality."
>
> (pp. 518–19)

It is ultimately paradox's lack of self-containment, its openness to a beholder, that allows paradox, nonetheless, to be the source of the development of a new principle of subjectivity, one involving a deeper sense of alienation and a negation of that alienation. The Renaissance created an autonomous third world between man and God, that of art, which gave it the second interpretation that it needed to question the first, and the sense of joyous self-affirmation and permanence that it needed to surmount time and death.

Bacon

What, however, is perhaps most interesting in the light of our pursuit of the genealogy of negation is that it was in this same Renaissance period, dominated by affirmations, that a critical conscious stance was first taken toward these subjective powers by Bacon. Bacon was the first to try to assess critically and to evaluate how and to what extent we negate and affirm and what the impact of these activities is on science and the pursuit of truth. It is not surprising to see that in Bacon's judgment we overvalue affirmation. He discovers that we lean toward it innately and uncritically.

> It is the peculiar and perpetual error of the human intellect to be more moved and excited by affirmatives than by negatives; whereas it ought properly to hold itself indifferently disposed toward both alike. Indeed, in the establishment of any true axiom, the negative instance is the more forcible of the two.[16]

We lean toward affirmations because we like to think we have the truth and its confirmation. We wish therefore to ignore the negative instance. We like the closed, the confirmed, the established. For this reason, as Bacon saw, we tend to stick to "first conclusions" and accepted opinions. Bacon saw that to discover the form of any particular thing we cannot apply a fundamental method, like that underlying Erasmus' work, of inclusion, of "and/and," of addition. Instead, form emerges as a consequence of following a procedure of inclusion and exclusion.

> To God, truly, the Giver and Architect of Forms, and it may be to the angels and higher intelligences, it belongs to have an affirmative knowledge of forms immediately, and from the first contemplation. But this assuredly is more than

man can do, to whom it is granted only to proceed at first by negatives, and at last to end in affirmatives after exclusion has been exhausted.

(p. 151)

God created without negation. We do not. We must proceed by a slower, more dialectical and indirect method of inclusion and exclusion. Bacon is the first philosopher of our ineluctable antitheticality of negation and affirmation, of positive and negative, of inclusion and exclusion, of presence and absence. If human genealogy differs from the account of the origin in Genesis, it differs in nothing so much as in that its formative, creative acts are dependent on a double, dialectical process of negation and affirmation. Whereas in God's creativity affirmation simply predominates, in our sciences and arts it is achieved. According to Bacon, our ultimate goal is also affirmation, only our lack of divinity makes us unable to attain the affirmatives directly. "In the process of exclusion are laid the foundations of true induction, which however is not completed till it arrives at an affirmative" (p. 155).

Bacon was the first to value negation and exclusion. He was the first to try to make practical and positive use of our merely human power. He saw how this unglorious power could be put to scientific use. He was the first in that sense to break through the weight of negative associations with negation. He saw negation in a neutral way because he was the first to take a critical stance toward affirmation. He saw that the imbalance in favor of affirmations and the lack of attention to negations is perhaps innate, but yet something that can consciously and critically be counteracted. He seems to have comprehended that man can, to some extent, control and change and influence the patterns of his ways of thinking. The attitude of favoring affirmations is not eternal and unchangeable. Affirmation is not a value or a necessity to which we must adhere. Bacon was the first to give us a new evaluation and picture of what the position of the powers of affirmation and negation were, and by critically stating what the situation was, he helped to change it.

Bacon has been called the most "modern" of Renaissance thinkers, among other reasons because he was indifferent to all that his world already knew. Whereas others were attracted to rediscovering what the ancients had known, Bacon was attracted to the unknown, compelled by the future, by change, hence "modern." Diderot rightly said that he "drew up the map" not of what men knew, but of what they did not know, "of what they had to learn."[17] Bacon wanted to increase our knowledge, "to bring into sight all that is most hidden and secret in the universe."[18] He was interested in "the resemblance of things" (which he still felt to be the chief point), but also in distinguishing their subtle differences. He had no use whatsoever for speculative philosophy, which he felt was out of contact with reality and unduly respectful of antiquity. He wanted to make known a portion of the unknown and he knew that an assault upon the unknown needed new methods that could not be merely methods of affirmation. What is important for us to note is that in Bacon, for the first time, the known comes to be linked to affirmation, and the unknown to a method that knows both how to negate and to affirm, to identify and to differentiate, to seize upon both presence and absence. Thus when Bacon outlined his scientific method by describing the three Tables of Investigation, he listed as the first of these the Table of Affirmation, or "the rule of presence." For him the rule of presence included a study of the rule of absence, the study of negative instances. His theory of forms echoes the same approach to objects.

Form is that which cannot be subtracted from an object without it ceasing to be an object. Form, he said, is the "true specific difference," (p. 121) and not to study forms is not to "touch the deeper boundaries of things" (p. 122). Form is the play of presence and absence.

> For the form of a nature is such, that given the form, the nature infallibly follows. Therefore it is always present when the nature is present, and universally implies it, and is constantly inherent in it. Again, the form is such that if it be taken away the nature infallibly vanishes. Therefore it is always absent when the nature is absent, and implies its absence, and inheres in nothing else.
>
> (p. 123)

Bacon knew that this is easily said but that the way of induction is "winding and intricate" (p. 152). One other aspect of his theory of form that makes it differ most radically from the Platonic notion of the eidos is the fact that at the moments when he speaks of it form begins rather to sound like force. Form is not a substance or an entity but a law of force.

> For when I speak of forms, I mean nothing more than those laws and determinations of absolute actuality which govern and constitute any simple nature, as heat, light, weight, in every kind of matter and subject that is susceptible of them. Thus the form of heat or the form of light is the same thing as the law of heat or the law of light.
>
> (p. 152)

The statement is important in the light of the future. Bacon prefigures a changed attitude toward form that is one with the revolution in attitude toward negation and affirmation. Form comes to be replaced by force or laws of force. The static model of form comes to be replaced by a dynamic model of force. As long as the model of form dominated, so did affirmation. When the model of force came to be foregrounded, so did the idea of perpetual dialectical negation and affirmation.

Montaigne

Montaigne complained in his *An Apology of Raymond Sebond* that the skeptical philosophers had "need of a new language. Ours is altogether composed of affirmative propositions, which are directly against them."[19] In other words, Montaigne perceived the old fundamental problem that true nescience, skepticism, would need a language of pure and unadulterated negation to maintain its ignorance, its open negativity, its skeptical self-irony or self-reduction. But we have no language of negation; ours is always a dialectical language of negation and affirmation; when we say "I know nothing," our opponents say "But then you know that you know nothing"—there is a positive in our negation. Or we say "Nothing is" and our opponents say "But that then is." This is the problem that leads some logicians to say that negation always only lives off the grace of affirmations, that implicit in every "nothing" is already a "something," and in every temporal presence or appearance, an absence or disappearance. There is no absolute nothing or negation, therefore, but only partial or relative negation. I want only to mention briefly here that the fundamental problem perceived in terms of language already in Montaigne is echoed by Derrida when he says that "we cannot utter a single destructive proposition which has not already slipped into the form, the logic, and the implicit postulations of precisely what it seeks to contest."[20] Derrida is repeating in a more comprehensive way the problems of the ineluctable antitheticality of language and consciousness with which logic, epistemology, and theology had always struggled.

Montaigne solved his dilemma by making only one affirmation: "only God *is*," and it is an affirmation that does not apply to this world (p.

246). In the world, one can only negate the affirmations, the infinite claims of reason or the senses to know. All that we "know," however, may be appearances. We may not ever know the substance or form of anything. All our experience may already be a distortion. It might, in sum, only be like the dream, which is also filled with subjects and objects. The negation of affirmatives helps one to stay in the human realm, the realm of ignorance, uncertainty, nescience. What is appropriate to man's reason is the form of the question, the proper form of doubt, for a question presupposes an answer of either yes or no. One must question and not try to answer.

Montaigne's essays are a return to the essay form of Plato, and yet not a return precisely because he questions and refuses to answer. The Platonic dialogue was conducted in a strictly logical and dialectical way where every thesis moved to its antithesis and where both were tested by the rules of logic. In Platonism, the dialogic–dialectic method had a goal, the logos or truth. Montaigne's essays are new and revolutionary because they are dialogues which do not pursue the logos, which do not end in affirmation, an answer, a known, but come to an end in a question, an unknown. "[N]othing is certain but uncertainty" (p. 170). Since this is so, Montaigne cannot pretend to be a formal and logical philosopher. He is "A new figure: an unpremeditated philosopher and a casual!" (p. 190). Since the mind is a "vagabond, a dangerous, and fondhardy implement" (p. 202), he, to be true at least to what he knows, his own mind, can only write according to whim, following no model.

What is different in Montaigne, compared to Milton and Spenser for example, is his tolerance for becoming, for incessant change. "Becoming is all"; becoming is a constant experience of dying, yet Montaigne is not afraid of it. Montaigne is able to face mutability without terror and bewilderment. He writes as if a spectator in a great theater of becoming, involved in change and yet disinvolved. He feels himself, his mind, and his body to be rolling and changing. He feels himself thus to be a surprising, original, and spontaneous being. He feels his own unknownness. But another part of himself *is* known. This is the part that is the repetition of custom and habit, and the certitude that there is something that is not becoming, but stasis. The self is still ambiguous but in a new way, by new acts of inclusions and exclusions. The temporal self—the unstable senses and mind—are examined and explored and recognized as being not merely a torment in which we inhere, as in Ficino, but our true, large reality. To comprehend this reality and this self new habits and methods of thought are necessary.

In Montaigne's single, unqualified affirmation—that of the existence of God and the necessity of faith—we find an echo of the old perfect Yes. But now it is clear that this Yes is applicable only to God and not to man, particularly not to man's mind. For Montaigne, to presume that the mind is in part divine, as Ficino did, is human arrogance. The scope of affirmation is thus vastly reduced. It applies only to the transcendent realm and not to the immanent. All of immanence has become a realm of skeptical negation. Immanence and transcendence are separated primarily by the fact that pure affirmation can be applied only to the one and not to the other. A new scheme leaves on the side of pure affirmation only God.

The power of affirmation appears reduced and limited. Affirmation is no longer an activity which bridges the gap between selfhood and divinity, making both one and coherent. To affirm divinity no longer necessarily means affirming selfhood. In this scheme, however, it must be stressed that this newly found world of negation is not perceived in a purely negative way. It is not experienced as a realm of loss and absence, alien to the self, outside it. The self and world are one in becoming, but this becoming is tantalizingly present, mysterious, engaging, interesting. Montaigne is obviously compelled by it, because it is new, unexplored, and unknown. The energies of his skeptical reason are employed to lay it bare rather than to ascertain the nature of God. In terms of what I said earlier about dialectical models, one can say of Montaigne that he is able to accept both models exactly in their aspect of negation. He can accept the many as a denial of the One, and time as a constant denial of the "now." One can say that he comes to crave a language of negation because he discovers pluralization and temporality as real presences. Or one can state it the other way around: perhaps he discovered negation because he had first discovered temporality and plurality. However one puts it, Montaigne clearly saw that negation is inevitable in a process that is open. If we are part of a process that is infinitely open and rolling, not applying an affirmation to any part of the process seems to be the logical conclusion. Montaigne's negative skeptical practice follows necessarily and logically from his new identification of man with the world of becoming. Scepticism keeps us true to the world of becoming and to our radically altering self.

Descartes

After Montaigne, as we saw in Bacon, the problem was perpetually to find the real source of affirmation in this world of becoming and negation. Was there anything in this world to which an affirmation could be applied? What could be affirmed with greater certitude, the subject or the object? And what in the subject or object? Had the self still a soul and the object still an eidos that could be affirmed? And could that soul or eidos ever be seized outside a practice of exclusion and inclusion? Descartes was caught in the midst of such problems. It is not surprising that the first source in which he searched for an affirmation was the subject, that old source of affirmation which had once been semidivine. Descartes assaulted the problem in a radically skeptical way. He decided to apply the method of which he felt certain, his power to negate, to doubt everything, including the presence and reality of his body. What remained at the end of this new version of the *via negativa?* What could he subtract from the self without its ceasing to exist? Or can one negate to the point of ceasing to be?

The *locus classicus* of modern doubt is the moment when Descartes, sitting by the fire in his winter dressing gown, decides to refuse his assent to what is because he may be being deceived. It is a demoniac moment in the history of skepticism because Descartes literally imagines that the world may be in the control of the devil.

> I will suppose, then, not that Deity, who is sovereignly good and the fountain of truth, but that some malignant demon, who is at once exceedingly potent and deceitful, has employed all his artifice to deceive me; I will suppose that the sky, the air, the earth, colours, figures, sounds, and all external things, are nothing better than the illusions of dreams, by means of which this being has laid snares for my credulity; I will consider myself as without hands, eyes, flesh, blood, or any of the senses, and as falsely believing that I am possessed of these; I will continue resolutely fixed in this belief, and if indeed by this means it be not in my power to arrive at the knowledge of truth, I shall at least do what is in my power, viz. (suspend my judgement), and guard with settled purpose against giving my assent to what is false, and being imposed upon by this deceiver, whatever be his power and artifice.[21]

This remarkable moment in Descartes echoes Plato's famous image of ourselves as the prisoners in a cave, deceived by mere shadows. It looks forward as no other textual moment I know does to the famous dialogues with the devil in *The Brothers Karamazov* and Mann's *Doctor Faustus*. As soon as Descartes determines to doubt and to dramatize the necessity of doubting, he has to suppose that all is a deception and has to conjure up the devil to make the possibility of the deception real. Thus, doubt comes to be a form of collusion with the devil, and yet we must doubt.

In Descartes' doubt, God is displaced by the devil and the world of substance by a bodiless self. In one moment of reflection the entire world of being, of presence and plenitude, is swallowed up. The cosmos disappears. In its place appears a deeply untrustworthy play of illusions guided by the devil. The devil is a deceiver who attempts to satisfy us with insubstantial, deceptive images. Reality may be like our unreliable imagination. Descartes seems to have feared that the imagination may be the truth. The negative as the devil, as the experience of total deception and distortion (which Descartes boldly imagined, though only momentarily so), is an extension and a darkening of doubt beyond the notion of a dreamlike deception. We do not find this in Montaigne; in Mann's *Doctor Faustus* it is part of the very structure of reality.

Descartes both fears the imagined deception and clings to it because consciousness in any form is an assurance against the void:

> Doubtless, then, I exist, since I am deceived; and, let him deceive me as he may, he can never bring it about that I am nothing, so long as I shall be conscious that I am something.
>
> (*Meditations*, p. 119)

Greater than the dread of deception, or that of an absent God or world, is the dread of personal nonbeing, of subjective nothingness, of death. Against this fear Descartes posited the certainty of his consciousness. Descartes' fear of death and his desire, above all, for certitude about the self's existence are at this moment his reason for shifting the subject to the center of the world.

Descartes rescues the self, or rather a flickering, unsteadfast awareness of self, from his doubt:

> I am—I exist: this is certain; but how often? As often as I think; for perhaps it would even happen, if I should wholly cease to think, that I should at the same time altogether cease to be.
>
> (*Meditations*, p. 121)

The self exists only on the occasions of self-awareness. Such a notion of existence was too precarious for Descartes to tolerate for very long. He saw that the actuality of consciousness is our first certainty. We can only affirm our peculiar capacity for self-awareness. Consciousness is. "It is a thing that doubts, understands [conceives], affirms, denies, wills, refuses, that imagines also, and perceives" (*Meditations*, p. 122). Consciousness is an experience; one cannot say that anything about it is valid, only that it is. Suddenly what we know about our mind is more certain than what we know of the outer world. Descartes examines his famous piece of wax and learns that he, the perceiver, exists, not the perceived. Knowledge—the subject, not substance as in Greece—must hereafter be the starting point of philosophy. Knowing, rather than being, moves to the center of attention.

Although Descartes systematized doubt, he clearly felt, as he himself admits in the *Discourse on Method*, that it is "a greater perfection to know than to doubt" (p. 64). He who doubts wants certitude, because he feels threatened, not by incertitude, but by deception. Descartes wanted certitude about his own existence. Ultimately, he simply assumed that he existed. I am a "thinking" thing, he claimed. "*I think, hence I am*" (*Discourse*, p. 63). The "thing" and the "I am" are inferences. All there is is thought. The thinking is true, but he does not know what or who it is that thinks. Descartes, however, makes of the ego's absolute certainty of itself a geometrical axiom. He assumes that essences, like mathematical concepts or his philosophizing ego, exist. He mixes logical propositions and existence as all philosophers using the old ontological arguments had done. Suddenly, we hear once more that if you deny the predicate, you deny the subject, therefore the predicate cannot be denied. Existence comes of necessity with God. If He is perfect, He must exist, for existence is one of the perfections and He has all perfections. God *is*, once again. Descartes' injunction to himself—*de omnibus dubitandum* turned quickly back into *Deus est* and *corpora sunt*.

Descartes' "I am" is a hankering after what had been and what he had known, the world of substance and plenitude. As soon as Descartes says "I am," the extraordinary boldness and novelty of his thought ends. What follows thereafter—the reestablishment of rationalism, of God, bodies, the world of the plenum—is all nostalgia. It is his desire for the familiar and the known. To bring back the known, he uses known methods, rather than methodical doubt. He proves the existence of God essentially on the lines of scholastic philosophy, although he had criticized these very methods:

On examination, I found that, as for logic, its syllogisms and the majority of its other precepts are of avail rather in the communication of what we already know . . . than in the investigation of the unknown.

(*Discourse*, p. 50)

Descartes knew that his doubt, not his logic, had led him to the perception of another reality, a strangely empty, obscure, and uncertain one which he himself could not tolerate for long. Descartes began by seeking the unknown, but then he turned back to the known. Ultimately, he explained away our sense of obscurity and incertitude in an old and established fashion. We exist, he argued, because we participate both in absolute existence and in nonexistence. The clear, distinct, true, and perfect in us is the consequence of our participation in God; the confused, obscure, false, and all error "proceed from nothing (participate of negation)" (*Discourse*, p. 67). Descartes did not value nothingness and the possibility of denying anymore than the medieval world had. He did not really like his thrilling experience of doubt by the fire. It made him extremely uncomfortable. Descartes was determined, as most of the men of the Renaissance, except for Shakespeare, to take the advice of Parmenides and "never let this thought prevail . . . that not-being is."[22]

Descartes did not ultimately value the very method of negation that he practiced. Negation is still strongly associated with nothingess, with the inability to found or establish, with the unknown, with error, illusion, evil, distortion, with the unclear and indistinct. In sum, it is for him an unproductive activity. He does not consciously acknowledge that his philosophy originated in negation and that it is a purely subjective and merely human philosophy precisely because it emerged from a purely human activity. This paradox exists in Descartes because of his desire for some kind of pure affirmative, something that he "could have no occasion to doubt," and because of his association of affirmation with the known, the substantive, the clear and the distinct. Descartes still finds God in his mind albeit only as an idea of perfection, an idea of nondoubt.

Descartes reduced the realm of the knowable, if only momentarily, as he reduced the scope of the self. Compared to the self that Faustus defiantly affirms in Marlowe, Descartes' self is almost a nothingness. Faustus affirms the self as an aspiring body-mind unity. Descartes' self is bodiless. It is a nondialectial self that has no other, not even a body. Or to put it another way, the body is its sole other, with which it has to try to reconnect itself. Descartes' consciousness is almost the nothingness in which Beckett's Unnamable struggles, but not quite exactly because Descartes cannot imagine his bodiless consciousness saying, as the Unnamable does, "I am not thinking," "I do not exist."

From the innermost sanctuary of consciousness, Descartes barred the idea of nothingness and the function of negation. This is the unknown that his method did not wish to know or to explore. Descartes' doubt is but a moment in a background of affirmation. It occurs in a context of certainty. He takes no pride in his doubting as a perfection. It is an imperfection. It is a method, a technique, and only momentarily foregrounded. He also does not see it as an inescapable necessity to which he is delivered over by language as the Unnamable is. He does not see it because he lives in a historico-philosophical period that still values certitude, the known, and the stable above their opposites. He had no method for living in incertitude.

Descartes extended the function of negation in the subjective realm as Bacon did in the objective realm. Both saw that a method which sought new knowledge in either realm had to make use of the power of negation, but both ultimately believed more in the activity of affirmation and the ultimate certitude and reality of affirmatives. In Descartes the power of exclusion is short-circuited particularly abruptly and harshly because, unlike Bacon, Descartes still wished for a totally unified system of metaphysics and science, for a system in fact that would have the qualitative effect of a philosophy (like Spinoza's) grounded on synthetic and deductive principles, but that would instead be based on analytic and inductive methods. What haunts Descartes as much as Bacon is the idea of "solid foundations," the indubitable that can only be affirmed. His "hyperbolic" doubt cannot be the end; it can only be the way to the indubitable primitive datum, which turns out to be only subjective. Descartes doubted, while hoping for certitude, and only because he wanted to find the indubitable.

Pascal

As the Christian myth recedes more and more, as the certitude of God turns into a certitude of his absence from nature within and without, faith loses its power to assuage doubt or to hold it in rein with doubt's opposite, certitude. Thus doubt proliferates, particularly from the sixteenth century onward, arrested here and there, but never for long. What was once a playful and predominantly fortuitous and "comic" awareness of the paradoxicality of our situation turns gradually into a permanent and tragic awareness of an existence within incommensurabilities, into a sense of condemnation to an ironic mode of existence. The stable and controllable ironies of an Erasmus, which are intentional and rhetorical, become senseless, absurd, and noninterpretable in a Pascal.

Erasmus doubted "all that he had come to know, as well as the methods by which he had come to know what he knew."[23] Yet, basically, his irony was purposive and teleological. Doubt is the method by which we reach our nescience, our ignorance. And nescience is our way to God and faith, for God cannot be known. In Pascal, by contrast, there is no grace in foolishness. Our ignorance is merely painful; it is no longer valuable; it is not a promise of paradise or the point in the self where the self dissolves in Christ. For Pascal, man is an incomprehensible mixture of greatness and abjectness, but neither our greatness nor our abysmal abjectness is a guarantee that God exists. We must always doubt whether God exists or not. This, for Pascal, is the worst of the ambivalences with which we must live. In Erasmus and Montaigne the ultimate doubt of God's existence is not a part of their doubt. In Descartes it is so only momentarily. In Erasmus' world only what participates in mortality is foolish and subject to doubt. Thus, his irony is fundamentally positive, fundamentally an act of fusion, rather than one of separation. In Pascal, however, irony is a realization of absence, a tortured awareness of division, disproportion, and dissociation.

To engage in doubt and paradoxes is, as Pascal discovers, no longer a possibility, a way of detachment in which one must engage for the sake of a more perfect perspective or a more perfect faith; rather, doubt *is* an actuality, our reality. The subjective possibility of doubt becomes the objective ironic condition in which we exist. The trust that was concomitant with a Christian world of plenitude changes into mistrust. Skepticism, which in Montaigne had been moderate, serene, playful, a source of enjoyment, becomes, in Pascal, immoderate, anxious, a source of torment. Certitude and affirmation are no longer in alliance. Affirmation is only a wager, grounded in nothing, but one we must wager.

In Pascal skepticism has become a more radicalized mode of existence, the mode of hope and despair. Every hope carries in it the threat of nonfulfillment. Pascal's wager is such a threatened hope. But we must make hope rather than doubt or resignation the fundamental category of existence. Pascal disliked Montaigne intensely because he realized that his form of open, moderate skepticism permitted the endless postponement of commitment to any idea of belief. It is a skepticism, therefore, that could in a godless world lead straight to nihilism or boredom or both. Pascal anticipates two primary experiences of negativity that come to predominance in the nineteenth century. He knew what the sense of the world without a God would be like. It is that first taste of a godless existence, and the accompanying ennui that Pascal wanted to combat. He did so first of all by not denying that the world "bears witness everywhere to a lost God."[24] And secondly he did it by proving that only uncertainty was certain, even in the transcendent realm.

Pascal did not hesitate to place uncertainty within the very act of faith itself. The wager is hope and uncertainty; it is a "yes" to an ambivalence, to an unresolvable yes/no. It is a submission to what we hope to be the truth. Like any commitment, it contains hope and hazard. The wager is Pascal's answer to nothingness, for it is no coincidence that it was Pascal's experimentation in particular which produced decisive confirmation of the existence of a physical vacuum. The idea of nothingness that had from earliest times preoccupied and puzzled man and which the Renaissance played upon in so many extravagant ways finally became a physical reality, a break in the world of plenitude.

Pascal complained that Descartes was "useless and unreliable" (297–78), but Pascal had imbibed the most radical moment of Descartes' doubt and extended it. Pascal went on to insist that we were all error, confusion, obscurity, and falsity. "We are nothing but lies, duplicity, contradictions; and we conceal and disguise ourselves from ourselves" (255–377). Between his great pain and his great faith, Pascal could tolerate the absence, emptiness, uncertainty, and possibility of deception that Descartes could not bear. To Pascal it was clear that the contradictions were inescapable and unsolvable. It was also clear to him that we were condemned to separateness and solitude. Radical doubt left us alone in an ironic world with our questions unanswered. The only remaining possibilities were subjective: "you must either believe, or deny, or doubt" (374–260). Since doubt led to the suspension of action and the will—since doubt was an inhuman abdication of our powers—for

Pascal only the two other possibilities were left: the affirmation or negation of the wager. To Pascal they represented hope or despair, the mode of existence that for him replaced the pompous and now impossible one of doubt and certitude that Descartes had pursued. The acceptance or rejection of the wager is a choice that is totally the responsibility of the subject. It is a test of our powers, and brings no objective certitude. It is a potentiated, radicalized skepticism, which wills and, in a sense, creates the affirmation for which there is no objective ground or reason. In Pascal affirmation is reduced to subjective willing, to faith. Montaigne was able to exclude God from his doubt; Pascal cannot. Doubt is all-inclusive, embracing transcendence and immanence. Affirmation is purely subjective, but the only way to reassert the existence of a permanently absent God. A new set of alliances has occurred. God is one now with absence and exclusion; He is outside. He has now been permanently severed from objective certitude, knowledge, being, and stasis. For this very reason, the need for affirmation is so imperative in Pascal. The felt presence of a whole lost world is dependent upon our power and will to affirm. Nothing is as clear to Pascal as his feeling that we cannot live humanly without affirmation. Without affirmation human society disintegrates into a state of nihilism. Every feeling of being alive in Pascal is one with the power of affirmation. We have this power and we must exercise it.

Pascal was the first to understand the limits of affirmation, the first to see what affirmation could not affirm or attain. He was the first to see that human affirmation, unlike the perfect Yes of God, was not synonymous with perfect and instant actualization, with substance, form, and light.

Racine's *Phaedra*

Timon's suicide issued out of his misanthropy, his discovery of the absence of binding human love in the world. Phaedra kills herself because she discovers that such a bond to others does exist, but it is a bodily, involuntary, and impersonal bond which she feels is dehumanizing. In Phaedra two selves speak and contradict each other, the involuntary sensuous self and the voluntary spiritual self. One gives her a sense of autonomy, a chance to guide her own fate; the other drags her against her will into the shade where Hippolytus is hunting.

Oh why am I not sitting in the shade
Of forests? When may I follow with my eyes
That racing chariot flying down the course
                        .   .   .   .
                Where am I? Mad?
What have I said? Where, where have I let stray
My longings, and my self-control?[25]

By language she displaces herself from where she is in the sunlight to
another place in the shade. She drifts from one reality into another, but
she always knows that she has drifted. She begins to speak the reality of
her conscious desire and shifts involuntarily into the language of unconscious desire. She is the "thinking reed" that would like to think, but
that discovers the reality of its "reedhood" to be an indomitable sensuous force, one which surges into consciousness, defiling thought.

Racinian tragedy, as that of Shakespeare, signals the rediscovery of
that kind of dramatization of interiority that seemed to have disappeared
with Greek tragedy, but interiority at the moment of its rebirth discovers itself as too monstrous to be revealed. Phaedra appears on stage
in speechless agony because what she knows of herself must be concealed. She is the epitome of the self-paradoxical, the self-oxymoronic—
a life that is a desire for death, a love that is a hatred, a desire for purity
that turns into an embodied, impure, unwanted desire.

Know me, then—Phaedra—in my madness, know
I am in love. But do not dare to think
That I—in love with you—believe that I
Am innocent, or of myself approve.
Nor that the mad love now deranging me
Like poison in the blood, is fed at all
By cowardly connivance of my will.
Unlucky object of the spite of Gods,
I am not so detestable to you
As to myself. . . .
                Can you believe that this
Confession I have just made to you—this
So shameful declaration I have made
Is voluntary? Can you think so? Ah!
Oh take your vengeance, do, and punish me
For such a hideous and illicit love!

Your father was a hero, be like him,
And rid the world of one more monster now.

[2.5]

Phaedra suffers dreadfully from the self-recognition of her impurity. "I hate my life; my love is horrible" (1.3). She is tortured by the realization and recognition within herself of the same unnatural passions and drives that raged in her monstrous family. She observes herself as mercilessly in the grip of the unconscious. Myth, in an act of Viconian recognition, becomes reality, a mirror of man's interiority.

Unlike Oedipus, Phaedra knows her capacity and desire for incest before acting it out, and she does not know how to live with it. She is torn apart by ambivalence, a *flamme noire;* as the granddaughter of Helios, she seeks light and purity, and no doubt also Hippolytus because he is pure, like the younger Theseus who killed the Minotaur, her monstrous half-brother. Thus, there is fidelity to Theseus in her very infidelity, and a desire for an impossible and pure love within that very passion which rages fiercely within her as a desire for an incestuous crime. Her only defenses against her awareness of this hideous, involuntary desire are silence and death. Only death is moral.

Ethically, Phaedra is above the world; she is pure because she condemns herself; she must die because she is a monster in the eyes of her own conscience. Speech is the only temptation to which she succumbs. Language itself is a *flamme noire;* it seeks to disclose, to reveal, and to set free what is secret and within. But language, by defining, betrays Phaedra's ultimately truly objectless love. Speech forces her to name the real Hippolytus as its object. Language betrays Phaedra into naming Hippolytus by its freedom to stray back into the past, into memory, and by its freedom to wish, to image, and to change what was. Phaedra, obsessed and haunted by the monster, the dark underworld of her father, and by purity, returns to the original scene of the killing of the Minotaur, the release from the monster by the combined forces of love and courage.

But no! In this design I would have been
Ahead of her, my sister! Me, not her,
It would have been whom Love at first inspired;
And I it would have been, Prince, I, whose aid
Had taught you all the Labyrinth's crooked ways.

Oh, how I should have cared for this dear head!
A single thread would not have been enough
To satisfy your lover's fears for you.
I would myself have wished to lead the way,
And share the perils you were bound to face.
Phaedra, into the Labyrinth, with you
Would have descended, and with you returned,
To safety, or with you have perished!

[2.5]

Language allows the optative and the conditional; Phaedra by a simple "or" substitutes Hippolytus for the young Theseus, and by a "would" she herself becomes Ariadne. Memory is altered by desire and she becomes the protagonist in that great adventure which she had missed. She strays into the labyrinth of the unconscious because she speaks. Language reveals the interior and hidden mythic dimension, the uncontrollable world of intensities. But language reveals it only in moments of madness, when the power of language possesses her and speaks itself and its archetypal desires out through her. Phaedra sees what is happening to her: "I recognize/My madness. I recall it all" (33.3). Phaedra's need to censure herself, to correct her speech, and finally to take back the impurity she has released from her being by self-negation increases as the play progresses. The play's action becomes her reaffirmation of her need to die.

Phaedra experiences love as a form of dehumanization. She can regain her humanity only through death or through understanding on the part of the world (Theseus). But the latter is impossible because he and she define the human in such a way as to exclude a Phaedra. Thus, her only way to freedom and purity is a tragic and negative way. To think that one can live in the world is an illusion and an error. In clear-eyed horror Phaedra realizes that one is oneself the source of all evil; one is unintentionally, guiltlessly guilty. And the world only connives with one's inner potential for evil by granting, thoughtlessly, as Theseus does, more evidence for the dark which is feared than for that which is hoped. In Phaedra's tragic, immobilizing vision, being fully human signifies recognizing simultaneously the necessity of the repudiation of the human. Phaedra's suicide is the consequence of her severe ethical self-doubt;

she is not what she should be. The petrifying question behind the tragedy is: how can we live knowing what we are?

In *Phaedra,* despite its intense interiority, the objective world is still present and meaningful. Phaedra's question, "Where can I hide?" (4.6) reveals a deep, open, and visible relationship to the universe. She sees it and is seen by it. It is a world of mutual recognition and responsibility. In herself Phaedra feels the pull of another world, the world of her own body that is her sign of connection to others, but she denies and represses this natural world in order to recognize and be recognized by the larger ethical, transcendent world. She refuses to relate to others by means of her instincts. Here the body is denied as much as it is in Descartes, and subdued perhaps for the last time for the sake of that larger affirmation and unity with the objective. But in the very process of being denied, the body becomes visible, a discovery made in the hatred and surprise of love: the discovery of being natural, beastly, instinctual. It is an undeniable that can yet be denied, but which continues to lie in wait for us. With the discovery of the sexual comes the discovery of the other. The sexual relates us to the other, even against ourselves, even in violation of our desire and need for autonomy.

Pure autonomy, however, is death. Phaedra chooses death because it is the only guarantee of pure autonomy, of unsullied self-possession, without that self feeling in turn possessed or impelled by the other. Phaedra exhibits an immense anxiety for the self. But she cannot live in the world with a self that is divided between two senses of the other— the otherness that her sexuality demands and the otherness that is the transcendence her spirit demands. She cannot live without exercising one or the other form of that otherness which her humanity demands. However, now to be more than the self means also to cease to be at all. Here the Promethean torment of the body that Ficino had been able to ignore while contemplating the unity of mind and God comes to the foreground as a power that cannot be denied except by self-annihilation. Phaedra's self-annihilation and self-loathing is also a desperate statement of self-love. The instincts oppose and mock the divine and pure aspirations of the mind. The body too has its goal and purpose, like the soul, like things. It has its own "sexual" eidos and its own methods of denial and affirmation. It is another world altogether with which the mind will unevadably have to deal in other than purely tragic terms.

Vico

The current of affirmation continues. The need to make affirmations is incessant. For Pascal, who is willing to live in incertitude, everything can still be gained by a subjective affirmation. For Descartes, only a small part of the self can be indubitably affirmed. Phaedra, to affirm and rescue but a small portion of her divine selfhood, pays the price of the loss of the whole self. The conditions under which an affirmation can be made grow more and more contradictory, perplexed, and poignant. There is no sure method of affirmation or a direct ground for it. As affirmation becomes subjective it becomes increasingly more complex and problematic. The object of affirmation wavers: is it something in the subject or something that is objective or is it both?

Vico, in a sense, simplified the problem by suggesting that the current of affirmation signifies only the need of the self to be and to persist. But then he immediately asked also whether our need to persist does not signify something larger, the need of the human race to persist. Finally, he asked whether the persistence of everything is not the indubitable testimony to God. Bacon had begun to suggest that our imperative need for affirmation itself needs examination, initiating specifically a critique of affirmation within his general criticism of the idols of the mind. Descartes argued that our strong need to affirm and to be is enough to prove that God exists and that he is not a deceiver who wishes to mislead us but one who guarantees that the most fundamental perceptions that we have about ourselves (that we exist) and the objective world (that it exists) are also true.

Vico approached these questions in a new manner. He seems to have understood that if persistence and being were our primary urges, one had a serious problem, and had to explain our urge to destruction and negation as well in a new subjective way without recourse necessarily to the old conception of sin and the devil. To this end Vico divided the world up in a new way between negation and affirmation. Our history, the history of the rise and fall of institutions, is a history of affirmation and negation, of creation and destruction. We can know it because we have made it. But it is God who guarantees the perpetuity and eternity of these cyclical *corsi e ricorsi;* He is the eternal persistence in being, a pure affirmation of history. Thus the perfect Yes still exists and guarantees our recovery from the wasteland we create, but our activity of creation is one mixed with decreation and destruction.

Vico perceived that what is at the core of our self-destruction is our power to particularize and pluralize, to create more and more clear and distinct ideas, laws, and rules. The pluralizing power of reason confounds and destroys us; the synthesizing power of the imagination recreates us and allows us to begin again, to be born anew. God gave us the seed of life, the mythic powers of the imagination, to preserve the race and the cycles of a seemingly linear history. The gift of imagination must be God's gift since men and institutions alone always run down into nothingness, destroying themselves.

Vico's "double" history, providential and human, is his way of answering Leibniz' question: why is there being and not nothingness? Or why is there affirmation and not only negation? The question indicated a new structure of perception, a reordering of categories. For whereas formerly nothingness and negation were a problem for the existence of which one had somehow to account, or that one had somehow to discount, and affirmation was self-evident and certain, now affirmation and being pose a problem that demands explanation, and negation and nonbeing are the realities that seem certain and unavoidable. In Vico's double system of history, eternal history is grounded in affirmation. It is static and nondialectical. The human history that we create is modeled on a dialecticism of negation and affirmation; it entails change and differentiation.

The critical division, echoing Bacon's, of immanence and transcendence, enables Vico to forge a new kind of link between man and God. This link is art or imagination, not reason, and it guarantees not certitude, but crude creative power and vision. The imagination is primary, creative, and totalizing. Reason is critical and pluralizing. Affirmation is no longer allied with reason, the powers of criticizing, defining, and particularizing, but with the unclear, embodying power of the imagination. Only that can be affirmed which has body and substance, and it is the imagination, not reason, which lends substance to things. In Vico's new set of alliances, affirmation is one with the body and the creative, mythic imagination; negation is one with reason.

Vico broke with the idea of a stable human consciousness. He believed in a changing and developing consciousness which could be known only if it was historically deciphered in its cultural embodiments and self-objectifications. The subject had now to be studied together with the objects that it made, transformed, and unmade. Men are fundamentally expressive. The self's negations and affirmations produce a palpable history. They are a productive activity, solid and visible. The other is now the self. The other is the self's self-objectification and expressivity. It can be studied and known. Vico forged nothing less than a new destiny for us by offering us a new source of self-identification: our history and institutions. Furthermore, he gave the becoming that Montaigne found tantalizing but bewildering a shape and an order.

We are no longer the dispassionate observers of change but its creators. Thus we are directly responsible for the change and, in a sense, in "control" of it. Vico does not as yet believe that we can through our own awareness influence our evolution. Our own critical awareness is sufficient only to show us that an evolution takes place, that history exists, and that we participate in making it. In other words, Vico does not see history as being wholly in the control of consciousness anymore than he sees consciousness as being wholly in control of itself. He makes quite clear that we do not in every instance know what we are doing, but that we do it, sometimes like clocks wound up by Providence, to preserve the race.

The moment of ambivalence in Vico is situated exactly in this moment of the full freedom and responsibility of consciousness. There is no question that Vico establishes that consciousness produces its objects, but he is not certain that we control or master them. He gives us our history without giving us control of it, without giving us the chance ever to change or revolutionize it. It does not occur to him to question whether consciousness could *not* produce these institutions, or whether it could produce others in another order, or whether man could, as in Marx, throw his weight behind a particular tendency or institution in a revolutionary manner. Revolution and criticism in Vico issue from reason, which is ultimately negative and divisive. The imagination is positive and synthesizing, but it has little to do with reality. It creates merely the mythic, fictive mold for reality.

In terms of our dialectic of negation and affirmation, Vico's work accomplished several things. For one, although it retains the idea of God, he more or less excludes the idea from human history. In Vico, God, though not unknowable, is more or less absent from secular reality. Thus his system focuses primarily not on a method or way of becoming unified with God once again (his system guarantees that unity), or on a way of reasserting His reality and our faith, but it focuses on a method—the axioms—by which we can refind ourselves and become unified with ourselves. The epistemological goal becomes the many, rather than the One. The knowledge of the many is foregrounded and affirmed. Our goal can only be the real, secular, immanent affirmations or negations that we are capable of making. In Vico's providential history we see an old model of form, the idea of the self-contained, the circular, the eternal. In his notion of history, we find a new model, linear (albeit not for long), evolutionary, and changing. The new model that is foregrounded is the model of form as force, a vision of evolution. This evolution lacks the dimension of an absolute unknown; it is not yet infinite, as it will be in Hegel, but it is the thing which we as men need to concern ourselves with. It is our proper object of study, and this study is furthermore clearly in large part a self-study.

The abstraction from history and particularity that Milton and Spenser still proffered as the model and ideal for ourselves is clearly by-passed now by the engaging reality of history. We can no longer practice the denial and negation of the historical world of radical particularity. The whole Platonic teaching of the denial of the particulars for the sake of the generals has now been overturned and in a sense invalidated. What we seek is an inverse method for finding the particulars. What is unknown and what we now seek to know and comprehend are the immanent subject and object. These are forms that are now subject to laws and forces in time. They are forms that have become forces. Forces participate in the dialectical play of negation and affirmation, creation and destruction. Forms participate in the play of presence and absence, inside and outside, included and excluded. Forms reveal and conceal. Forms displace. But forces do not merely conceal; they transform and cancel, creating the new and leaving the old permanently behind. Forces are forms in time and participate in its destruction and irreversibility.

Vico displaced permanently the former primacy of our concern with the perfect affirmation that was one with stasis and rest. But what we gained was the tremendous affirmation of the subject as a creating, persisting, producing, instituting force. In the light of this powerful self-affirmation, self-expression, and self-duplication in which the subject engages, making history, institutions, and art, even the fact that this subject cannot ultimately triumph and persist alone seems not to matter. Though Vico is deeply skeptical about the history he describes, which always ultimately flounders, and although there are moments when Vico himself sees only our madness, and hence, our need for providence, what triumphs in *The New Science* is not the note of skepticism and despair, but Vico's wonder and amazement at the spontaneity, power, creative energy, and will of man. If Montaigne was surprised by his own originality and ingenuity, Vico was amazed at that of the entire race of men. The history of the race was for him, for all its failures and discontent, for all its lack of critical self-awareness, a magnificent history of achievement.

Vico's discovery of historical perspective transformed and ordered mutability; it is no longer the great flow of absence, destruction, and death that it had at first appeared only to be. History is a flow of irreversible absence, but nonetheless an orderly, meaningful, and intelligible flow. Man too is a great flow of absence and destruction, but he makes himself a persistent presence in his monuments and institutions. We know man was different in the past because the monuments are qualitatively different. Or because they are qualitatively different we can assume that man was, and that time and historical change are. Historical perspective dramatizes and foregrounds all the things evolved in time. It shapes time and death into meaningful, special units. However, historical perspective is perhaps more than any other single factor (if one had to name one) responsible for the closure of the Renaissance world and its project of a total and pure appropriation, integration, and inclusion of all of the past into the present. The past can no longer be made wholly present as Pico had attempted to do in his philosophy of syncretism; and his faith in its validity as truth and knowledge is shattered. In Vico, each age is locked into itself, into its own conditions, differences, and originality. These differences are interesting and valuable, and they can be understood, but they cannot be synthesized into a new, more complete truth.

Kant

Kant's analysis of the beautiful and the sublime is in many ways a perfect summary of what the Renaissance world had tried to achieve by affirmation and negation. It is significant first of all that Kant relegates the very possibility of achieving, especially the affirmations, to the aesthetic realm. Secondly, it is important to remember that in Kant the aesthetic experience is not confined to works of art alone, as in Hegel, but takes place also in man's subjective experience of himself within the objective world of nature. The subjective experience of the beautiful echoes all that the Renaissance Platonists, mystics, and Christian humanists had craved when they pursued the vision of the One or God. The beautiful is a feeling of radiant stasis and animation, an intuition, ultimately, of perfect accord between the self and the world. We feel that the mind and the world were designed for each other; they are one, capable of comprehending each other. The beautiful is thus a feeling of vibrant stillness, of animated rest.

It is, as Kant's analysis lays bare, a paradoxical feeling which produces a sense of the All, of one Form, of unity precisely because in catching all the paradoxes and opposites at once, it escapes dialectical oscillation and partiality. Kant's critical idealism defines us as limited, but a state of paradox is as if an escape from these limitations. Paradoxes produce a sense of totality, of all-inclusiveness. In paradoxy we are both free and unfree, limited and unlimited, nothing and everything. Our state echoes the Renaissance world of paradox so ably described by Rosalie Colie. The beautiful is a feeling of radiant stillness and completion—a set of paradoxes and opposites brought to a momentary balance.

In this moment of the beautiful, the mind feels nothing but itself as the other, as form. The feeling of the beautiful is noncognitive, idealess, and conceptless. The paradoxes that spellbind the mind—disinterested interest, subjective universality, nonpurposive purpose, exemplary necessity—paradoxically also give the self a sense of form, of the bounded and unified. The free subject (free of its own usual mental activity) is as if one with the free object, the object purified of its phenomenal nature. The purified formal subject and the purified formal object are one. The distilled contentless subject and object are indistinguishable.

Kant defined us as conditioned and limited, but in the aesthetic experience he sought to recover a formal, unlimited freedom. He believed that at the core of the aesthetic experience such an unconditioned experience of freedom and totality was available to us. But it was available to us only formally (and therefore in an experience of form) only when we cease to be psychological, emotional, epistemic subjects and become pure, playful aesthetic subjectivity.

The reward of our momentary distillation and abstraction from the phenomenal world is an enhancement of our feeling of aliveness, our feeling of vitality. The great gift of a sense of the possibility of the fusion of subject and object, now as before, seems still to be that great sense of perfect life and self-affirmation. The perfect affirmation still only comes when the subject affirms both itself and the other, the objective. The aesthetic experience is purely subjective; it gives us no objective knowledge, and yet it is deeply suggestive of objective knowledge, so much so that Kant did not escape putting it to devious use as a testament to the noumenal world. The contentless pattern or form of music, *Hamlet*, or a sunset incites the purely formal play of our own minds, giving us a sense of their reciprocity, their harmony, and beyond that intuitions of the possibility of the deep intimacy of subject and object, their intercourse. The supreme pleasure of the formal accord makes us leap to the intuition of noumenal reality. Beyond the phenomenal world is one world of formal accord of which we are a part. Here again the self finds itself by losing itself in the pleasure of the other.

Kant's beautiful is a pure experience of affirmation of the self and the world. It is an unambivalently pleasurable *feeling* (rather than an emotion), the essence of which is the experience of form as such: the world and the self are as if designed for each other; they are in perfect accord. Or it is certain that at least our faculties are in perfect correlation with each other: the imagination appears freely to conform to the lawfulness of judgment. Beauty is a free, inexplicable, almost absurd experience of subjective purposiveness which induces intuition of objective purposiveness.

The aesthetic experience of the sublime is a more complex feeling of simultaneous affirmation and negation, of pleasure and pain. The sublime includes a moment of alienation, pain, fear, "bewilderment" and "perplexity," and it produces "a momentary checking of the vital powers."[26] We experience an arrest of the will to live; the power of self-preservation is threatened. The sublime is therefore an "earnest" rather than a "playful" experience, "a negative pleasure" (p. 83). Hence it is an emotion, for emotion has to do with movement (*emovere*); what the mind experiences is not stasis, but movement. Thus the essence of the experience is not form but force, movement—this movement in the self of emotions.

The fundamental emotion—action and reaction—is similar to what

Pascal described in his famous passage on the "thinking reed." Man feels his frailty, his smallness, his insignificance, his impotence, his nothingness. Man feels this nothingness, for example, when confronted by a hurricane or the Milky Way. In Pascal man maintains himself because he has thought, which elevates him above all of nature. By thought, Pascal said, "we must raise ourselves, and not by space and time, which we could never fill" (391–347). In Kant man similarly conquers the vastness (magnitude) or power (might) of nature by thought, which is more vast and powerful than either. By thought man also conquers the pain, fear, and confusion that these phenomena produce within him. But in Kant, clearly, something more interesting is stressed than the fact that thought is more vast than space and time and stronger than inner pain and fear. Thought has the special ability to make something nothing. It really conquers the vast mountain by making it nothing, by saying "it is nothing" and "I am." Thought has the power to "kill" the object and assert the subject. What, consequently, the sublime experience gives us is an infinitely pleasurable and heightened experience of ourselves.

In the sublime we do not feel an intuited accord between the self and the world, but only the noumenal power of the self. This heightened experience is bought at the price of an experience of dissonance, discord, and disjunction between the self and the world. One feels a degree of alienation (the mind and the world were not designed for each other), but one also feels in the self the power to withstand this alienation and dissonance and to surmount it.

The sublime thus entails a new consciousness of negativity, put in the service of subjectivity rather than in the service of the other, as in mysticism. We have the ability to turn all to nought to maintain the self. In the beautiful we distill the world but we do not negate it. In the sublime we negate it in order to affirm ourselves. This negation is killing for the objective but benign toward the subject because it enlarges and elevates the subject above the object. In one the subject and object are not in discord; in the other they are. In the sublime we negate the power of the world over us. We sever our connection and bond with nature.

Kant says that nature is sublime when it "calls up that power in us . . . of regarding [things] as small" or as "without any dominion over us" (p. 101). Thus, Kant does not speak as yet of the mind's negativity, as Hegel will, but of its power to make something that is large small, or something that is powerful powerless. The mind has the power to turn into the opposite, to reduce. But when he goes on to comment on our admiration for war and soldiers, it becomes implicit that Kant sees this power to reverse and reduce in the context of our power to destroy and kill. To make small or powerless is almost to undo, to make something nothing.

Thus at their core the powers of reason are antithetical powers; we have the idea of the all because we have the idea of nothing. We have the power to totalize because we have the power to diminish. They are one and interdependent. And by this power of reason to make all and nothing, "we are superior to nature within, and therefore also to nature without us," (p. 104), whereas for the imagination alone, the transcendent is "like an abyss in which it fears to lose itself" (p. 97). The sublime is a more complex experience because we feel a dissonance not only between ourselves and nature but within our own faculties.

The beautiful is the subjective experience of the representation of the *form* of an object; it is an experience of boundaries. The sublime is the experience of the representation of "a formless object"; it is an experience of *"boundlessness"* (p. 82). The perplexity and displeasure that is part of the experience of the sublime is the consequence first of all of the imagination's confrontation with the boundless. Formlessness gives imagination the experience of its inadequacy and limitation: the imagination's function of synthesis proves unequal to grasping the totality of the representation, albeit the idea of totality is available to us in thought.

As Kant says, it is an experience where violence is done to the imagination and the subject, particularly to the subject's sense of purposiveness. "We must seek a ground external to ourselves for the beautiful of nature, but seek it for the sublime merely in ourselves and in our attitude of thought, which introduces sublimity into the representation of nature" (p. 84). But the recovery of a sense of wholeness within ourselves, between the imagination and the reason, gives us our first sense of our own radical boundlessness and power—without God.

Without God our infinity is a negativity, a boundless force and power to make all great things small and powerless. "It is for us a law (of reason) . . . to estimate as small, in comparison with ideas of reason, everything which nature . . . contains" (p. 96). Kant does not foresee our exercising this sublime power over God himself, but he sees how the subject, a part, can substitute itself for the whole. The sublime is a metonymic act. The beautiful is synthesis; it is a metophorical activity and substitution. The terrible and seemingly small and powerless, Lilliputian perspective into which nature puts us, which frightened Pascal, is not something that we have to accept or tolerate passively, but a vision that we can reverse by our own positive negating powers. Swift's Gulliver feels captured and undone by the other; in Kant's sublime, consciousness undoes the other by negation. The sublime experience entails the experience of negation but it concludes in self-affirmation. Both experiences, that of the beautiful and the sublime, are descriptions of how we feel alive and life-affirming, and descriptions of conditions under which (and ways in which) we earn our sense of self-preservation.

In the sublime, to experience what we are, we have to experience what we are not. We have to experience severance and separation by negating and affirming, including and excluding. Kant clearly situates this power of severance in reason. The imagination initiates a passive and painful perception of alienation, but reason turns it into a positive act of intellection. The feeling of the beautiful is by comparison a pre- or irrational experience in which reason is not exercising its special powers. Thus in the beautiful we as if are what we are not; we include in ourselves what we are not. Or another way to put it would be to say that we do exclude particularity in the old Neo-Platonic manner in so far as we distill the eidos, form, or general from the particular, but we do not practice separation from the eidos of the object.

By comparison, the negation practiced in the sublime is far more radical and of a different order altogether. Now we can say that the practice of negation for the sake of the eidos, form, or essence, is but a partial or mild negation because nothing that essential is really excluded. In fact, it is a negation that makes possible an inclusion of subject in object, whereas in the sublime, negation produces a permanent sense of exclusion, severance, and difference. If we compare sublime negation to mystical negation, we can say the former causes the self to appear, the latter the self to disappear. What is different in the sublime is that the activity of negation no longer takes place at the expense of the self but the other, the nonself. Thus, the sublime is in a sense a form of reversed mysticism. The self comes to know only itself, but, as in mysticism, as more than itself. The sublime ends in a supersensible sense of selfhood. We are more than we are, an infinite power to create and destroy.

The self, suffering under time and destruction in *Timon, Doctor Faustus,* and *The Revenger's Tragedy,* which did not know what it was or how to assert itself—that self, trembling still for its spiritual existence in Descartes, Pascal, and Racine—has now developed a multiplicity of new ways to affirm, delight, preoccupy, study, and view itself, in becoming, history, art, and science. In Kant's sublime, furthermore, it can begin to enjoy its negativity as a power given to it for self-enlargement and self-preservation, rather than for self-destruction. The sublime experience tells us who we are and what we are. The aesthetic experience becomes a powerful form of self-knowledge and self-recognition. The question for the nineteenth century will now become: is this sublime self the truth, or did Kant perhaps exaggerate the powers of subjectivity?

Goethe's *Faust*

Kant knew that without moral ideas, the sublime is merely terrible. In Act One of Goethe's *Faust*, Faust evokes the Earth-spirit and feels merely crushed. The Earth-spirit makes Faust rediscover not his reason but his nothingness. Faust feels what he is not, but also what he is: this fundamental nothingness that is mere need and lack, an ability to nihilate the objective world that appears to be annihilating him. Faust wants to die, but in his nothingness he gives birth instead to the figure and symbol of his nothingness, Mephistopheles, the spirit that negates. Mephistopheles alone can defeat Faust's sense of nothingness in relation to nature by also calling that nothing. Thus Faust at the moment of being nothing is inseminated by the primordial negative, the devil, and paradoxically acquires the will to continue living via negation. Clearly, the spirit of pure negation has restorative powers. It is only by the aid of this spirit of absolute negation that Faust is reborn into his new life.

Nature awakened in Faust what Hegel called the general consciousness. This awakening is also an awakening of the inner dialectic of affirmation and negation, of identity and difference. Consciousness of the objective world develops in Faust the idea that he is like nature, a god, and then the perception that he is different, a mere worm. The Earth-spirit tells him that he is not equal, not the same, but "only equal to what you think I am."[27] He has only, as Hegel argues, a concept of nature; he can only grasp nature in thought. The realization that he is only equal in thought without the power and substantiality of objective nature makes Faust collapse. He feels the Spirit has made "a dwarf" of him, "a nothing" (p. 12). He is a mere worm in the dust that can be crushed to nothing. "What a reversal. . . . A worm and now this," he exclaims as he contemplates suicide as the only heroism open to weakness and smallness (p. 13).

General consciousness is an affirmation that ends in self-negation. General consciousness makes us go in a cycle from a sense of godhood to a sense of insignificance. "Along with this rapture . . . I am given a companion, who with his cold and withering words, humiliates me continually and turns your gifts to nothingness with a whisper" (pp. 56–57). Consciousness of the objective world gives him a sublime sense of a-liveness that ends in a perception of difference, of self-conscious nothingness. He discovers that he is nothingness in relation to it, but he is saved from suicide by discovering that it also is nothing for him. The closeness and divine oneness with nature in which he temporarily believed is an illusion. But in realizing that it is an illusion, he is thrown back upon himself and forced to discover what he alone is without it. As a worm, he gives birth to himself as a new nothingness, as Mephistopheles, as a power to make the sublime objectivity nothing. The world is nothing and he cannot do without this nihilistic attitude toward God because out of it his own self-consciousness is born. He is saved from nothing because he gives birth to it. His nothingness by becoming his own creation is something: the activity and thought of Mephistopheles. Consciousness can be won from the objective world, but self-consciousness can only be won by the self in relation to itself, in discovering the self as an activity of negation, and in discovering the need of the self to relate to another subject—here the woman, the fair form that Mephistopheles shows him in the mirror.

Mephistopheles is the negative that is the great positive in that it is also the spirit, which by showing us our own nothingness, not only as the ability to defy all, but as a need, a lack, an absence, leads us to the other and the experience of love. Mephistopheles is the spirit that makes Faust see the fair form in the mirror, the woman, the other, the answer to our emptiness. Faust's discovery of his nothingness, as a need for or a lack of another, for Gretchen, echoes the negation in Genesis—"*it is* not good that the man should be alone"—which produced Eve.

Thus Mephistopheles, born of the will to die because we are nothing, gives us a new point of departure for consciousness. Faust discovers consciousness in its nothingness to have a double aspect: it is the spirit of negation that by accepting nothingness survives it, and it is the nothingness of absence that teaches us that self-consciousness is only given to us via another consciousness. Mephistopheles enables Faust both to live and to love. The two protagonists of self-consciousness are hence Mephistopheles and the woman. Faust is the man who is the combination of these two. The one leads him to the other. Negation leads him to affirmation.

The devil is "a part of the force that always tries to do evil and always does good" (p. 21); it restores to Faust his sensuous bodily nature, his need for the other, his need to seek not only Gretchen, but Helen, beauty, and art. Goethe's work examines self-consciousness, not consciousness. It is about our relationship not only to the objective other, but to the subjective other, the woman or the things made by man, the things that are like him, that resemble him.

The devil is negation, the ability to say no, perpetual skepticism, nihilism, despair, and emptiness. It is all these things at once, and also the need and lack that drives us once again to seek to experience love and hatred. The devil is also inanity, frivolity, unseriousness, wit, and boredom. He tells the witch not to call him Satan; that is so old-fashioned (p. 41). He is really a Renaissance man with a new secular attitude that escapes the confines of mere morality. These characteristics are not merely lesser advantages of the spirit of negation, enabling us to lose ourselves in other ways than in love—in frivolous pastimes, distraction, wit, indifference, immorality, and unseriousness—but important defenses of our unavoidable guilt and criminality. For another great danger besides suicide that threatens our self-preservation is our becoming guilty in regard to others, in hurting and killing not ourselves but them. In guilt, we feel like Phaedra that we are so bad we do not wish to live.

The devil is the voice in us that separates us from others and lessens our sense of responsibility toward them. As Mephistopheles says of Gretchen, *she* asked for it, and there have been countless others like her. He is the inner voice that says, "Take it lightly; don't be so self-critical." He is the balm of irresponsible moral indifference to others, the voice of egotism that says each is responsible first to himself. This voice which does not identify with others is a necessary voice, a life-voice, not a death-voice. Mephistopheles and the woman together represent Faust's discovery that he has a need for both indifference and identity. He is also the balm of nonsense, gibberish, meaninglessness, mere sexuality, and absurdity. He is the nonfeeling, rationalizing voice without which we would go mad. He is the "reason" that says, "It is all so absurd and nonsensical, how can you apply moral ideas to it?" He is the truth that life goes on despite morals, that these do not encompass it. He is a liar or the truth of our having often lied.

Over! A stupid word.
Why over?
Over and pure nothing, there's no distinction.
What good is eternal creation!
Creation is subject to annihilation!
"Now it's over!" What's its meaning?
It is the same as if it had never been,
And yet it circles as if it were.
For myself, therefore, Eternal Emptiness I prefer.[28]

This is Mephistopheles, pure negation. He equates *vorbei*, the temporal, with nothingness, and his wager is that Faust will also. Faust will renounce striving because nihilism, this constant perishing or dragging of creation into decreation is the truth. But the difference between Faust and Mephistopheles is exactly that the man refuses to equate *vorbei* with nothingness. For Mephistopheles, becoming is nothingness acting "as if" it were something. It is a trick, an illusion of temporality which makes inane, vacuous movement appear purposive. For Faust impermanence is a kind of nothing, but it is all we have.

The grand affirmations, connecting to eternity, such as those that Pico, Ficino, Milton, and Pascal made, are no longer possible, but impermanence, too, is an invitation, an opportunity to make momentary, temporary, incomplete affirmations. Temporality, *vorbei*, is not "ein dummes Wort." "Over" is not nothing but something. The temporal dialectical model is affirmed for its potential, although ungraspable, positive moment. For us there is neither complete, infinite satisfaction nor complete, infinite despair. There are moments of supreme satisfaction where we wish to arrest time, but we are never satisfied to the point of death, to the point of wishing time to cease altogether; we are never, even in bliss, certain that there can be nothing more. It is a certitude that the mystic could have, but not a temporal man like Faust. Affirmation is no longer merely subjective; it is also temporal. Pascal's wager has to be reiterated daily.

The overplus in *vorbei* is the experience of love, and that is the something which saves Faust. The greatest positive that Mephistopheles produces is yearning. Love, that overplus of man's sexuality, saves him because it prevents him from giving in to the voice of indifference and criminality within him, even in a world without God. Goethe affirms that we can, even in a godless world, experience life and meaning without becoming wholly evil, skeptical, or nihilistic. Yet Faust is to the end devil enough to ignore both death and guilt, forces which could make him despair and cease striving.

The great saintly figures, like Christ and Buddha, resisted the devil's pact. Goethe's Faust does not resist it because he experiences it as part of his nature. Yet he escapes it because it is not only his nature to say no. Man, as Marlowe also saw, is in a new alliance not with Christ but with the devil. The spirit of negation is inalienably a part of him, but Goethe makes the first great effort to comprehend this spirit amorally, outside a religious framework. Thus he gives us the first literary analysis of the birth and diverse activity of the spirit of negation within us. Goethe's morality is one of self-realization and self-actualization. Goethe knew that every soul that strives makes a devil's pact. The desire to persist entails the need to change and to negate what one is. The need to be more than nothing produces the need to be. The need to be more than you are provokes simultanously self-hatred and hatred of the objective other, self-destruction and a need for the human other.

Faust opens with the rejection of knowledge and language because man can never comprehend his being purely rationally, contemplatively, cognitively. Man can only know his nature in experience because man is his experience and his becoming, a dynamic, restless, incessant activity. Experience adds the content, the meaning to concepts and to empty words. For language alone is empty and contentless.

The world in *Faust* is not a form, but a force. We are in a temporally sublime world rather than a beautiful world. It is a boundless world, which no reader can even begin to synthesize on first reading. The boundlessness of it is an important aspect of the imaginative experience of this world. The world as becoming can almost not be represented, but here it still is represented as an apprehendable synthesis in formal images of weaving, of the rainbow, and the waterfall. As a synthetic world it echoes the formal presentation of totality in the past, as in the work of Erasmus and Milton. What is different about this synthesis is that it is confusing and contradictory and man can never experience it "clearly and distinctly," without error, misapprehension, distortion, and perplexity. It is a sublime temporal world which, by synthesizing the finitely temporal with the infinitely temporal, produces a vast spatial sense as well. It is an immense, confusing, and overwhelming world of perplexity and pain. *Faust* is the poetic counterpart of the *Phenomenology of Mind*. There is no being here, but only becoming, unrest. Man's nature or essence, in so far as it still makes sense to use such words in this context, matches this unrest of becoming. Mind and world are identical again but only in idea, only as equal dialectical forces.

Faust could only lose his pact with the devil for either of two reasons: one, if he ever ceased to strive because he was satisfied and at rest; or two, if he ceased to strive because nothing he ever achieved was permanent or lasting. But Faust does not lose his pact because he is never either wholly desperate or fulfilled. If Faust could say "linger on," if he could only affirm, then he could release Mephistopheles ("then of your services you would be free"). And thus, he, in a sense, goes to Heaven because he fulfills the ambivalence, the limitation, that God gave him, the limitation of being becoming. Faust's salvation is Goethe's bow to the power that once belonged to objectivity. In the salvation a reversal occurs of the power of striving. Faust is drawn onward. It is not the fact that he aspires which Goethe stresses, but that he is drawn. Our aspiration, so Goethe allows at the end, may be in some kind of alliance with the objective, perhaps even divine other. Our aspiration and striving may merely be a symbol of its drawing power. In the secular world the concrete other that draws man is the erotic–sexual other, but it may merely be a sign of a greater, expectant, erotic force, the *Ewig-Weibliche*. It is finally not there to be had, to be seized and expropriated; finally, it is given, received. We strive, but finally we are met. Even merely temporal satisfactions contain in them a sense of grace which may be a reflection of an ultimate grace. When we are fulfilled, we not only feel that we have attained something, but that something has been given to us.

Hegel

The first great philosopher of negativity and human negation is Hegel. He initiated the age of negativity of which Kierkegaard, Marx, and Nietzsche became the heirs. Like Goethe, he positivized our power of negativity, showing that it is the key to the comprehension of all conscious human activity. Negation makes possible the development both of history and of human consciousness, and is the very reason why the conception of an elaborate and chequered, though rational, evolution had such a flowering in Hegel's philosophy.

What Vico saw as the particularizing and pluralizing power of reason, as its ability to create and proliferate more and more clear and distinct ideas, and as ultimately divisive, confounding, and destructive for the race, is what Hegel calls negativity and is what he celebrates. Negativity is the process and the result of the activity of negation, which is a positive pluralizing and multiplicatory power. Negativity is the diachronic consequence of the activity of negation, which could in Hegel almost be, but never quite is, a synchronic activity and principle. Negation splits and doubles, causing an opposition, and giving birth to an otherness. This otherness is not simply the mean between two extremes, a harmony of opposites, but the new, diachronic creation, off-center, devious, imbalanced, which negativity rescues from negation for the advance of historical development. What Hegel calls mediation is precisely this moment and movement from synchronic negation to diachronic negativity. Hegel explored primarily the diachronic rather than the synchronic possibilities of negation. This is one reason why the concept of a non-centered, dispersed totality was inconceivable to him. Nonetheless, Hegel's world contained in itself, in the idea of negativity, the seed of its own future destruction. The idea of negativity, with its power to particularize, objectify, and produce otherness, disjoined from the idea of a rational evolution, leads toward Nietzsche's vision of a dispersed totality.

Mind itself is for Hegel both total and absolute, and radically particular. Its great "unrest" is its disinterest in the same, the identical, the unified, and the self-enclosed. For Hegel, truth is born when unity is "torn asunder." The moment of the "tearing asunder," not the moment of the "gathering together," is what interests Hegel. This is also why the negative is no longer in Hegel the derived or the secondary, in the sense that the negative sentence is often considered as derived from the base, declarative sentence.

The negative can never again be merely backgrounded because the origin, Absolute Spirit or Mind, is itself already dual and complex, both a something and a nothing, for nothing can in a rational, organic vision grow out of a single point, an unbreakable unity. The beginning is negated at the beginning, in order for it to begin, and *only* thus, in such an action, in such a movement, can it begin, or is there a beginning, a process. This perception about the origin makes Hegel in a sense the precursor of the genealogist proper as defined by Nietzsche and Foucault, the genealogist who sees differences and disparities and for whom the origin is not only dual, contradictory, and dialectical, but multiple, random, and accidental. Yet he is no more than a precursor because, fundamentally, Hegel is a rational historian, concerned with both the continuity and the synthesis that emerge from the diachronic dynamics of negativity.

Each idea is inherently one-sided and inert, until its antithesis, the germ of its own death, is elaborated; it comes alive in its antithesis. What matters to Hegel is the inalienable fact of this antithetical activity of negation, and the idea of mediation. The mediation is what happens with the negation, or the consequence that is negativity. It is a resolution that is not an easy harmony or intermingling. It is not like the predictable orange produced by the mixing of yellow and red, but more like the at first somewhat surprising green produced by the mixing of yellow and blue. It is a new and different creation because it participates in time and reason. Nothing that is temporal can be mediated on a synchronic axis because even while the mediation occurs, we are moving, diachronically, to another level beyond, in time. "Science," as Hegel says, "is not found complete in its initial stages," because the ideas on which it is founded are not static.[29] As soon as we say anything about one of the stages we have designated en route to the acknowledgement of the whole, we alter the nature of that stage, giving it an otherness that differentiates it from itself.

The "catness" produced by cat is not merely a mediation of the particular and general but is the birth of the idea, a new phenomenon added to the particular and the general. It is the idea born in the subject and reborn out of generality. It is the rebirth both of the particular and of the general, the Spirit reborn in the idea and the idea reborn in the subject. The idea is the creation of the mind, and as the mind creates the idea, it creates itself. This is the otherness of reason that always exists in Hegel. Reason seeds the mind; it comes to itself in the particular human mind that discovers the idea in itself. However, the appearing of the idea in the particular mind would, for Hegel, be inexplicable if Absolute

Mind did not exist. The idea is both subject and substance, particularized from the perspective of Absolute Spirit, but from the perspective of the particular subject and the particular object, "catness" is the general or the Spirit reborn out of the particular. Hegelian mediation is never either the particular or the general, but a turning from one to the other, a reaffirmation forever that the two are united and one, that there is one Spirit in its negativity which always points only to itself in its infinite diversity.

Negation establishes an object in its objectivity even in and by conceptualizing it. The concept "cat" "kills" the real cat, but also establishes it as an empirical reality in and by this very act of conceptualization. A double negation occurs here. As the mind thinks "cat," it negates itself in favor of the object; the mind is dominated by its apprehension of the object. Further, the real object is negated by the conceptually apprehended object. This is the double loss or absence of negation. But the concept or predicate into which the subject and object rush or into which they are displaced by the activity of negation is itself not abiding, because the mind will retrieve the concept, an empty generality, and by reflecting on it once again will also split or double itself and its object once again.

Negation splits, doubles, divides, differentiates, and distances; it discovers a break, gap, or suspension in thought itself. Hegel calls the event mediation, and says that our "horrified rejection of mediation . . . arises . . . from want of acquaintance with its nature" (p. 82). For negation or mediation is the unrest or self-movement of thought itself, its becoming, to which the ancients and the modern idealists do not pay enough attention. However, the fact that thought by thinking cannot remain identical to itself or in-itself, that it moves from self-identical generality, which is nothing but an abstraction, to a content, a definition, a predicate, an otherness, is precisely what strikes Hegel as miraculous and astonishing and what makes him think that thought is alive and organic.

> The living substance, further, is that being which is truly subject, or, what is the same thing, is truly realized and actual [*wirklich*] solely in the process of positing itself, or in mediating with its own self in transitions from one state or position to the opposite. As subject it is pure and simple negativity, and just on that account a process of splitting up what is simple and undifferentiated, a process of duplicating and setting factors in opposition, which [process] in turn

is the negation of this indifferent diversity and of the opposition of factors it entails. True reality is merely this process of reinstating self-identity, of reflecting into its own self in and from its other, and is not an original and primal unity as such, not an immediate unity as such. It is the process of its own becoming, the circle which presupposes its end as its purpose, and has its end for its beginning; it becomes concrete and actual only by being carried out, and by the end it involves.

(pp. 80–81)

In Platonic dialecticism the other, the opposite, the remainder, was always either excluded in a true-false logic:

Is Love of something or of nothing?
Of something, surely, he replied . . . .

And does he possess, or does he not possess, that which
he loves and desires?
Probably not, I should say.

or it was mediated or harmonized as a mean between two extremes:

'Hush,' she [Diotima] cried; 'must that be foul
which is not fair?' 'Certainly,' I said. 'And is
that which is not wise ignorant? Do you not see
that there is a mean between wisdom and ignorance?'[30]

The classical mind discovered opposition and differentiation, the fact that the mind breaks naturally into extremes and opposites, ruining the single and self-identical, but it did not dwell long enough on the significance and meaning of the negative. It did not discover the negative as a temporal process of negativity nor as a real moment of objectification. For the ancients and for mere idealism, the negative is synonymous with the lesser or the false. Hegel redefines "falsity" as "otherness," as a crucial dissimilarity. "To know something falsely means that knowledge is not adequate to, is not on equal terms with, its substance. Yet this very dissimilarity is the process of distinction in general, the essential moment in knowing" (pp. 98–99). It is becaue they granted no reality to negativity as otherness or estrangement that the ancients could not establish or constitute the object. They were too anxious for the general, the universal. Therefore in their dialecticism, in so far as it was a subject-object dialectic, the object or the particulars always disappeared.

Theirs was a dialecticism of distillations, an upward movement from particulars to generals, in which the world of the many turned into mere appearance, into phenomenal unreality. Hegel, by stressing the miracle and self-movement of negativity in dialecticism, showed that the world does not merely vanish or become devalued. It is estabished as an objective, empirical reality, and it "disappears" only in the mind because the mind has conceptually understood it as an empirical reality. Hegel's negative dialecticism does not abolish the real object as classical logical dialecticism had. "The real is the universal" is in a sense a true proposition, but it does not mean that the real has ceased to be (p. 121). Rather, the mind has acted on it, making it move from the subject into the predicate, from an in-itselfness into an otherness. Negation is a way of mental domination, but not of derealization or destruction. The ideal negates the real, but without abolishing it, without denying it. In Hegel's negative dialecticism the particular object is established, albeit only conceptually.

With negativity Hegel discovered that what appears to be joined and one, circular and tautological, is only loosely connected, or connected in such a way that it is amenable to disconnection and separation. Negation discovers or uncovers the disconnectedness, disjunction, separability, dispersibility, or "splittability" at the heart of things. For Hegel every split is a positive, an enhancement of Absolute Sprit, and the way to a further split and objectification. He never loses his sense of control over the process of splitting, and it never occurs to him that the ideal, developmental temporal stages he describes may not be necessary nor the activity of an Absolute Mind. Hegel also fails to see that the pluralization produced by his Spirit's negativity creates a mediation that is always a structure of domination. For though the ideal negates the real without abolishing it, his system forgets that the real also remains to negate the ideal. Adorno, for one, quite rightly objects that Hegel's negative dialectics left behind or ignored too much that it relegated to mere nonmind. Hegel is too engaged by the productivity and pluralizing self-movement of the mind to consider that these actions depend upon an original substitution. For actually, negation produces a substitution, a metaphor or, from the perspective of the real cat, only a metonym, a conceptual part for a vital whole. Hegel was concerned only with the organic movement and multiplication of mental substitutions.

The whole, the becoming that is unrest, is only possible because of negativity, and is, therefore, itself negativity. Not to be aware of the negative from the beginning, not to think of the beginning as negativity, is to lack "the seriousness, the suffering, the patience, and the labour" that are all attributes of the negative (p. 81). The idea of a first principle "*is* defective because it is merely the universal, merely a principle, the beginning . . . . The really positive working out of the beginning is at the same time just as much the very reverse, it is a negative attitude towards the principle we start from" (p. 85). The circle (form, unity, self-identity) is a notion that in Hegel "arouses no sense of wonderment." What strikes him as astonishing and great is the negative activity of separation and estrangement, and thus, he makes this activity the basis of his world.

> The action of separating the elements is the exercise of the force of Understanding, the most astonishing and greatest of all powers, or rather the absolute power. The circle, which is self-enclosed and at rest, and, *qua* substance, holds its own moments, is an immediate relation, the immediate, continuous relation of elements with their unity, and hence arouses no sense of wonderment. But that an accident as such, when cut loose from its containing circumference,—that what is bound and held by something else and actual only by being connected with it,—should obtain an existence all its own, gain freedom and independence on its own account—this is the portentous power of the negative; it is the energy of thought, of pure ego. Death, as we may call that unreality, is the most terrible thing, and to keep and hold fast what is dead demands the greatest force of all . . . . But the life of mind is not one that shuns death, and keeps clear of destruction; it endures death and in death maintains its being. It only wins to its truth when it finds itself utterly torn asunder. It is this mighty power, not by being a positive which turns away from the negative, as when we say of anything it is nothing or it is false, and, being then done with it, pass off to something else: on the contrary, mind is this power only by looking the negative in the face, and dwelling with it. This dwelling beside it is the magic power that converts the negative into being.
>
> (p. 93)

Hegel permanently fractured being—that once wondrous circle—because he saw thought as "fracted" and as energized by fracture. Thought is like time, seemingly a continuous, organic stream, but actually punctuated by a series of deaths which produce separations and release autonomous beings. In thought, negativity acts like death, allowing a similar autonomy and independence of concepts and ideas. Death is at the heart of life, but it is also death that creates or allows being. The mind's natural negativity is a formidable and deadly, but productive, power. Death, therefore, in Hegel, is rational, meaningful, and purposive. In a sense, each moment is parent to a child. There may be pain in death and disruption, but there is also meaning in them. By contrast, death in Nietzsche is arbitrary, irrational, violent, and nonpurposive.

For Hegel, continuous death is at the basis of becoming, but death is also inevitable because nothing can be done with the One. Activity and thought can only begin with the two, the split, the separated and doubled, the dismembered and divided. What Hegel laughs off as an impossible beginning for Mind in his metaphysics, Lacan echoes later in his discussion of the ego: "It is autonomous! That's a good one!"[31] It seems that the One, which once was, is an impossibility. One is two. For Lacan the self is the discourse of the other. For Hegel the mind is the otherness of its negativity. Hegel concludes the world of the One and Form, that once beautiful and desirable tautology, by discovering "the portentous power of the negative," the very energy of thought itself, its independence, its egoism.

Nothingness is mere form; negation is force. Nothingness recreated as self-creative negation is the very precondition of our being mind or human. Negation in Hegel is never primarily a way to hide the truth (or rather, to the extent that such an awareness is present in Hegel, it is backgrounded), but a way to seek the truth. For the truth is not one truth, but a continual movement of multiplication in which single truths appear and disappear. The continuous movement of truth, which Hegel called Absolute Spirit, is a form constantly moving within itself. In Hegel, negation is always conscious, patent, and benign. What is negated has been understood. It is not something hidden, repressed, or unconscious.

In Hegel the world roots itself in negativity. It makes negativity its beginning, for it is only thanks to negativity that it can have a pure beginning, that it can be itself and come out of itself and out of nowhere else. In a sense, in Hegel even God no longer creates without negation. An isolate perfect Yes would be meaningless because it would be pure unrecognizable identity, a pure in-itselfness and unawareness.

In Hegel, dialecticism becomes a universal law which embraces both thought and being. Hegel turned the flat, two-dimensional triangle of traditional logical dialecticism into a three-dimensional pyramid. Hegel's transformation of the old dialectical model is a leap like that the Renais-

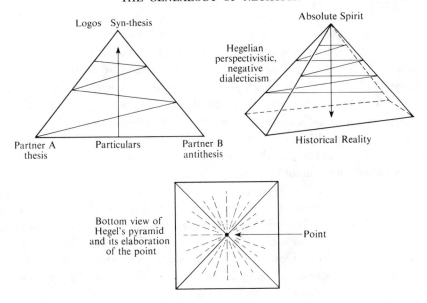

Logos Syn-thesis

Partner A   Particulars   Partner B
thesis   antithesis

Hegelian
perspectivistic,
negative
dialecticism

Absolute Spirit

Historical Reality

Bottom view of
Hegel's pyramid
and its elaboration
of the point

Point

sance made when it transformed the flat, medieval canvas into a canvas with perspective and depths. Just as the Renaissance artists added perspective, so Hegel added negativity, and by doing so he discovered process, self-movement, or temporality. He is the inventor of perspectivistic dialecticism. In him thought turns inward to discover its own depths and dimensions. Before him, so Hegel saw, when the Absolute had been thought of as subject (God, or being, or the One), it had been taken to be a fixed or static point, which assumption had in fact made the realization of the Absolute as subject impossible (pp. 84–85). Therefore, Hegel's task became the elaboration of the Absolute as concrete historical and cultural reality, the elaboration of the point that the ancients had not understood.

The self is now more than a single self even as becoming is more than one truth or stage. The problems of otherness, of multiplicity, of difference, divisiveness, doubling, and selflessness that had formerly appeared as problems between a subject and an object (or the object versus the eidos) are now replayed as problems purely on the inter- and intrasubjective levels. Many of the traditional experiences of man's nothingness, vanity, emptiness, and insubstantiality in relation to an objective other, experiences to which man had responded with self-humiliation, self-reduction, self-negation, self-hatred, self-irony or occasionally by self-glorification, are now analyzed and ordered by Hegel into sequential and temporal stages of consciousness, indicating various degrees and levels of self-awareness. Thus these various theological and theoretical moments in which the self appeared as nothingness compared with being are partial moments of truth, moments eclipsed in the course of the mind's movement to ever-new self-realization. All these moments are positive and comprehendable, but they are also insignificant and irrelevant in that they are superseded by new stages in a potentially infinite movement of truth.

It never occurred to Hegel, as it did to Kierkegaard, that this progressive, forward movement was merely possible and not also necessary. Nor did it occur to Hegel that this movement could be irrational and haphazard rather than rational and systematic. The notion that the development could seem less than a joyous adventure because it could entail an arresting degree of fear and dread is one that he also did not entertain, because those who were worthy confronted death and turned death into being. But we are also afraid to become. We dread to become. Hegel simply overlooks arrested development or regression, very much as he does the case of the suicide, by declaring that the latter is of no interest to him since one who commits suicide ceases to be a world-historical figure.

Thus in Hegel there is no explanation for neurosis, or arrested development, or fixation of any kind. His world is too temporal to allow the elaboration of a stasis, a dialecticism of a stationary and circular kind. Thus there is also no account in his "world of unrest" of boredom, ennui, desirelessness, or idealessness. Rather, the great opposite to the self becomes the self's idea of itself.

The negative in Hegel has in it pain, shock, loss, renunciation, death, and error—but none of these experiences are lasting, nor do they win dominion in this world. Inevitably, rational self-assertion and self-actualization dominate. The self's very becoming is seen as this negativity, a necessary unhappiness from which the self can never be free. Unpleasure, such as Kant discovered in the sublime, is now a permanent part of self-experience. However, in the world-historical figure this unpleasure will never lead to self-condemnation, as it had in Phaedra, but to renewed, rational self-actualization.

The mind, in a sense, is always unhappy in its negativity, its doubling and distancing. But, at the same time, in this double alienation the mind is itself and, in a sense, happy in its own exercise and energy. The self's doubling would be senseless if mediation would not simultaneously be the opportunity of recognition. Hegel's most incisive analyses focus on the dialectical processes of mutual recognition. In Hegel's world, unless we enter into relations we have no meaning.

What is important for us is that the negative moment becomes a constitutive element in Hegel's system, and that now the different interpretations of negativity as contradiction, contrariety, opposition, and polarity become important. However, Hegel opposes the dialecticism of negative reason to the speculative mode of positive reason in which negation is superseded. Speculation is the positive result of negative dialectics, the affirmative that comprehends the differentiations and dissolutions in their totality, and "the ultimate truth not as Substance but as Subject as well" (p. 80). Negation in this system is always definite or *bestimmt*; it focuses on a particular relation. Thus, primary here is no longer the being-nonbeing dialectic, but the something–other dialectic. It is a negation that has to do with plural relationships and objectifications. Our negativity produces the objectifications of history and culture, the substitute worlds that relate to us and recognize us as nature never can. The mind's negativity allows us to fulfill ourselves in Hegel. In Freud, reason distracts us from the "natural" world that continues in ourselves in the id and that makes us seek only the pleasure that the mind forbids us. In Hegel negation is part of the force of reason and not of the id. Organic destruction and creation produce a sense of incessant transience. A sense of self based merely on nature's transience would make the self appear merely as incomprehensible, shifting, fickle, relative, and uncertain, as in Montaigne and Pascal. But the self's negation in Hegel has a telos because the individual self preserves its self-actualization in historical and cultural monuments, those signs of its seeming death. Individually and collectively we do not destroy the child that we are today, but we gently negate our childhood to become something more and something more rational tomorrow.

There is no true-false in Hegel's thought. There is only elaboration and completion. The opposite of the more and of the more complete is the less complete. Hegel's system is without anger, resentment, or hostility toward what has preceded him. The kind of impulse that will surge up in Feuerbach, Marx, Kierkegaard, and Nietzsche for radical criticism and reevaluation, for deconstruction and destruction, is absent in Hegel. Compared to what these thinkers came to believe, Hegel's vision of negativity is innocent. For Hegel, each past age knew itself and knew Spirit in a whole and spiritual way, but each age did not yet know all of itself or of Spirit because Spirit is endlessly flowering. Hegel knew nothing of unconscious negation.

Consciousness begins as an intercourse with objects and comes to know itself as a sensuous awareness of the "here" and "now." That something "is" is all that sensuous consciousness can say. It is born to witness that "it is," only immediately to experience the anxiety of separation, its capacity to feel the difference between the "it" and "I" and the difference between the many "its" which it has to classify, name, and arrange.

There is no development without the experience of separation. The perceptive consciousness negates our sensuous oneness with things in the world, our feeling of being close to them, of merging with this sand on this beach. Examples of the sensuous consciousness occur at moments in Rousseau's reveries when he feels the self almost as a nothing, as a sensuous sensation, but where it is the consciousness that is felt and not nature as such. The perceiving consciousness codes, orders, classifies, and categorizes its new-found distance from things. Sensuous consciousness is our sanity, a state of absolute certitude, a state of receiving rather than perceiving. The perceiving consciousness learns the difference between things and their definitions until it becomes capable of understanding the idea of force and of saying "it—all of nature—is" and "I am," and "We are different."

General consciousness is object oriented. It is more aware of the objective world as such in itself than of itself. At the end of this phase of consciousness we know that nature is and that I am, but the I has no idea precisely what "I" is. However, now consciousness can say: What am I? and by this very question it initiates a stage of self-consciousness, consciousness's desire for itself. Consciousness feels its painful separation from nature and its power to say it is nothing, but simultaneously consciousness also knows that it itself is nothing or nothing more than negativity and negation. Consciousness can say that something is nothing; it feels itself as a deathly force of negation. It is the not-yet-realized, the empty, and yet already a dreadful power. Keats's sonnet "When I have fears that I may cease to be" is an example of the empty "I am" exercising its negative power over all of temporal nature:

—then on the shore
Of the wide world I stand alone, and think
Till Love and Fame to nothingness do sink.[32]

The mind discovers its powers to void all of nature, to make the transcendent all itself a nothing.

This moment of Hegel's description of desire recurs in almost all preromantic texts. In Chateaubriand's *René*, for example, we have the typical case of a hero who desires a self without knowing what this self that he desires is. His very torture is his experience of undefined, indefinite, uncertain selfhood. He is a set of contradictory opposites, energetic and lassitudinous, striving and fickle, hopeful and desperate. What threatens him is not exterior danger but his inner impulsiveness, fickleness, spontaneity, and above all self-destructiveness. The opposites that call René are the vision of the immense creation at the top of the volcano and the infinite abysses below. René's self-image is violent and natural: a volcano is dangerous, destructive, disruptive, unpredictable, and uncontrollable. In this image there is a double vertical pull downwards to nothingness (the world is nothing and the volcanic abyss is nothing) and only a single horizontal line upwards toward infinity. The story fulfills the law of this image: it is imbalanced toward death, the mediating point between these two forces of all and nothing. The death instinct comes to dominate because life is experienced as too unpleasurable, complex, and empty. René's one desire, for suicide, remains unfulfilled, but later it gives his life an interpretation: it is a punishment for this sin of suicide.

René is self-consciousness in a state of desire for itself, knowing itself only in its own negativity. Again and again we have René going out into the world or nature and discovering only that all is nothing. This is part of his sentimentality, his lack of concreteness, his ideality and generality. He asks himself what it is that he seeks and finds he has to answer, "I did not know."[33] His self is permeated by a new dimension of the unknown. All his desiring is a kind of dreaming for which the objective world is not enough. The world is a dream and his own sense of self is but as vague as a dream. Nature is, as Hegel says, but this "dark void of the transcendent and remote super-sensuous" (p. 227) which brings no fulfillment. Thus desire turns itself into a narcissistic, symbiotic love, often born out of nature itself. Nature turns into a woman, a subject. And this ambivalent apprehension of an object as subject is the first sign of self-consciousness's turning to its own needs, to another subject, not to an object. René admits:

> I felt I needed something to fill the vast emptiness of my existence. I went down into the valley and up on the mountain, calling, with all the strength of my desire, for the ideal creature of some future passion. I embraced her in the winds and thought I heard her in the river's moaning. Everything became this vision of my imagination—the stars in the skies and the very principle of life in the universe.
>
> (p. 96)

Thus nature becomes strangely feminized and subjectivized before we break with her completely. Beautiful examples of this feminization of nature occur everywhere in Romantic poetry. Sometimes, however, it is the poet who becomes feminized by the power of this embodied, subjectivized nature.

> Oh! then the calm
> And dead still water lay upon my mind
> Even with a weight of pleasure, and the sky
> Never before so beautiful, sank down
> Into my heart, and held me like a dream.[34]

Wordsworth is compelled by an ecstasy that has weight and substance, death and beauty. Yet the love that he is learning is that for his selfhood. The first other whom we desire is but ourselves.

Preromantic love like that of René is so often incestuous or symbiotic because it is really self-love, self-desire. René's despair turns concrete the moment his sister admits from the tomb her forbidden passion. The tomb turns out to reveal not "some great vision of eternity" (p. 88) but Oedipal sexuality. René is given self-consciousness, but at the same time the possibility of its development is snatched away from him. The plot is almost sadistic in its denial of self-understanding, self-fulfillment, and self-synthesis. René is denied suicide (simplicity, innocence, the inert) only in order to suffer more, to feel guilty and fated, to learn that interiority is negative, dark, and sinful, and that Amelia (his anima) also wants to die because she feels a love that can only be repressed by death or religion. Amelia attains a sense of transcendent selfhood, but she never succeeds in drawing René up from his sense of suffering disjunction.

The secret of selfhood has been revealed to him; it is narcissistic, autoerotic, and incestuous because it is not really desire for the other but for the self. However, as in Hegel, it is the other which reveals to self the object of its desire. Self-consciousness can only develop in relationship to another subject. For Hegel the mind's goal is its own self. But this phase of desire, as we can see especially in romanticism and in the novel's subjectivity, is a dangerous and threatening stage for selfhood because it is a powerful experience both of the self's negativity and of the nothingness of nature, even in its transcendence and sublimity. The stronger romantics were able to convert the negative into being by two different processes: either they dominated nature by feminizing and subjectivizing her or they asserted the power of imagination over the transcendental void of nature. But the weaker romantics and preromantics often either drifted in the vagueness of desire without discovering its goal, or they succumbed to the fearful experience of nothingness and the power in the self to negate.

Another example here is Werther, who moves from his perception of being embraced by the all that is nature to the perception of nature as a devouring abyss. Werther also perceives that in reaching for infinity in either direction man is checked and comes to feel his limitations instead.

> Does he [man] not lack force at the very point where he needs it most? And when he soars upward in joy, or sinks down in suffering, is he not checked in both, is he not returned again to the dull, cold sphere of awareness, just when he was longing to lose himself in the fulness of the infinite?[35]

Werther experiences the fall into the abyss in himself and nature that René barely escapes. He comes to feel only his negativity, his desire to die.

> I want to die! I lay down to sleep, and this morning, in the calm of awakening, that thought still remains firm, still quite strong in my heart: I want to die!—It is not despair, it is the certainty that my sufferings are complete, and that I am sacrificing myself for you. Yes, Lotte! why should I conceal it? One of us three must go, and I will be the one! O my dear! in this torn heart the frenzied thought has slunk about, often—to murder your husband!—or you!—or me!—So be it then!
>
> (pp. 135–36)

Werther is no longer concerned with the options of life or death, but with alternate forms of death: murder or suicide, to kill the other or one's self. Suicide becomes the heroic avoidance of the possibility of murder. Werther dies not in despair over life, but with a sense of sacrifice, of honor, and of martyrdom. To live means to have to be able to tolerate hostility toward others, and Werther, unable to tolerate his murderous thoughts, turns upon himself. Werther's death conforms in large part to the classical Freudian explanation: suicide is murder in the 180th degree; it is unconscious hostility directed toward the introjected (ambivalently viewed) love object. Nonetheless, at its core Werther's suicide is an adventure, a daring exploration: "Look, we are dreaming when we speak of dying. I have seen many a man die; but mankind is so hemmed in that it has no feeling for the beginning and end of its existence" (pp. 149–50). Suicide is part of Werther's search for the boundaries of his identity, the boundaries between himself and others, himself and nature, the boundaries that for him give way everywhere so that he is left without a self.

Phaedra kills herself to rescue a portion of her divine selfhood. Werther kills himself to prove that he feels—his pain and emptiness. In *Werther* time is feeling. Werther's suicide is the consequence of his doubt of the existence of his self-identity as such. "Oh, this void!—this fearful void which I feel here in my breast!" (p. 108). Werther experiences his interiority not as guilt or evil, but as a felt emptiness. This void attracts and obsesses him. He comes to desire it. Werther is not certain that he exists without the other—without a dialectical exchange with the other, whether that other be Lotte, or nature, or God.

> And why should I be ashamed, in the terrible moment when my whole existence is trembling between being and not-being, when the past shines like a flash of lightning over the dark abyss of the future, and everything about me is sinking, and the world going to destruction with me—Isn't it then the voice of the creature which is being driven back into itself, fails to find a self, and irresistibly tumbles to its fall, that groans from the inner depths of its vainly aspiring powers, "My God! my God! why hast thou forsaken me?" And should I be ashamed of that saying, should I be afraid of that moment, seeing that he who rolls up the heavens like a robe did not escape it?
>
> (pp. 112–13)

Werther divinizes his weakness, powerlessness, his lack of selfhood. He gives way to the abyss. Should he be ashamed or afraid of his failure to find a self when there was a moment when Christ himself doubted his innermost sense of self, his being one with the Father? Perhaps all our relations, to God, the world, nature or the other, are the sign of our inability to be separate, to sense and experience existence at all except in mistaken symbiotic relationships? Every authentic separation precipitates mourning, desire, and sorrow. Every real divorce is like a death. Werther sinks into that sorrow and death.

The self's negativity exercises itself on itself. Werther does not have enough self to engage in a battle of domination and submission. He considers briefly the possibility of murder or suicide, but he does not have the strength of self to act on the other, only the strength of self to act on himself. Werther in his self-desire lives in the ambivalence of identifying himself both with the other that is nature and the other that is a subject (Lotte). He experiences both the identity and the separation, but he has not enough strength to tolerate the separation. Losing Lotte and nature, he feels he loses himself. In him, separation does not as yet develop a sense of difference sharp enough to give him a sense of separate being, so he commits and defends the one act that does objectify his interior sense of self: suicide. Suicide here is the symbol of his sense of separation and of the fact that he has no autonomous, separate self. He only feels differentiated suicidally. This is also why he cannot function as an artist; he has no ego, no reality-based sense of self. He has only a mythic, ideal, generalized sense of self, a sense of selfhood dependant on identification with a supportive, substantial otherness, an identification which nature and the other cannot and do not permit. The artist, however, must be able to submit the merely emotional creativity to a medium, an alien, objective material. Werther cannot tolerate any separation, so he is one only with his emotions, running their course, unchecked, in him.

Werther dies of the experience of negativity in desire. He does not have the strength to confront death and to turn it into being, albeit he does glamorize his death as an imitation of the divine sacrifice. But Werther also demonstrates Hegel's point that human desire is more than a desire for self-preservation. It is a desire to be recognized as an autonomous, free independent spirit, even if this desire can only be demonstrated in self-negation. For Werther, suicide is a demonstration, a final word, a communication of the fact that he has felt; it is not merely a skeptical demonstration of the world's vanities, as Timon's suicide was, but an act of self-assertion. Werther dies, dressed in the costume of his desire, demanding recognition for what he was, even while his suicide declares that his desire went unrecognized.

The first desire is a desire to be recognized. This is the very precondition of any kind of human relationship. Any situation in which this is not a given or in which this is denied is alienating and intolerable. At the origin of self-consciousness Hegel posits want, this fight for the recognition of ourselves as human, as spiritual rather than animal. Lovers will want each other to desire not only their bodies but their desires, even if they cannot as yet define these. And indeed these desires can be authentic and strong, as are those of Don Quixote, albeit he initially borrows his desire from a model, or they can be inauthentic and weak if we borrow our desire merely from another's desire, as Werther partly does from Albert. And if the model, whom we imitate or echo, is not a hero or a model of admiration, our desire can come into dreadful conflict with the desire of the other, creating a sense of resentment and superiority, as in the case of Werther. Thus desire cannot only be deflected and perverted by another's desire, as René Girard has amply demonstrated, in a way that never allows your own desire to develop, but your conflict with another can lead you into an empty, destructive self-conflict. Don Quixote, who admires his model and rival Amadis, experiences a rich and original development and elaboration of his desire. Werther, who despises his rival, ends only in self-hatred and self-conflict.

To establish human rather than animal reality, Werther would have to combat Albert spiritually, but Werther escapes the domination–submission struggle by trying to assert an untouchable superiority in death, a superiority that is merely empty and abstract. We need confirmation by another of our desire, because otherwise our idea of ourselves may be wholly false, imaginary, or demented, as Don Quixote's idea of himself would be if Sancho and everyone did not come partly to share it and participate in it. And it is exactly because Werther fails to impose himself or to be recognized except in death that the inauthenticity of death clings to his aspirations. Werther's weak superiority is even more empty and bitter than that of the master, whose domination is also tragic because finally he is only recognized by an unequal, a slave.

The activity of negation and its constant presence in the development of self-consciousness will become more evident when we move to the nineteenth-century novel and the historical era proper of subjectivity. It is not possible to speak of the novel's subjectivity without speaking of negation. But is is in Hegel that the genealogy of negation is made one and equal with the genealogy of affirmation, and that negation is given the power of making history.

However, it is perhaps also right to conclude a chapter that begins in the Renaissance with Hegel because his system as a whole looks both to the past and the future. Paradoxically, Hegel, like Vico, manages to retain the notion of the One, of unity, and of totality by transforming being into a dynamic becoming that is both subject and substance at once. However, unlike Vico, his One is not a stasis, a stillness, a rest. Rest and stability are conditions that Hegel finds neither possible nor desirable. This is simultaneously an achievement and a limitation. For all of Hegel's radical awareness of difference, which he achieves only by granting negation an important place in his system, his ultimate stress is not on difference but on synthesis and identity. Where he can no longer stress identity, he still stresses synthesis. Subject and substance are one and identical. Hegel cannot renounce his belief in totality any more than the Renaissance world could, although these totalities are different in kind. However, he ultimately makes the subjective mind equal to this whole (though not identical with the whole in time) by giving it infinite powers of rational synthesis. Ultimately, there is no struggle for domination between subject and substance: "Spirit is alone Reality" (p. 86). This gives tremendous new powers to the mind—powers no earlier thinkers envisioned—without, however, giving the mind autonomy from substance, as Descartes briefly envisioned doing. In Hegel's world, subjective solipsism is theoretically simply not possible.

Hegel's overall system is a rational affirmation which at its core defies the potential irrationality of negation's pluralizing power. The multiplicity of negation produces ultimately not a world of radical nonidentity and disparateness, but an orderly and unified world of development. Finally there is but one evolving, systematic, and in a sense, monological Spirit. There is a whole to which perfect affirmation, but not negation, can be addressed, because the human subject cannot negate a totality which is both subject and substance at once. Thus Hegel's dialecticism entails negation and historical elaboration, but ultimately this negative dialecticism is surpassed by a positive speculation that reincludes and unites all that has been elaborated and multiplied. He envisions mind as oscillating between inclusion and exclusion, presence and absence, in ever more comprehensive conceptual spirals. We exclude the subject to comprehend the object, then we exclude the object to comprehend the subject, but then we move back again to the object to comprehend it in a new way. The oscillations and the return, on ever-new levels, between the subjective and the objective order are what Octavio Paz sees as the pattern of our recent history. He predicts in his work on Lévi-Strauss that the present structuralist glorification of the objective is bound to end as had the glorification of the subject that began in the seventeenth century. We are in a new era of structual objectivity which can itself not last.[36]

Perhaps the new era will end precisely when we realize once again that negation is like a scissors which cuts our attention, including and excluding, but that the cut need not produce a form or design and its remainder, but merely a set of infinitely explorable, nonidentical possibilities. Negation is empty. It's negative. When I say "it is not raining," I say nothing positive or definitive, but I open up a set of nearly infinite positive and negative possibilities. Or at least this is one radical way of viewing negation. A more conservative way is to say that the negation is circumscribed and limited, opening up only a circumscribed set of logical alternatives.

Hegel himself was not fully aware of the double possibility within dialecticism itself, the fundamental possibility of stressing the dialogos (or dialogue) that is geared toward the logos, or the dialogue that is bound to the Indo-European root *legein*, meaning to gather, sort, read, count, speak, interpret. The more primary root of *leg* is not yet associated with logos and gives us the notion of a nonlogical, open, free, meandering conversation.

The first great example of a nonlogical dialogue is Diderot's *Rameau's Nephew*. Hegel understood the importance of this work, but finally subsumed it under his dia-logical movement. He saw, but could not grant autonomy to, the importance of an open, nonresolved dialogue. Rameau's nephew's mind freely cancels and explores, negating and affirming, as if for the sheer joy of it. Hegel's system as a whole gives us a constant feeling of absence and presence, but finally there must be a reason for the absence and all must be comprehended in a presence. What is ultimately true is the synthesis, the whole, the centered, organic totality. Hegel refuses to renounce the idea that we can grasp it. Despite his importance to the future, Hegel himself was too tied to the past to imagine or foresee that his dearest idea, the astounding power of negativity, would give birth to a totality alien to his own, the concept of a non-centered, dispersed totality. Hegel reversed the direction of classical dialecticism; he stood their logos, as it were, on its head, but he did not reject their logos. He gave it vital, organic characteristics.

There is no dialecticism without negation. There is no dialecticism without exclusion or the remainder, but Hegel wants no exclusion or remainder. Hence there has to be a way of thinking that is superior to negative dialectics. Negation entails a loss, a sacrifice, an absence, to which Hegel, too enamored of totality, ultimately paid no attention. Hegel loved negation because he loved the strain and tension of the remainder, but he did not love it as much as the idea of a totality. Hegel loved the truly dramatic situation of the mind's negativity, but he preferred the for him even more dramatic situation of a totality. Hegel speaks of this drama as one of death and birth, but it is really a drama of presence–absence. Dissimilarity and differences are crucial to the development, but ultimately there is synthesis, and the oneness of totality. Thus in Hegel we culminate in a paradox, we have a new model of the human consciousness based on difference and multiplicity, but this new model is subsumed under an old model of Mind as such as synthesis.

In Hegel, as in Kant's sublime, the mind finds the ground of unpleasure and pain in itself. The sources of its sense of painful alienation are no longer exterior, the result of moral or theological preconditions of sin and guilt. The mind creates unpleasure for itself by itself, autonomously. The pain of life is a relation of the mind to itself. Thus every novel hero must confront himself in his search for the sources of his perplexity and disillusionment. Pain is no longer avoidable by faith or the ethical life; it can only be transmuted into self-awareness.

After Hegel there is no poetics that is not also simultaneously a poetics of negation. Hegel himself initiated such a poetics in his aesthetics, the first comprehensive theory of art, which explains art's evolution as emerging from the mind's evolving need to duplicate its spiritual self-awareness in sensuous objectivity. Primitive, symbolic art pushed its awareness of its subjective power into stones and huge external forms, reaching perfection in architecture. Here spiritual self-awareness is awesome and powerful, but dim and confused, as is the spiritual sense evoked for example, by Stonehenge or the Sphinx. Classical art found the perfect sensuous object in which to represent itself, the human body. Greek sculpture is the perfect example of the mind expressing itself in sensuous materiality. In romantic art, the human spirit feels alienated from the natural, sensuous body. It is a stage of art that necessitates a negative portrayal of nature, the body, the sensuous. Here inwardness triumphs over the world and seeks to express itself in media in which externality is already abstracted, in painting, language, and music. For Hegel, the latter two arts in particular negate sensuousness by converting visibility into audibility. Thus music and poetry, insofar as words too are merely sound, allow the mind to reflect its inner time of ideas and feelings, its living movement and operation.

At the end of the introduction to *The Philosophy of Fine Art*, Hegel speaks of the wide pantheon of art as an essentially infinite enterprise, "to complete which the history of the world will need its evolution of centuries."[37] But at the same time, he speaks of art as "a thing of the past" which the reflective culture of his time makes more problematic and difficult. "The present time is not . . . favorable to art" (p. 13). What Hegel meant by that was, first, that the living, sensuous creation which defines the existence of a work of art is unlikely ever again to be as exterior, as molded into reality, as Greek and medieval art had been. Second, the very reflectivity and inwardness of the mind, which now make necessary a theory of art, lead the mind away from sensuousness toward scientific theory as such. Artworks become infected and over-burdened by thought and no artist can abstract himself from his reflective culture. Hegel seems to be doubting the capacity of the mind to continue to forge its sensuous opposite, the mind's power, as it were, to give birth to sensuousness. And possibly that is because Hegel's whole system repressed the sensuous as such. However, when we turn to a highly reflective work like Beckett's *The Unnamable*, what we find is a new sensuousness discovered in language itself. What carries and em-bodies both the sensuous and the spiritual now is the sign. The signifier is its body; the signified is its spirit. And one cannot escape feeling the weight and reality of the other. Beckett uncovers a new body, a new sensuousness within language, but because of negation, the activity that separates, and pluralizes, and manages thereby here to flood language with sensuousness.

Hegel employs negation to explain the evolution of art, but, finally, as in the *Phenomenology*, he abandons his faith in the activity of negation, because the ultimately real is rational. Unlike the case of Kant's sub-lime, the feeling here of our noumenality in the face of art or nature is not something static, but something evolving and changing. Further-more, Hegel does not think that we merely feel something in relation to the work of art, but that we know something because we have made the work of art, which in turn knows what we know and can reflect it back to us. Hegel as yet could not see that the conceptual world which he built rested on language, which was itself a body (a substance, a signifier) and a signified (a meaning, spirit), and which itself entailed negation and affirmations, inclusion and exclusion, and that therefore his ultimate affirmations were subject to language's play of presence and absence.

In Hegel, the activity of negation institutes a temporal, secular world. Negation establishes what will turn out to be an unhealable world of differentiation and difference, radically particularized and plural. The potential discontinuity, dissonance, and disorder of such a plural world is what Hegel did not want to recognize. Instead he wanted to achieve something sublime and almost Biblical—a world of separate, free forms, a whole in which creation is not an experience of alienation. To achieve this, negation grows, as if demented and omnipotent, into a belief that Mind itself can dominate and synthesize the huge brood of the differentiated that is its own achievement and creation. The ultimate war of domination in Hegel's system is fought between his negative dialecticism and his positive speculation, and in this war negation is used against itself, as it were, as a totalizing idea to establish the speculative synthesis. This final use of negation which underpins Hegel's faith in an absolute, rational synthesis cannot but be a delusion, a delusion of the mind itself.

CHAPTER 2

The Novel
and the Self's
Negativity

I am characterizing this agency [the ego] here not by the theoretical construction that Freud gives of it in his metapsychology . . . but by the phenomenological essence that he recognizes as being in experience the most constant attribute of the ego, namely, *Verneinung*, the givens of which he urges us to appreciate in the most general index of a prejudicial inversion.

Lacan

The novel is a great discovery: far greater than Galileo's telescope or somebody else's wireless. The novel is the highest form of human expression so far attained. Why? Because it is so incapable of the absolute.

D. H. Lawrence

God created *ex nihilo*, but without negation the novelist cannot. His creation *ex nihilo* presupposes negation. Austen's *Emma* begins with an ideal, hyperbolic authorial affirmation, instantly qualified and almost withdrawn. The novel's process turns into the process of the negation of its initial affirmation, the positive that is suspect from the beginning.

> Emma Woodhouse, handsome, clever, and rich, with a comfortable home and a happy disposition, seemed to unite some of the best blessings of existence; and had lived nearly twenty-one years in the world with very little to distress or vex her. . . .
> The real evils indeed of Emma's situation were the power of having rather too much her own way, and a disposition to think a little too well of herself; these were the disadvantages which threatened alloy to her many enjoyments. The danger, however, was at present so unperceived, that they did not by any means rank as misfortunes with her.[1]

The word "seemed," and its connection to the problem of appearances and reality elaborated in the subsequent paragraphs, introduces the reversal.

The dazzling opening dream-image of happy, independent selfhood in

Emma dazzles no one more than Emma herself. It is a generalized self-image of how she would like to appear to be in her own eyes and in the eyes of others. It is a positive image produced by self-love and substantiated by the recognition and unqualified admiration of others. The image is Emma's self-objectification, her self's idea of itself. It is supported and guaranteed reality by her father's uncritical recognition of her as perfect or by his demand that she be perfect: "and never, never could I expect to be so truly beloved and important; so always first and always right in any man's eyes as I am in my father's" (p. 58). Emma is handsome, clever, rich, seemingly untroubled, free, powerful, and independent. It does not occur to her to question the value or real-life possibility of being "always first" and "always right"; the condition is too pleasurable for that. Nor can she morally or emotionally question the value of being "first" and "right" in the eyes particularly of her father, a man who is himself, ironically, rather imperfect.

Austen, however, questions immediately whether such a notion of selfhood is surface, illusion, appearance: a "seeming" rather than a reality. She suggests that it may be a fairy-tale, dream-image of autonomous selfhood, containing "dangers," "evils," and "disadvantages" which Emma cannot see or does not wish to see, and which she comes only to see, in a sense, with the help of a false "artistic" creation.

Emma's problem is not like René's or Werther's. They do not know who they are. They are the empty sublime self, severed from nature. Emma, by contrast, thinks she knows who she is. She is the "sublime" social self. She is the "master" who is recognized by others but who feels little need to recognize them. She maintains herself at the expense of those others, whom she negates and whose condition she claims not to share, who are her "slaves," and who submit to her. She only recognizes those who recognize her as the one she believes herself to be.

Emma thinks of herself as a self-sufficient, self-contained form, a unity, a perfect circle. The self's first idea of itslf is imperious, absolute, and autonomous. In order to be, the autonomous ego must be distinct from other egos, centric, and rounded in itself; it cannot really recognize others. The social "sublime" is a sense not of coexistence but of autonomous superiority. "I am I," unlike anyone else, and superior to everyone else. The belief rests on a disbelief that anyone else is equal to the self or shares the powers that the self believes itself to have. The self is felt to be unique, and this sense of uniqueness must be maintained and asserted. Above all, this self refuses the idea that it itself is in any way enslaved, as Emma obviously is by her own idea of superiority.

An ego ideal such as Emma's can only be maintained by denying any identity with others. The self is itself; it is not like others. Any similarity with others has to be violently negated, for this self rests on its sense of difference from all others, and this difference is a superiority to others. Others are regarded in terms of what they are not or have not compared to what she is and has. If there is anything that another has or is not, that something has to be relegated immediately to the status of the unimportant, indifferent, or inessential. The self has to repudiate it strongly. To be what she is, to maintain her identity, Emma has to negate or make irrelevant what she is not at that moment.

Emma is unmarried. That is the one thing she is not and has not. And the need to be married in this society, paradoxically to maintain one's autonomy, power, and superiority, is one outstanding factor that contradicts from the beginning Emma's dream of selfhood. Marriage is, in this society, essential and basic. Emma has to break the autonomy of the self, if not for instinctual reasons, then for social reasons. For marriage is the only way to maintain the "sublime" social self.

The self is largely negative. It rests upon and maintains itself by exclusions. The novelist's labor is partly the activity of finding ways to reinclude and reinsert into the self what it excludes and negates. The novelist must move the self from a position of self-affirmation that rests largely on negation and that is mere in-itselfness and unawareness to a new position of self-awareness and self-affirmation where at least some of the self's self-defensive negations can be abandoned. This is Austen's primary task and the technique that she uses to accomplish her end is itself a technique of negation, a way of making present by consciously allowing and accentuating denials.

Emma's initial, glamorous self-affirmation hinges upon the denial that she will ever marry. It is out of this denial that Austen builds the rich irony and drama of her novel. "And I am not only, not going to be married, at present, but have very little intention of ever marrying at all" (p. 57). Austen knows as well as Mr. Knightley that this declaration of never marrying "means just nothing at all" (p. 26). The very certitude and absoluteness with which it is stated makes it suspect, as do the elaborate, defensive rationalizations by which it has to be proven.

Emma's declaration is a classic example of Freud's definition of the function of conscious negation. Conscious negation is, for Freud, a kind of miracle, a leap from unconsciousness to consciousness which allows us to release material from the unconscious on condition that we lie. When the patient says, "It is not my mother" (or "I will never marry"), we can ignore the "not," argues Freud, because the unconscious association is more primary than negation. Conscious negation and negative judgments free us, at least indirectly, from repression. We can at least speak about what is not or is not to be. Emma's declaration is a "symbol of negation," in Freud's sense, because it reveals the truth (Emma must marry) by denying and hiding it.[2]

Austen, knowing this, makes her novelistic form a drama of conscious negations and revelations in which every sentence and scene has behind it the weight of something denied and negated by consciouness. Austen uses conscious negation to illuminate unacknowledged affirmation or desire. Austen's irony is this very sense of the presence and pressure of the excluded and negated. The systematic, orderly, and coherent character of this irony, and the effect of ironic restraint that this coherence produces, derive from the monadic and simple characteristics of the negation and from its conscious aspect. The humor, however, lies largely in the repetition of the negation in situations that point ever more to its unconscious, symbolic aspect.

Austen's use of traditional ironic negation is new because she stresses and plays upon the psychological dimension of conscious negation. Emma's negations, which are synonymous with her youthful blindness and self-deception, rest not upon objective facts that are concealed or hidden from her (as Oedipus's heritage, for example, is from him), but upon the subjective concealment of deeper motives and desires of the self from itself. Emma cannot allow this other self to emerge because it contradicts both what she consciously thinks she is and what she consciously must be, the dutiful daughter to a father whose ideas on matrimony are purely negative and who cannot be abandoned. The self's conscious negativity is a power of self-prohibition which systematizes and organizes the self, but never adequately or permanently.

Austen's ironic knowledge of the mechanisms of conscious negation makes itself felt from the beginning when she lets Emma appear as a matchmaker, but seemingly only for others, not for herself. To do it for others, however, is clearly a vicarious way of exploring the idea of a suitable partnership for the self. It is the subjective aspect that obviously makes the play of matchmaking both so pleasurable and necessary that it cannot be renounced. When Knightley questions her success or demonstration of power in this role, his criticisms have to be quickly deflected both for her own sake and that of her father. The self's idea of its perfection has to be maintained and fought for. And her father's partnership in this idea is equally important, albeit narcissistic: "she would not have him really suspect such a circumstance as her not being thought perfect by everybody" (p. 5).

Again and again, the dialogic scenes, such as the opening one with Knightley, are Emma's chance to see a larger truth and to modify the dream-image of selfhood; yet repeatedly Emma repudiates the annoying other voices because she cannot renounce the image of her self constructed jointly by her father and herself in their narcissistic partnership. Knightley's rational criticisms have no effect on her because what she needs to realize and to incorporate into consciousness is something repressed, unknown, and semi-conscious. The conscious errors she commits in her matchmaking activities have their source in her drivenness by an as yet unacknowledged and unconscious necessity.

The self that she has constructed is clear, certain, and functional. To tamper with it seems nothing less than to lose certainty and the pleasurable reverence, even idolatry, of her father. Nonrecognition of the self in its idea by others puts it in jeopardy and doubt. Thus Knightley, the nonrecognizer, is the one who is recognized last. He is the final possible marital partner whom Emma singles out and identifies, and identifies only thanks to her alter ego, Harriet, her negative artistic creation.

The self's negativity in the social world is a power to turn others to nought, to dominate them, and to invalidate their reality. Emma's self-affirmation rests upon this negative power. Emma makes Harriet her "slave," one who believes in her and her self-image of superiority and perfection. She enjoys Harriet's deference and gratitude; it is essential that she be shy, grateful, impressed, and malleable. Emma's interest in Harriet seems like "kindness," but it is also an exercise in power. Her domination of Harriet is benignly authoritarian but total. Then, after making sure of her dominion over Harriet, Emma, paradoxically, does the reverse: she tries to make Harriet a "master."

Emma willfully distorts Harriet's rank, abilities, experience—even her physique. Emma makes Harriet more than she is, excluding and ignoring her deficiencies and social inferiority, in order to make her a surrogate self. Harriet is not merely a puppet, she is a dramatic double, as much like Emma as self-deception can allow, and one whom Emma makes play the game of courtship for her. Emma duplicates herself in order to explore her own possibilities and to find herself. Harriet is a self-substitute, a self-projection, a way for Emma vicariously and imaginatively to flirt with the idea of marriage that obsesses her. She is Emma's subjective creation, her narcissistic "work of art." But this artistic creation is false and negative because it does not capture the real Harriet. Nonetheless, even a deficient and defective fictional creation has the power to evoke recognitions and detachment. Ultimately, Emma's distortion of Harriet, her energetic enterprise of imagining and creating her, serves her (Emma) in ways that she cannot anticipate. Harriet discovers for her whom she loves and respects, sparing Emma all declarations of love and marriage. Emma discovers, ironically, not whom *she* must marry, but whom *Knightley* must marry. Emma's road is an ironic *via negativa* all the way.

To appropriate Harriet and to secure her for her own experiments, she has to cut her off from other influences and possibilities. She severs her ties to others by an arbitrary and willful misinterpretation of the Martins: "they *must* be coarse; they *must* be doing her harm." The "must" here connotes a nonexistent necessity that is but Emma's own— her exigency, her willfulness, her convenience, her urge to control, imagine, impose, and discover. Emma "rewards" Harriet for writing an answer of "no" to Martin's proposal by telling her that as Mrs. Robert Martin she would have lost her friendship: "I could not have visited Mrs. Robert Martin, of Abbey-Mill Farm" (p. 35). It is an ugly form of emotional blackmail and social domination, prompted by unconscious personal and selfish ends.

Emma's need of Harriet makes clear the problem of the "sublime" social self. No ego can develop and find itself except by risking itself in the struggle with another self or ego. Since Emma cannot, for various reasons, risk her autonomous selfhood directly, she needs another, like herself, to play out her own fantasy life, fears, and possibilities. She flirts with Elton for Harriet—so much so that everyone, including Elton, thinks of him as a match for her. When he proposes, she is shocked, outraged, and bewildered, and she attributes the error largely to him. "His manners, however, must have been unmarked, wavering, dubious, or she could not have been so misled" (p. 91). The ambiguity of her own behavior is quickly projected onto him. Emma cannot acknowledge that Harriet is an emotional outlet, a way for Emma's own emotion to slide ambiguously between the self and another, appearing and disappearing there in the other.

The tantalizing play of a conscious negation that is so obviously a need for self-affirmation (Emma's conditional playing with marriage) continues.

> Now, it so happened that in spite of Emma's resolution of never marrying. . . . She had frequently thought . . . that if she *were* to marry, he [Frank Churchill] was the very person to suit her in age, character and condition.
>
> (pp. 80–81)

She imagines that she "must be in love" (p. 178), as the need to be in love and to marry becomes somewhat more clear and conscious to her. Finally, she discovers not so much whom she loves and must marry, but who *must* marry her. "Knightley must marry no one but herself" (p. 280). Knightley is the truth of Emma's social soul and conscience. He alone is the equal with whom she can maintain her autonomous social self while extending and securing its power and superiority. To marry Knightley is not really to marry another but her own rational, ethical, and social potential. Knightley is the same, higher self, not another self.

Comically, Knightley is the ideal replacement for Miss Taylor, lost at the beginning of the novel, whose presence Emma cannot do without. For the absence of Miss Taylor put Emma "in great danger of suffering from intellectual solitude. She dearly loved her father, but he was no companion for her. He could not meet her in conversation, rational or playful" (p. 2). The truth is that out of conscience and duty she could not consciously consider abandoning her father. And the truth is also that his companionship is in actuality often a trial and an unpleasure. So Emma is unconsciously torn and ambivalent, divided between the narcissistic pleasure and the unpleasure that her father gives her. Knightley, however, is a new companion for herself and, no less important, for her father. Emma's conflict between duty to a father who adores her, but who is crochety, valetudinarian, and difficult, and to independent self-affirmation are resolved by Knightley's offer to move to Hartfield. Now an unstated anxiety that lay repressed beneath her conscious negations, an anxiety which duty, propriety, and narcissism united to bid Emma conceal, can be voiced: "Such a companion for herself in the

THE NOVEL AND THE SELF'S NEGATIVITY

periods of anxiety and cheerlessness before her!—Such a partner in all those duties and cares to which time must be giving increase of melancholy!" (p. 310). Emma's marrying entailed from the beginning a double problem and the need for a double solution, both that of her own self and her position and that of a dependent parent. Hence she could indeed never marry unless a number of conditions were first met and a number of problems were first resolved. The real, but hidden, problem of the parent is moved to the foreground only when all the other problems are finally resolved.

Emma discovers whom she must marry by discovering whom Knightley must not marry, not someone beneath him, not Harriet, not a social unequal. In discovering this she also rediscovers the difference, the social inequality between Harriet and herself which she had tried so hard to deny, and had continued to deny despite Knightley's warning, because a substitute self was temporarily so necessary to her unconscious drive. When this drive finds its expression and goal, she can see consciously, clearly again and face the errors, social and moral, (or, to put it less severely, "imaginative") that she has committed during the time of her self-deception. Now Emma can abandon what had previously appeared so necessary (never marrying) because she discovers a new necessity. It is in that quick substitution of necessities that Emma salvages her old self-image. Emma does not change. In fact rather than denying her self-image, she reinforces it and her narcissistic pleasure in it. She includes Knightley in her partnership with her father. Thus, whereas he may reprimand her and correct her imaginative excesses, her father will continue to praise her and, unbeknownst to her, to manipulate her and to "enslave" her, paradoxically, to her idea of herself as unenslaved. Emma rescues her narcissistic pleasure in herself by securing her union with her father. She merely adds Knightley to guarantee that her social sense of selfhood, which she has never abandoned, will predominate over her wayward imaginative, "artistic" leanings.

Notable in the moment of her recognition is her use of the word "must"—that word of necessity, of certitude and order, that she had used and misused so often before. The word expresses her desire for the necessary, indubitable, stable, certain, formal, and proper. It expresses the whole social and moral world of *Emma* (and also the neoclassical artistic world of Austen) and simultaneously its limitations. Ironically, when Emma had said earlier "it must be so," it was precisely not so. She was precipitous in her desire, and deceived. This time she is right in the context of her narrow social order with its narrow conception of self-hood. "It must be so" if there is fundamentally to be no change. In Emma's world the goal is not change but stasis and form. When any disequilibrium appears, calling for a reordering and a restructuring of relationships, the new order and relationships have to recreate and reestablish the old order as closely as possible. The ideal of this social world is to minimize change. Her father is an extreme and ironic example of the fear of change, but Emma is nonetheless part of the world of her father, and she knows its rules as well. Her use of the word "must," albeit earlier misapplied, reflects her fundamental mentality. There are "musts," there is a right and necessary order, and there is certitude. Her repeated use of "must" gives us a sense of her identity, her persistence in time, and it also tells us that her whole world is one of identity, of the recreation of the same and similar because the great advantage of the same, of the identical, is that it can be known and recognized. Emma's recognition is a taking cognizance of what was already known and there. The truth is not new and different, but the old and familiar. The world and the heroine appear to be fundamentally epistemological, in the realm of the consciously knowable and recognizable. Emma's recognition does not change her, for that would be registered in a change of language and vocabulary, in the discovery of the new, the unknown.

Samuel Johnson, whom Austen so much admired, wrote in *Rasselas*, "If that which is known may be overruled by that which is unknown, no being, not omniscient, can arrive at certainty."[3] Johnson's statement is paradigmatic for the conservative principle of adherence to the known, the preexistent, the established. To adhere or even to conspire with the established, the known or knowable, or by extension with the palpable, present, perceivable, the empirical and rational, in the widest sense, has its rewards and advantages; primary among these is the sense of certitude, form, order, and stability. Johnson had no method or way of dealing with radical incertitude and the unknown. He thought these would lead to madness and disorientation. He did not wish to push his thought to the point where it would inherently come to entail the unknown, but we can say that, in a sense, to think about the known does not entail thought. Johnson's ideal was the domination of life by reason. He feared the imagination and the unconscious with its drives, wishes, and desires, for reason, as he saw, could not in fact always dominate them.

Hence, Johnson's rather dark, dreary, and pessimistic humanism, his failure to appreciate the imagination (based on rational fears), and the arrest of his thought in the known because the known can be affirmed. As Bergson thought, one problem with the unknown is that it can never be affirmed.[4] To affirm the unknown appears impossible or like making a substanceless, empty affirmation.

Austen understood somewhat better than Johnson that the very processes of consciousness as well as language entail both negation and affirmation, and that they function not only to make something present to us but to exclude us from something else. We seize a portion of reality, of the known, and affirm it only on condition that we exclude, or repress, or negate something else. Austen allows her novel to be impelled and haunted by the excluded, and she employs a vocabulary of negation to illuminate the excluded, the consciously and verbally negated and unknown. Austen does not let the unknown overrule the known any more than Johnson did, but she does, as an ironist, allow a break and a disjunction between the known and an unknown knowable. Her irony allows her to acknowledge that a change in the known is to some extent inevitable, and that imagination or "appearances" are as much the consequence as the cause of this change. She sees that there is no stability in conscious knowing, but she does not fully understand the implications of this insight.

The unknown with which Emma has to deal is, to borrow Bachelard's term, a "precise" or limited unknown.[5] Emma does not have to deal with an infinite negativity, an open and infinite unknown, and her negations make no such infinite unknown available to her. She is arrested in the epistemologically knowable, in a social self and in a fixed set of relationships to others. She reidentifies herself as the same self she was at the beginning, as the socially "sublime," as the master whose errors of self-deception were limited. The "humility and circumspection" (p. 328) Emma "learns" entail, for example, knowing now what she should have remembered earlier, that "the intimacy between her [Harriet] and Emma must sink; their friendship must change into a calmer sort of goodwill" (p. 333). In the course of the novel, the fundamental stage of selfhood described is not surpassed; it is merely clarified and secured.

For Hegel the explanation would lie in the fact that the self that sees itself as the master cannot change; this self can only reaffirm itself in its domination over others. In Hegel only the self that has recognized its enslavement must change, for the "slave" is the first in history who has to study his own condition for the sake of his survival. He is the first to really recognize and know another or to know that others exist, to come to know the true problems of coexistence and, with that, the full force of negativity in the self both toward oneself and others. The greater novelists of the nineteenth century all focus on the "slave" (not on the "master"), on him who discovers his interiority together with his negativity, as Emma never does. The narrow sense of selfhood portrayed here fundamentally lacks the need of the others, the anguish of necessary coexistence.

Knightley can attempt to criticize and correct Emma in her temporary aberration and self-deception (though not succeed, because as a mere moralist rather than a psychologist he cannot see the deeper, hidden motives for her distortions of Harriet, for example), but ultimately there is really no one in the novel to negate or change Emma. In fact, the entire novel is as if constituted of one character, Emma herself. All the other characters merely *appear* to have an autonomous existence; structurally, they all function as elaborations and clarifications of Emma herself. They are all as if emanations out of Emma herself, parts of her being become full-fledged, independent characters. Each reflects or mirrors an aspect, habit, condition, or characteristic in the heroine that Austen wishes to stress, ironize, or make especially visible. Thus Miss Bates reflects her condition of being an unmarried daughter; Mrs. Elton her snobbery and dilettantism; Frank Churchill her domination of others and her capacity for concealment (ironically, by manipulating her), and so on.

Each of these mirror-images stands in a dialectical relationship of opposition, similitude, contradiction, or contrariety to Emma and to each other. Together they are a "speech" that articulates Emma. Their primary purpose and function is to deepen the portrayal of Emma and to make evident that her innermost self is social, as theirs is. All the characters are linked in this way because this is not yet a social world of radically differentiated and autonomous individuals, a condition which would make the idea of social harmony utterly problematic. This formal coherence of characters, which is simultaneously social and psychological, also declares that Austen did not as yet know or have the need for a deeper conception of interiority. Austen uses the surface of the novel to elaborate one of its points in depth. And in a sense, Austen also uses the method because she has no other alternative, because Emma herself lacks the depth of interiority that can portray itself or, we should say, that needs to portray itself. The master cannot know himself. Thus the multiplicity and diversity of independent character creation is ultimately controlled and restrained in *Emma* by an idea of character coherence. A radical differentiation of characters cannot and does not take place.

On the one hand, complete, dramatic character coherence, the mirrored interreflection of all characters, is a special formal and structural achievement of Austen herself. It is a way in which she surpasses Fielding, who managed to dramatize the novel by giving it plot coherence, and it gives her novel its famous neoclassical economy, that absolute sense of a lack of excess. On the other hand, Austen's character coherence reveals her lack of artistic freedom in relation to the creation of autonomous characters, and further, the limitations of her creativity as a whole. Secretly, the formal character coherence is in collusion with Emma's sense of her identity, an identity that rests on a difference merely of social superiority. The structuration of characters both confirms her importance and centrality and ironically negates the degree of superiority and difference from others that Emma assumes. She *is* the most important person in Highbury, albeit not the only one. The reaffirmation of her social place guarantees the lesser places of all the others. To negate Emma in her fundamental identity would be to negate the society as a whole.

The social order, like the order of the self here, is closed and narrow; the possibilities for displacement and dislocation are inherently limited. The society, like the self, can be criticized and corrected, but not changed. It is a social order disconnected from the truly changing and temporal historical forces. In this novel the social world substitutes for the lost world of being, of stasis, and presence. It is the world toward which affirmation is directed and in which it is sought. Austen can question the subject as a knower and ironize and negate its self-assurance, but she does not question the object to be known by the fully socialized self. This object and the self that knows it may be in error, but they can never be portrayed as contingent, unnecessary, and dissolvable. The individual inheres in a fixed social matrix and its fate is derived from that matrix. Thus Emma's autonomy is merely her given social place. She is not yet an individual free in relationship to society and historical forces.

What Emma attempts to negate, what is unconscious in her character, is therefore from the beginning conscious and ironically present in the structure of the novel: her marriage, her full social destiny or fate. It is this social structure or being that her character finally unites with and in which she finds her resolution.

The self is finally and still "ex-centric" to itself. It now affirms itself by affirming its social rather than divine ex-centricity. Emma was deluded only in thinking that she could maintain her social superiority purely in her independent autonomy. That social superiority entails, however, a full recognition of society and its codes. Emma is the form, the unity, the circle that she had believed herself to be, only this form and unity is the larger circle of her being in society.

Austen's novelistic form, despite its neoclassical perfection and closure, is less closed than the closed society and closed sense of selfhood that it represents. This paradoxical aesthetic opening in closure is the gift of her irony.

> Seldom, very seldom, does complete truth belong to any human disclosure; seldom can it happen that something is not a little disguised, or a little mistaken.
>
> (p. 297)

Austen's irony is epistemic. She knows that the mind, with its limitations, ignorance, and imaginings, cannot, in the final instance, be closed, a "must," a certitude. Her irony, by ironizing the possibility of self-knowledge, of epistemological truth, also ironizes indirectly Emma's earned sense of necessity and certitude. And her structure, which is a pattern and process of disclosures and revelations right up to the end, makes a small break in her own world of artistic, formal being. Every reality or truth (or, by implication, formed fiction) turns but into another surface, hiding yet another reality or a deeper motive. Our knowledge of reality (our portrayal of it) and of ourselves is always potentially illusory, inadequate, and ignorant. For her heroine this means, as Austen finally suggests, that Emma's conscious negations have their basis in an unconscious repression, an ambivalence toward her father that Emma truly knows consciously nothing about. However, the potential problem of the autonomy and independence of the unconscious is not and cannot be addressed, for Austen's irony extends only to consciousness and glimpses the unconscious as if inadvertently and without recognition.

For her as a novelist, this self-succession of "truths" means that only Socratic irony is wisdom. By this irony Austen is "above" the content and even the form of her novel. Irony allows her both to structure it as she has, by negations, and to escape from it. The negativity of irony gives her freedom from establishing an ultimate, final knowledge because, as she says, this knowledge can never be perceived. We are never illusionless.

Irony is a metasubjective posture, a release from the subjective need for truth, closure, and form. Hence, it is an escape from art, the formed and finalized. But it is also the realization of the novel form as fiction because as fiction the novel is the perfect objective correlative of epistemic irony. Neoclassical irony permits a detachment from the novel as an art form, a detachment which the post-romantic, realistic novel will find far more difficult to achieve.

Austen's irony lends her novel an epistemic temporality, a sense of becoming in knowing, but not a sense of social-historical temporality. The *process* of knowing is disjunct from the social-historical stasis, and does not truly affect the latter. The stasis of the latter, however, infects the former and is the ultimate source of the sense of ironic restraint in Austen. For the negativity of irony is potentially infinite, a dissolution of all into paradoxy. Austen's ironic negativity is finite, a balance of the known and the potentially knowable unknown. It is a limited epistemic negativity, a vision, not of radical paradoxy or of potential meaninglessness, but of the postponement or delay of knowledge. Another way to put it is to say simply that her irony is rational and not Kierkegaardian.

This postponement of knowledge creates a gap between Austen and her characters, who seek a realization in knowledge. It is the experience of a force hovering above the stasis of her created world, and yet it is ultimately not disconnected from this world. The shock of the negative in irony troubles Austen's known world without its ceasing to be a known and knowable world, just as it troubles her aesthetic form without its ceasing to be form. It illuminates this world without destroying it. The self's epistemological nature is more opaque than neoclassicism had assumed. It has a new dimension of hidden selfhood which did not exist in Fielding, for example, but this new, less accessible level of selfhood can still be exteriorized and the hidden dimension of the self can be brought to light by the processes of conscious negation.

Like all true ironists, Austen is spellbound by contradictions, but the ones she cares most about are conscious and psychological. She is limited to reincluding only those revealed by the symbol of negation—the strong, excessive negation that carries its own opposite in its shadow. Austen labors to make the shadows evident in order to achieve a balance of knowing and nescience, of self-knowledge and self-deception. Her irony leads to immobility, balance, and detachment, to a moderate but not radical becoming of knowing. In Emma the negated, the seemingly extrasystematic, is reabsorbed into the social self. This is possible because Emma's recognition reveals her negation to be, in fact, a denial. A denial refers to the field of action, and Emma can heal her denial by marrying the right man. A negation, however, also has reference to the field of meaning and to the unconscious. And it is to these deeper breaches in meaning and in consciousness, so much more difficult to heal and to balance, that Austen's irony has no access because her unknown is progressively knowable. It is not a radical unknown. Emma's submission to the social self has its formal counterpart in Austen's submission to epistemic irony. It is the very limitation of this irony that allows her to create a fiction and to give her novel formal completeness, the immobility of perfected form.

Georg Lukács' *The Theory of the Novel*

To produce an authentic novel form, the novelist must actualize subjectivity and objectivity in the novel in a particular way, a way which strikes Lukács as necessary and predetermined. Subjectivity must ultimately be rendered in the form of irony because irony is "the sole possible *a priori* condition for a true totality-creating objectivity."[6] Objective reality must be portrayed as devoid of God or a logos.

> When the peak of absurdity, the futility of genuine and profound human aspirations, or the possibility of the ultimate nothingness of man has to be absorbed into literary form as a basic vehicular fact, and when what is in itself absurd has to be explained and analysed and, consequently, recognized as being irreducibly *there*, then, although some streams within such a form may flow into a sea of fulfilment, the absence of any manifest aim, the determining lack of direction of life as a whole, must be the basic *a priori* constituent, the fundamental structural element of the characters and events within it.
>
> (p. 62)

Objective reality must be represented by the novel because this representation was also the goal of the epic, but "the present," as Lukács says in his 1962 preface to the *Theory*, is, despite the general Hegelian tenor of the work, "not defined in Hegelian terms" (p. 18). It is not, as in Hegel, a world of rational becoming under the dominion of Absolute Spirit or Reason, but an unintelligible and meaningless becoming lacking any kind of "manifest aim," goal, or evolutionary direction. The present is nihilistic, purposeless, and impermeable to reason or ethics. The novelist's impossible task (because this is what the genre demands) is to form and represent a world that is inherently formless and nonrepresentable, fractured, contingent, heterogeneous, a nothingness of inessential particulars.

Obviously, this kind of irrational and absurdist interpretation of objective reality is no longer valid for the Marxist Lukács of 1962. It is the kind of defeat and abdication to the "Grand Hotel Abyss" that he sees in Adorno, Ernst Bloch, and French existentialism, which seem to him merely theoretically outdated. Thus, he calls his exegesis of reality "traditional-conventional" (p. 21), and says that his conception of the present in the *Theory* represented "a 'Kierkegaardisation' of the Hegelian dialectic of history" (p. 18). By this he means that he put the burden of any kind of dialectical actualization of Spirit on the solitary, passionate, and demonic existential subject, in this instance the novelist. Just as Kierkegaard had centered his dialectic on the subject and God, so Lukács centered his on the novelist and his form. He admits that in the *Theory*, like Kierkegaard, he turned away from the objective order to concentrate upon the subject on which he pinned all his revolutionary and ethical hopes. Lukács suggests that it was his despair over the war which contributed to his acceptance of such an absurdist interpretation of objectivity and to the "ethically-tinged pessimism" which pervades the *Theory*. Nonetheless, one can say that such an ethical and subjectivist orientation toward a nihilistic reality is common enough in the genre as a theme or a problem. One finds it, for example, in Levin in *Anna Karenina* or in George Eliot at those moments when she forgets her meliorist faith in an underground current of positive, ethical biological movement and sees only the humanly nonsupportive and unintelligible chaos of particulars.

Lukács' approach to the novel is in Foucault's sense historical rather than genealogical. The novel has an origin, namely the epic. Yet, the continuity between the novel and its origin has been strangely disrupted, and the origin itself, though it is there, is voided. The novelist has only the aesthetic form or category given to him and not the world that produced and supported it. He has the empty form, but above all not the subject-object identity that made up the heart of this epical aesthetic form. The novelist is then a historian in a world ideally made for a genealogist; he is in a world of disparities and differences, in a dissociated subject-object world. The novelist finds himself in the position of trying to fit a non-Hegelian world into an essentially Hegelian form. He faces a contradiction that may at any moment destroy the possibility of form as such.

For Lukács in the *Theory*, God or the logos has retreated into form. Thus, although the objective world is no longer Hegelian, no longer a manifestation of Absolute Spirit, aesthetic categories still are. They preserve their aim or telos. Forms or genres still have an "*a priori* origin or 'home' " (p. 40) which they seek to attain and with which they seek to be reunited. In a present voided of God or Spirit, the aesthetic epic category alone reminds the novelist of what totality is. By totality Lukács means a system immanent with meaning, a world like that of Hegel, at once coherent, systematic, organic, and meaningful. The form still glows with Hegelian rationality; in it resides a God and truth. The novelist's only access to an apprehension of God is via the detour of form. God, truth, and meaning have contracted into aesthetic form. It is this passionate overloading of form with significance, with in fact the entire Western spiritual heritage, that explains Lukács' passionate theoretical concern with mere aesthetic form to begin with. To epic subjectivity this totality was given or, as Lukács says, epic subjectivity simply "received" it. Thus, in the epic, totality was objective or metasubjective (p. 50). Objectivity and receptivity are absolute characteristics of the form (p. 74), characteristics which the novel must also seek to attain.

The novelist's task is dual. He must make his creative subjectivity receptive to or identical with the fractured, dispersed present. Simultaneously he must also affirm his identity with a now empty, teleological form. He must recreate two utterly contradictory and opposed totalities: one, the epical, the centered, organic totality; the other, a non-centered, dispersed totality. The novelist must fracture and splinter his subjectivity to reflect accurately the new dispersed totality, and then he must negate this fractured subjectivity to reaffirm his affinity with the organic totality. It is in the midst of such self-reversals and self-negations that a new kind of creative subjectivity is born, that of the novelist. Lukács calls this new subjectivity ironic, "profoundly inartistic," and "the deepest melancholy of every great and genuine novel" (p. 85). It is melancholy because it is so purely negative.

The only affirmation possible to this subject is its awareness of multiple dissonances—between the novel and the epic, the subject and the object, and both in relation to epic subjectivity and objectivity. The "affirmation of dissonance . . . is [in the novel] the form itself" (p. 72).

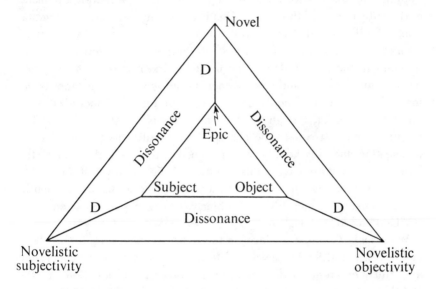

Novel

D

Dissonance   Epic   Dissonance

Subject   Object

D   Dissonance   D

Novelistic   Novelistic
subjectivity   objectivity

Only by the affirmation of its multiple dissonances with the epic, only negatively, can the novel assert its connection with the epic and with the logos that has taken refuge there. Subjectively, the only mental state that can express perfect dissonance is irony. Irony is the totalization of dissonances. It is a coherent presentation of the lack of coherence in the novel, and the only way the novel can achieve epic objectivity.

The novel's form "constitutively coincides with the world as it is today" (p. 93). Lukács' conception of the dialectic between genre and history is, as he states in the preface, only "formally" similar to Hegel's because, in fact, his non-Hegelian interpretation of the present has produced an aesthetic crisis inconceivable in Hegel's world of Absolute Spirit, where aesthetic forms were a representation of Spirit in sensuous form. Whereas in Hegel the actualization of Spirit does render the function of art problematic, the goal of all art, despite evolution, is not obscured. For Lukács, both this goal and reality are thoroughly obscure and nonavailable.

"The novel is the epic of an age in which the extensive totality of life is no longer directly given . . . yet which still thinks in terms of totality" (p. 56). Lukács tries to demonstrate what thinking in terms of totality entails when this totality is no longer given. First the temptation is to pretend that the totality still *is* given, and that it is not merely a demand of the subject and of the genre. This is a utopian and romantic temptation, a falsification that the novelist may try to perpetrate by his structural and compositional powers. But "all the fissures and rents which are inherent in the historical situation must be drawn into the form-giving process and cannot and should not be disguised by compositional means" (p. 60). Lukács holds fast to the demand for the concretization of the objective order, though it is here non-Marxist, nondialectical, static, negative, and abstract. In the *Theory*, Lukács calls this demand for objectification and this fidelity to the objective as it is a demand of the form's logos. Before leaving this question of the portrayal of objectivity in the novel, one can just add that there is in fact no major nineteenth-century novel in which historical objectivity is represented as anything but God and logos-forsaken.

What seeks God and the logos in the novel is the subject, both as hero and novelist. But for Lukács the pattern of the search and its conclusion are utterly different for the hero and the novelist. Lukács allows for the fact that some individual novelistic hero may seem to find fulfillment, as a Levin does at moments, or as Zosima and Alyosha do in *The Brothers Karamazov*. But the novelist will always be aware that all such fulfillment is purely subjective or, in Lukács' sense, "abstract" (i.e. lacking concretion, objective reality). Lukács uses the word "abstract" in the same sense as Hegel does. The novelist always knows that

the elements of the novel are, in the Hegelian sense, entirely abstract; abstract, the nostalgia of the characters for utopian perfection, a nostalgia that feels itself and its desires to be the only true reality; abstract, the existence of social structures based only upon their factual presence and their sheer ability to continue; abstract, finally, the form-giving intention, which, instead of surmounting the distance between these two abstract groups of elements, allows it to subsist, which does not even attempt to surmount it but renders it sensuous as the lived experience of the novel's characters, uses it as a means of connecting the two groups and so turns it into an instrument of composition.

(pp. 70–71)

The novelist knows that it is he who is making the novel. He is, paradoxically, the source and the basis of a form whose fundamental orientation is the representation of totality as objectively given. His own purely subjective structural powers, his ethical and conceptual intelligence, constitute the form. The system or structure that he constructs is "abstract" because it is merely subjective. The novelist must make patent the subjective basis of the form by pointing to its merely fictional and private character, "by recognizing, consciously and consistently, everything that points outside and beyond the confines of the world" (p. 71).

Because the novel must gesture toward what it excludes, incompletion is as endemic to the novel form as it is to the world it represents, a world which lacks the completion of meaning. The novel must point to the extrasystematic and extrastructural, the negated, the larger reality that no form can any longer comprehend because this reality is too fractured and formless to be formed. Thus, the novel is a form caught in pathos, a form that negates its own artistic enterprise and logos, eradicating its structural affirmations by a negation. The novelist composes a whole "which is then abolished over and over again" (p. 84).

The novelist is, for Lukács, the first artist who self-consciously experiences his artistic negativity. He suffers the irreparable dissonance between the idea of form as the completed and the reality of form as the incompletable. The novelist faces an artistic dilemma and paradox that had never before existed: he has to exclude form from form itself. Thus he becomes painfully aware of the aspect of form-creating that has to do with exclusion. Many of the essays in *Soul and Form* had already been precisely about this new artistic dilemma. In a meaningful, whole world, art had seemed to be a problem (only or primarily) of acceptance, inclusion, and openness to what was there. Now it is a self-conscious activity of inclusion and exclusion. Lukács' elaboration of artistic negativity, of the new and acute way in which the force of exclusion and inclusion were felt in the form-giving process starting in the nineteenth century, is one of his original contributions. Given the new conditions, the novelist becomes an ironic creator and destroyer. Irony is itself, for Lukács, a pathos, a demonic, passionate excess, almost a madness that arraigns the world and the strained artwork it makes possible because it demonstrates the inadequacy of both to the soul. Because, for the novelist's epical soul, the form that he makes is never adequate. Irony is the novelist's way of indicating this adequacy, by revealing the negative and inconclusive result of the whole.

For Lukács, the centrality of the hero and the inner biographic form of the novel follow inevitably from the subjective basis of the form. The hero and the fact that he is, inevitably, "a seeker," a man whose destiny and meaning is not given to him, demonstrate the dissonance between the subject and the given reality. The novelist, beyond that, demonstrates the dissonance between the form of the novel and the form of the epic. For this reason the novelist's ironic wisdom exceeds in breadth and depth such wisdom as the hero may acquire, the knowledge that his ethical demands and ideals are purely subjective and psychological, and "that meaning can never quite penetrate reality, but that, without meaning, reality would disintegrate into the nothingness of inessentiality" (p. 88). The centrality of the hero is for the novelist but a reflection or mirror-image of the problematic centrality of his own subjectivity in the form (p. 83). It is for the novelist but a disheartening reminder that the craving for meaning and objectivity which lies equally in the soul and in the epical form is inaccessible to the novel, but a reminder also of the truth that the struggle for totality can never be abandoned.

Irony is the novelist's demonic assault on a God who has taken refuge in the epic form, who is available only aesthetically. It is an ultimate dialectic between the godforsaken novel and the spiritual epic. Irony is demonic because it is an overreaching that has "no reason and cannot be explained by reason, challenging all the psychological or sociological foundations of [the novelist's] existence" (p. 90). Paradoxically, the Lukácsian novelist is finally both the Kierkegaardian demonic genius who, like Ivan in The Brothers Karamazov, defies the spirit to rant and rave against the injustice and inadequacy of the world as it is, and also like the Kierkegaardian Knight of Faith who believes (or, in this instance, tries to believe) the absurd and the impossible. The novelist's ultimate leap of faith, however, is not to God but to the affirmation of God in the epic form.

The novelist's irony is demonic, because only to the demonic spirit is the godforsakenness of the world fully revealed "as a lack of substance, as an irrational mixture of density and permeability" (p. 90). But the novelist corrects this ethical perception and condemnation by a higher, spiritual ironic stance of resignation and ignorance.

> The writer's irony is a negative mysticism to be found in times without a god. It is an attitude of *docta ignorantia* towards meaning, a portrayal of the kindly and malicious workings of the demons, a refusal to comprehend more than the mere fact of these workings; and in it there is the deep certainty, expressible only by form-giving, that through not-desiring-to-know and not-being-able-to-know he has truly encountered, glimpsed and grasped the ultimate, true substance, the present, non-existent God.
>
> (p. 90)

The novelist, like Kierkegaard's Abraham, makes the movement of resignation which suspends all ethical and merely rational demands, and which brackets the finite, but he cannot complete the second movement of faith and believe that he will get back Isaac, therefore getting him back in fact from the infinite as a gift in the finite. Lukács elaborates on his "faith" at the end of the *Theory*, where he speaks of a "new world" and a "renewed epic," but where he also says that such a new world is glimpsed only if at all in art and "art can never be the agent of such a transformation" (p. 152).

"The present, non-existent God" is glimpsed by the novelist in the epic, because by irony the novelist announces his disjunction from the epic but also his tenuous connection to it. By saying this novel is *not* the epic, he makes the epic totality negatively present. Lukács' irony, thus, is Hegelian negativity without the ultimate synthesis. The epic here represents redemption, but the novelist's "constitutive relation to redemption—remains inexpressible" (p. 91). In Kierkegaardian terms, the novelist can only say that he believes that he could get Isaac back, not that he *has* gotten him back. The novelist's whole way to God is a detour, "by way of category to essence" (p. 91). Only through the category of the novel can he get to the essence, the God who resides only in the category of the epic. The novelist's faith and allegiance to the epic must be absolute and his own novelistic form must be perfectly achieved as dissonant with the epic in order for him to achieve freedom in relation to God.

> For the novel, irony consists in this freedom of the writer in his relationship to God, the transcendental condition of the objectivity of form-giving. Irony,

with intuitive double vision, can see where God is to be found in a world abandoned by God; irony sees the lost, utopian home of the idea that has become an ideal, and yet at the same time it understands that the ideal is subjectively and psychologically conditioned, because that is its only possible form of existence; irony, itself demonic, apprehends the demon that is within the subject as a metasubjective essentiality, and therefore when it speaks of the adventures of errant souls in an inessential, empty reality, it intuitively speaks of past gods and gods that are to come; irony has to seek the only world that is adequate to it along the *via dolorosa* of interiority, but is doomed never to find it there; irony gives form to the malicious satisfaction of God the creator at the failure of man's weak rebellions against his mighty, yet worthless creation and, at the same time, to the inexpressible suffering of God the redeemer at his inability to re-enter the world. Irony, the self-surmounting of a subjectivity that has gone as far as it was possible to go, is the highest freedom that can be achieved in a world without God.

(pp. 92–93)

Irony is the novelist's way of rejecting the very coherence and totality that he has created, but perfect ironic technique is also the novelist's only way to affirm and constitute his spiritual nature once again. By means of irony the novelist indicates his allegiance to form by indicating that neither his subjectivity nor reality is formed or absorbed by the structure that he has created. Irony is the novelist's way of keeping what Kierkegaard called "the wound of the negative" open.[7] It is a way for the novelist to contradict his very achievement, to leaven his novel with the unformed and unconditioned and with the totality that once was in the epic.

Irony is a standpoint from which the novelist can negate (in the sense of criticize) his own novelistic world. It is heightened self-negativity. But ironic negativity is also the only stance that seems to offer the novelist, within the becoming of his own subjectivity, a stasis, a seemingly stable, asubjective pole within the self. The novel's "nature as process excludes completeness only so far as content is concerned. As form, the novel establishes a fluctuating yet firm balance between becoming and being: as the idea of becoming, it becomes a state" (p. 73). Irony is the novel's form, correcting the self's and the world's incompleteness and turning becoming into a state. But this stasis, completeness, and form which irony lends to the novel come from the stasis of nothingness and not from the stasis of God.

The vast structural effort of the novel represents man's ethical-spiritual nature as now reduced to and visible only in technical, aesthetic form. Unlike the ethical man, whose norms are "rooted in the existence of the all-perfecting God" and in "the idea of redemption," and whose norms remain, consequently, "untouched in their innermost essence by whoever dominates the present, be he God or demon," the novelist cannot free himself of the empirical present; he cannot renounce the world and his "realization of the normative in the soul or the work cannot be separated from its substratum which is the present" (p.91). The novelist can only feel free in relationship to God when he achieves technical or formal, rather than ethical, perfection. His ethical duty is to aesthetic form, a vast detour to God.

The novelist abolishes his subjectivity in favor of his technical achievement. The perfection of technical form, when achieved, mimics for Lukács the stasis, accord, and stillness that once was being. But this being is a stabilization and totalization of dissonances, the perfection of the self's negativity in irony. Irony is not an experience of faith, but merely the apprehension of a possible, pale, and distant relationship between the novelist's present formative urges and the form of a past totality in the epic or a future totality to come.

For Lukács, nothingness is the world's secret and the novel's secret. Irony, whose productivity is the making of everything into nothing, is the only subjective stance that can match and balance the nothingness of reality. Irony is a destruction that dissolves actuality and its meaning and also the actuality of the ironist himself. Positively, it recognizes only paradoxes, irreconcilable oppositions, and alternatives. Irony or nothingness is the singular "meaning," the one negative truth that gives unity to the novel's form. Irony is the subjective counterpart to the objective nothingness. It is the only way to make the subject and object identical once again.

Lukács saw the novel as a new kind of form, threatened by incompleteness, dispersal, insubstantiality, and disjunctions, but it was still a form, a unity, and hence the mystery of the possibility of such a unity had to be explained. The answer to this mystery lies for Lukács in the constructive powers of the self's negativity in irony. For Kierkegaard the self's negativity led to irony and then, by a leap, to faith. For Hegel it produced rational self-objectification. In Lukács it produces only irony, neither reason nor faith. The constitutive potential of negativity is reduced.

It is this ironic negativity that guarantees the truth of the form and that validates and makes possible the very paradox of a subjective form which claims to represent totality. In the epic, form was structure plus meaning. The novel is the epic form, the sign, emptied of the signified, having become a mere signifier. This cannot be. So the novel's form becomes structure plus the "meaning" of nothingness. Thus, "the immanence of meaning required by the form is attained precisely when the author goes all the way, ruthlessly, towards exposing its absence" (p. 72). The novel's meaning lies in the absence of meaning. Irony is the ruthlessness of the self's negative capability to void itself. By irony the novelist demonstrates that his ignorance, his meager knowledge, his ethical duty, and the meaning of his existence are only about form and in form and can only be form. For his perfect duty to form, the novelist is rewarded by a glimpse of what was once the essence of the category.

It is when Lukács discusses the ultimate relationship between the novel's form and that of the epic that the intense palimpsest effect of his vision—perhaps of any vision based in an origin—becomes clearest, but also most anxious. The novel occupies the same aesthetic space or place that the epic did; hence the palimpsest effect. But the novelist cannot be self-sufficient or free because he must read this prior form, because this is the only place where what was once written can still be traced or deciphered. The novelist assumes that what was, though it no longer exists, is terribly important, and therefore, our last glimpse of him, as a writer, is as an enslaved and anxious reader. He is the reader of a barely discernible, and perhaps indiscernible origin from which he is disconnected and which is no longer either generative or actual.

"The novel" is "the form of the epoch of absolute sinfulness" (p. 152) and hence it is a form that cannot be redeemed by totality nor can it represent redemption, but it can indicate our need for redemption. The novelist's highest freedom lies in irony precisely because he does not and cannot make the Kierkegaardian leap to faith. Irony is incompleteness and paradoxy. It is the opposite of faith and certitude. Thus, Lukács' " 'Kierkegaardisation' of Hegel" stops at the point where subjectivity seeks to satisfy itself by leaping solitarily toward transcendence while certain that it is one with immanence. Lukács has lost Kierkegaard's faith in the conjunction of the finite and infinite, and therefore the leap is abridged.

It was somewhat but not much of an exaggeration when, looking back on the *Theory* in 1962, Lukács found it to be essentially a piece of oppositional literature, a work in which "a left ethic oriented towards radical revolution" was coupled with a right epistemology or ontology (p. 21). The apolitical spirit of the *Theory* hardly warrants such terms as "left" and "right," but it certainly makes evident that Lukács' primary ideological mentors or guides could no longer be Hegel or Kierkegaard. What comes closest to anticipating Lukács' conversion to Marxism in the *Theory* is his unwillingness to renounce objectivity no matter what the cost, and his willingness, in fact, to allow the dominion of subjectivity by objectivity. The objective order is nothing and hence the novelist makes himself nothing, by developing his powers of negativity and irony. Although Lukács seeks a subject-object union, and achieves it, there is an inequality. Objectivity appears in the last regard to be the model for subjectivity, or, at the least, Lukács will not allow any subjective arrogance or self-celebration. Thus, given the two major critical responses to the Hegelian world and its rational illusions offered by the nineteenth century, that of Kierkegaard and Marx, Lukács opted in the *Theory* for the subjective response offered by Kierkegaard. Since he saw that it led to an impasse: the subject alone could never hope to transform historical actuality—he turned next (so it is logical to assume) to Marx and his solutions.

For the Marxist Lukács, the *Theory* can obviously not serve as an ideological guide. Ideologically it can only stand as an example of his own intellectual development at a given moment and of the possibilities and currents of his epoch as a whole. Another question, to which Lukács does not address himself as fully, is whether the *Theory* does or does not (in very general terms, granted) accurately characterize the nineteenth-century novel. By "accurate" I mean in a way that is functional and useful, a way that can be guiding theoretically, although it is obviously not the only way the form can be approached or interpreted. Useful in the *Theory* I would call Lukács' stress on the novel's fictional nature, his emphasis on its subjectivity or "abstractness." Useful also is his accent on the absolute negativity of this subjectivity, its self-reflexiveness and self-negations, potentiated to an absolute irony, which as a state of becoming becomes form—a form based absolutely on nothingness and dissonances. Useful, above all, is his definition of irony and fiction as incompleteness, nonmastery, loss, inadequacy, lack of accomplishment, unreason—almost a madness, whose very energy is a decentralizing and displacing one. I can think of no major nineteenth-century novel in which the dynamic force of such a displacing and dissonance-evoking ironic energy is not felt.

I think we can say that Lukács' vision of the negativity of novelistic subjectivity is fundamentally correct for the nineteenth century. The nineteenth century novel *is* ironic, often demonic, dissonance-obsessed, even melancholic, but it is harder to go along with Lukács' ultimate displacement and submission of novelistic form into epic form, or the idea that it issues its cry for redemption from the perspective of the epic's logos. There is a relationship to the epic in George Eliot for example, but it is not an enslaved relationship between the novel and its master and predecessor, the epic, such as Lukács sees. In Eliot, there is an awareness of the epic which produces a sense of difference, but not commitment. The novelist knows that he must seek new resolutions. Furthermore, what we see is that a tradition develops of self-delight in mere fiction-making, in Sterne and Lewis Carroll, which continues, for example in Dickens' *Our Mutual Friend*, and which flowers in twentieth century formalism. Gradually the novelist seems to come to what Blanchot has called "contestation"—the making of affirmations that affirm nothing. Lukács' concern with the epic origin was certainly a sign of his inability to do that—make affirmations that affirm nothing—perhaps it was also a sign of his inability as yet to renounce completely the totality or perfect affirmation that Hegel called Absolute Spirit and Kierkegaard God.

George Eliot's *Middlemarch*

In her "Prelude" to *Middlemarch*, George Eliot, like Lukács, sees the epic as resting in being, and the novel's substratum as nothingness. The novelistic is perceived, by contrast, as the loss and absence of something that the epic had. In her miniature presentation of her theory of the novel, the epical is the experience that reaches God. It is aspiration leaping, unshackled, to fulfillment. The epic is the genre of unity, coherence, and transcendence. Here there is no break or disjunction, no barrier between the self and God, immanence and transcendence, the deed and its realization. Eliot concretizes her vision of the epical by giving us a complete, abbreviated biography of Saint Theresa, who fulfilled her "passionate ideal nature" by founding a religious order. The novel, by contrast, is an antiepic, constituted of the breakdown of the epical conjunctions. The novelistic heroine is a repetition of the epical heroine under new, unpropitious conditions. Her life is one of "mistakes," "tragic failure," a matter of "dim lights and tangled circumstances," incoherence, inconsistency, and formlessness. The lack of coherence in the social order is echoed within the subject in its own indefiniteness, vagueness, and ambivalence. And therefore Dorothea will be the "foundress of nothing."[8]

Dorothea is ardent, theoretic, and inspired, passionate, rash, eccentric, and severe, seeking martyrdom and eager to spend herself on others. She will have to discover above all the emptiness that can exist in the heart of coexistence, and the endless possibilities of mutual alienation, solitude, and noncomprehension. Eliot introduces her by making clear the contradictions within her and those between her and others. She is like "a fine quotation from the Bible . . . in a paragraph of today's newspaper" (p. 29). In the first dialogic scene with Celia, Dorothea's manner of self-domination by puritanical ethical principles becomes clear in contrast to the more mundane and reality-oriented sister. Dorothea governs herself by moral, hierarchical conceptions: the spiritual is real and superior, the bodily or aesthetic is inferior. We learn that she delights in a pagan way in horse riding but that this is something in which she can indulge herself only because she plans soon to renounce it. She rejects her mother's jewels similarly as pleasure and frivolity, although she demonstrates that she, not Celia, is capable of the deeper aesthetic response to them.

Dorothea distorts her own interiority. By her selfless and ideal conceptions, she blinds herself to her own physical and emotional realities and possibilities. She achieves her ideal self of spacious generality only by self-negation. She attempts to shape herself tyrannically by her ethical-spiritual superego ideals, allowing the expansion of only certain aspects of herself and violently crushing other impulses. She also tends to tyrannize others by this same vision of transcendental selfhood, but the others invariably escape her domination. Celia, in her sanity and balance, her capacity to differentiate between jewels and religion, and her simultaneously detached and lovingly defensive attitude toward Dorothea, is Eliot's way of ironizing the latter from the beginning. In the voice of the townspeople, however, there is more than irony and detachment.

A young lady of some birth and fortune, who knelt suddenly down on a brick floor by the side of a sick labourer and prayed fervidly as if she thought herself living in the time of the Apostles—who had strange whims of fasting like a Papist, and of sitting up at night to read old theological books! Such a wife might awaken you some fine morning with a new scheme for the application of her income which would interfere with political economy and the keeping of saddle-horses: a man would naturally think twice before he risked himself in such fellowship. Women were expected to have weak opinions; but the great safeguard of society and of domestic life was, that opinions were not acted on. Sane people did what their neighbors did, so that if any lunatics were at large, one might know and avoid them.

(p. 31)

There are the sane and the insane; the sane do what everyone else does. Clearly, Dorothea who, as Celia says, "does what no one else does," must be relegated to the insane, erratic, troublesome, and unpredict- able. The voice of the townspeople may be superficial, but they are the real community, the tradition, the others with whom Dorothea's life is inevitably one. Dorothea's hidden inner conflict is also the sign of her potential conflict with those others whom she censures just as she cen- sures aspects of herself but who also censure her.

Dorothea's choice of Casaubon completes the conscious negation, the disregard, the intolerance that she has shown for her own young, physi- cal, aesthetic, and autonomous selfhood. The choice guarantees that her marriage will be a trial of self-negation and self-repression. Dorothea's blindness is not like Emma's, who admires herself too much; Dorothea admires others too much. Everyone else is able to criticize Casaubon, to reduce him to an equal or inferior, because no one else desires his con- dition. But for Dorothea, his imagined knowledge is a dream and a desire. Casaubon appears to her cognitive aspirations as a hero of knowl- edge. Like Don Quixote she sees not the barber's basin but a fascinating gap between what she imagines he is and has, and what she feels she lacks. The difference between herself and him, and others and him, becomes a difference of inferior and superior, master and servant. Ca- saubon emits very few signs that correspond to her inner dream, but Dorothea makes him the object of illimitable interpretations; she con- nects him to her own deepest internal needs and dreams. She makes him special; she grants him an interiority like her own. "Signs are small measurable things, but interpretations are illimitable, and in girls of sweet, ardent nature, every sign is apt to conjure up wonder, hope, belief, vast as the sky" (p. 47). Dorothea seduces herself into loving by transferring all of her unreleased yearnings onto Casaubon, as if he were a god of knowledge, the source and ground in which she can complete herself.

It is in the midst of these dreams of self-totalization and self-completion that Eliot turns the perspective on Casaubon himself. We learn that he feels nothing; "a blankness of sensibility, a flatness" makes him feel frightened, lonely, and disappointed in love. His private world of pain, fear, and hope takes no cognizance of Dorothea whatsoever. If anything she is the enemy, the source of a sense of heightened misery, because he does not feel what he is supposed to feel. She makes him conscious of not feeling, of his sterility.

Mutual fear and even hatred, then, rather than love, communication, and self-enlargement are what the great nineteenth-century dream of coexistence, human mutuality, and social unity turns out to produce. Two consciousnesses, the "I" and the "Thou," left to experience each other, come instead upon the chaos of the solitary, agitated self. Dorothea in Rome is too confused to understand what is happening to her, but she was "becoming more and more aware, with a certain terror, that her mind was continually sliding into inward fits of anger or repulsion, or else into forlorn weariness" (p. 228). Dorothea is depressed because she has nothing to do, because her life is not beginning, and because her energies are utterly sapped in her pointless inner struggles. She begins to hate Casaubon in flashes and to resent his cold, distant, offensive treatment of her; but more, she hates herself for hating anyone and anything, and for not being able to elicit love. If she were herself not deficient in loving, would she not elicit love? So she tries to love more, but a vindictive element has crept into her love, and her struggle with that element makes her lose her own ground and sense of herself: she appears wrong, guilty, inadequate, impotent, and afraid. She is frightened by her own rising capacity for anger and resentment, and tries to allay her anxiety by longing and loving and glorifying Casaubon once again. The other is but an experience of intense self-anxiety, for which the self has no resolutions.

Dorothea feels "humiliated to find herself a mere victim of feeling . . . all her strength was scattered in fits of agitation, of struggle, of despondency, and then again in visions of more complete renunciation, transforming all hard conditions into duty" (p. 230). Dorothea becomes the victim of her own feelings because these are not accepted but repulsed. Casaubon keeps her at arm's distance. Feelings can be transformed into hatred or anger, but they cannot simply be excised or amputated. Hate is love made angry, love negated. Indifference, not hate, is the opposite of love. But Dorothea can neither hate nor be indifferent. So she must repress the hate and anger and it is the repression of her feelings that brings on her depression, forlornness, despondency, and sense of solitude. Eliot's is a classic description of a familiar emotional pattern. Love is a feeling of expansion, of receptivity, and acceptance. It is a yes and an affirmation. Hatred is a feeling of contraction, of confinement, and narrowness. It is a negation and reduction of relationship and of the sense of relatedness. Eliot's images, such as those of the lake and basin, dramatize these oscillations of affirmation and negation between the self and other, which resound deep in the self as its own negation and affirmation.

Dorothea's self-repression, her loyalty, sympathy, and capacity for "direct fellow-feeling with individual fellow-men" are largely for nothing. With Casaubon and even with Rosamond, Dorothea experiences the negation of the very best part of herself by the other. The mature, ethical ego, which recognizes the independence of the other's ego and sees it in a sympathetic perspective, is fundamentally no match for the psychologically real: narcissism and its mechanisms of defense. The "self-identity by exclusion of every other from itself," said Hegel, "takes its essential nature and absolute object to be Ego." The other is for this ego an "unessential object," an object with "the impress and character of negation" (p. 231). One's relationship to another to whom one does not appear as essential can only be a sham relationship. Except for one moment of communion in the library when Casaubon accepts and returns sympathy, Dorothea's interpersonal experience with him is purely negative. Casaubon trusts no one. He is wounded, insecure, and hides his condition by a display of false strength and self-sufficiency and, above all, by distance and coldness. Dorothea's sympathy merely threatens him and makes him feel paranoid, suspicious, and afraid of being discovered in the failure that he must conceal. Thus Dorothea's efforts are in vain; she can neither penetrate nor change Casaubon's consciousness, and his distance creates arrestment in the interpersonal realm. His defense mechanism is like an unyielding fate against which

Dorothea runs up, a fate which ends the dream of mutual contact and exchange.

Casaubon is one of the many failed masters in Eliot's work. He fails to master the cultural-historical world, just as Lydgate fails to master the natural world, Bulstrode the moral-religious, and Brooke the political. None of these characters proves equal to the complexity of objective conditions. Unlike the master systematizers of the nineteenth century— thinkers like Hegel, Marx, Darwin, Wagner—who managed to impose a genetic and structural order on the world, her ambitious men fail to subdue the chaos in an order and system. In a sense, with them Eliot writes the tragedy of totalization and totalizing—the impossibility of the domination of radical particulars by an organic whole. In that way she makes us more aware that her novel too borders on the edge of the chaos of particularity, a chaos that she knows no one can see, because they see only by the light of their ego, which is an act of radical exclusion. It is this great fact of the limits of the self, of the self as a nearly infinite power to exclude, which Eliot, far more than Austen, made the center of her novelistic drama.

She presents this drama in her famous image of the pier-glass and the candle. The "mirror" she holds up to nature is fundamentally opaque, filled with nothing but scratches. The scratches are the events, the mystery of the objective order in its minuteness and multitudinousness. They stand for chaos, for the absurd, opaque, mysterious, explosive, unknowable character of reality. Reality is dense, impenetrable, and unintelligible because it is so vast and so particular. This is why her intellectual heroes who venture forth into this reality flounder. It is a chaos without meaning and order, but it is overwhelmingly and oppressively present; it is the fundamentally nonrepresentable reality that Lukács speaks of, equivalent to nothing. How does one write a novel on the background of nothingness? Eliot also can do little more than indicate the presence of the scratches and briefly speculate that perhaps it is the minute, invisible changes taking place within this chaos that ultimately control conscious life; otherwise, she, like Lukács, focuses on the primarily negative, limiting powers of the subject. The ego can make a world because it excludes.

The ego, because it is blind and limited, acts like a candle and makes the world a clear image. The fundamental distortion and untruth of the ego is a reduction of the complexity of the world. Rosamond's ego, mate-rial, appetitive, pleasure-seeking, conventional, is the most reductive of all. It wards off all complexity, particularly that of others, making her in-capable of any kind of sympathetic identity. She lives in blissful indiffer-ence to others, feeling misunderstood in her suffering of inadequate self-gratificatory fulfillment. Her ego functions self-protectively, allowing her to hold tenaciously on to what she seeks. She is, as Hegel says, "cer-tainty of self" without truth (p. 232).

But even those with larger, less instinctual egos fail to master the world in Eliot's novel because they fail to master themselves. They fail to attain the self-knowledge that can only be gotten from another. Lydgate, for example, fails to understand that he will experience the need for a real, other consciousness, a wife who would be more than an ornament.

> He went home and read far into the smallest hour, bringing a much more test-ing vision of details and relations into his pathological study than he had ever thought it necessary to apply to the complexities of love and marriage, these being subjects on which he felt himself amply informed by literature, and that traditional wisdom which is handed down in the genial conversation of men.
>
> (p. 193)

Lydgate does not see that the rigor applicable to scientific discovery is needed to comprehend human relations, or that the clue to his own pas-sionate nature will be provided by another. Eliot herself makes such problems, and particularly the marriage relationship, the very center of all her conscious, intellectual, and scientific effort. She knows that the self must move in cycles from itself to the other for the sake of self-knowledge, and then back again to itself to master the new chaos of anx-ieties produced by the other in the self. But how is this new crisis of anxieties to be resolved? Eliot herself here appears uncertain and am-bivalent about the very nature of the crisis and problem. Is it fundamen-tally ethical or existential? Are there problems deeper than those touched by ethics? Eliot appears to perceive that there are, and yet she would like to make every problem yield to an ethical resolution, the res-olution of mutual sympathy and coexistence. This becomes the limit of her art, and is at the core of its self-contradiction, non-resolution, and incompleteness.

Lydgate is defeated by his "spots of commonness," his aristocratic carelessness, his lack of a proper stewardship of what is his based on an egotistic sense of deserving only the best, but ultimately he is defeated by his own psychological fear of distance and alienation from others. Like Dorothea he is willing to give up being loved but afraid to stop loving himself. He fears hatred, and sees only the alternative of hatred, of ruthless criticism and domination of the other, or of love, a surrender to the other. He submits to Rosamond as much as to his own fear of domination, hatred, and alienation. This fear of alienation, this lack of a proper vision of alternatives, this dread of outright conflict and the full expression of negative feelings—which produces self-repression and depression as much in Lydgate as in Dorothea—are fears and lacks that in some ways govern Eliot herself as much as her characters.

Eliot's consciousness too appears so much to be governed by certain positives that the negatives cannot be adequately explored. They can only be pointed to as tragic and inevitable. The old ideal and aspiration of harmony, unity, and accord, transferred now to the interpersonal sphere, seek recognition and fulfillment still. Conflictlessness, the sympathetic comprehension of one consciousness by another, is so desirable that in a sense it justifies self-negation, self-repression, and even self-destruction. Eliot clearly sees that the comprehension is not mutual, yet her heroes and heroines are invariably those who attain the inner sympathetic vision of another soul. Thus her moral heroes are invariably slaves—they understand without being understood in return. They are dominated by the inadequacies and failures of others.

Eliot sees the failure of the dream of coexistence and mutual recognition; she sees the dream of the fusion of I and Thou turn into a nightmare of domination of the stronger by the weaker, but her art remains fundamentally uncritical of this condition. Tragedy functions to accept the situation rather than to criticize it. There is a tragic waste, avoidable, perhaps, in a far-distant future of nontragic coexistence. Eliot's acceptance of a radically unequal condition of coexistence rests upon her own fear of dissociation, alienation, and solitude. Thus she allows enormous sacrifices to be made to achieve her positives—communion, sympathy, unity, social cohesion, harmony—and to escape the negatives.

What is the point of conscience in a world of radical egotists and criminals? Why do Mrs. Bulstrode, Dorothea, and Lydgate submit to a demanding, self-destructive, and self-arresting faith in others which these others do not deserve? What makes them even capable of this faith? Ultimately, it is an anxiety over the death or possible collapse of the other that compels their acts of compassion. The threat to the self-preservation and survival of the other activates the sympathetic and life-protective instincts in the heroes and heroines. Their conscience is born out of death—out of a shared fear of death. The heroine and hero intuitively know that the negativity and contingency of the other is but a reflection of their own. Lydgate sees Rosamond threatened by the collapse of her dream, and the healer in him responds to her terror. Dorothea understands the plunge that Casaubon has made from "we must all die" to "I must die," and she reaches out her hand to help support his existential terror. Her sympathy and ethical nature develop under the impact of death, not God. Ethical, for Eliot, is the instinctive erotic force that reaches out to combat the anxiety of death. Coexistence is actual, is achieved only and momentarily in the face of death. But can coexistence alleviate in fact the problem of existence, the problem raised of the singular existence and its death?

As in Lukács, it is not the objective nothingness of meaninglessness and disorder but subjective nothingness that constitutes the crisis in her novel. It is the nothingness, the horrid emptiness in the self, that seeks resolution. And ultimately Eliot in a sense evades the anxiety of death by making it analogous to the anxiety of solitude and otherlessness, the anxiety over the absence of the other. The absence of the other, the nothingness of solitude, is potentially healable by the presence of that other, whereas the actual nothingness of selfhood, the absence of the self to itself, is not. Eliot's vision of tragic coexistence partly disguises the fundamental problem. It is as if contact by feeling could alleviate every problem, even death and madness.

Eliot's view of insanity is like her view of the objective chaos, as something filled and present though unmasterable. Madness is the presence of many other hallucinated voices, and not an experience of deathly emptiness.

> Mrs. Cadwallader said, privately, "You will certainly go mad in that house alone, my dear. You will see visions. We have all got to exert ourselves a little to keep sane, and call things by the same names as other people call them by. . . . I daresay you are a little bored here with our good dowager; but think what a bore you might become yourself to your fellow-creatures if you were always playing tragedy queen and taking things sublimely. Sitting alone in that library at Lowick you may fancy yourself ruling the weather; you must get a few people round you who wouldn't believe you if you told them. That is a good lowering medicine."

(p. 581)

Mrs. Cadwallader's advice echoes that of Samuel Johnson in *Rasselas*. Madness can be avoided by the necessity of direct, feelingful, sympathetic contact with others. Communion is the answer to the nothingness of solitude that can cause madness, and indirectly also to the nothingness of death, simply because Eliot gives no other answer to the latter. In her world, one conscience reaches out to another who exhibits at heart a horror of nothingness and emptiness. But Eliot can never make that response of conscience a mutual one.

Eliot's novel is itself a symbol of negation, oscillating between concealment and revelation of the objective and subjective conditions of nothingness. The oscillations, her own ambivalence, become especially clear once again in her "Finale." The very fact that she writes a "Finale" is, first of all, an indication both of the fact that her artistic world is not terminable, closed, and rounded off in itself, and that she wishes it to be so. This is in some ways an unnecessary gesture toward the reader in whom she assumes she has built up a biographic and affective interest in the fate of her characters, an interest which she feels called on to satisfy. Here the strong sense of community—this time between the reader and the author—in a sense morally dictates that she go on. Her faith in realism, the idea that the novel is in a special way coextensive with and attentive to lived moral experience, makes her yield her formal skill to the reader, her extension of our experience of consciousness. But into this extension she introduces a little shock for the moral consciousness when she expands upon the fate of Dorothea. She tells us that according to Middlemarch tradition Dorothea does not have the reputation of being even a "nice woman." Thus her heroine is not only obscure, "the foundress of nothing," but in no way even exemplary, as Clarissa and Emma had been. On the contrary, for the community she is a negative model. She has not only no wider communal influence, she does not even have their respect. Her reputation is the very opposite of the minimally acceptable, the "nice." Here Eliot demonstrates once again a critical realism—one that, in fact, surpasses her own realism and meliorism—by pointing to a radical alienation between the individual and its society. Her highest individual ends up as no more than an outcast and ostracized being. Instead of communion and coexistence, there is a level at which there is total misunderstanding, alienation, and remoteness between the "us" and the "them."

But also characteristically, this glimpse of a gap between practice and her own theoretical hopes is quickly covered up. Although Dorothea's life is absorbed in that of another, although the "determining acts of her life were not ideally beautiful," and "her great feelings" were error, her great faith an "illusion," she is part of the invisible good active in the world (p. 896). Eliot's faith is in some ways a private mysticism like Dorothea's own, only in Eliot it finally takes on a coldly objective and scientific form. She moves from conscience to science, acknowledging an infinite progress, mutation, and change that is beyond our control. Eliot felt the presence of an unknown, ungraspable force that eluded all conscious control, an unknown she did not recognize as the unconscious but as an exterior Darwinian-type force. She sees that conscious, moral mastery is not enough and yet she believes in it. She relegates to nature, an objective force, the task of mastery and resolution. The unknown is objective. But in this yielding, she also indicates that she is not sufficiently aware of the unconscious as a subjective unknown inherent in man. She cannot abandon the idea of genealogical order or the notion of development. Somehow, the good conscience was in collusion with this objective unknown, for somehow those types that fail to adjust to the new social conditions of coexistence will not survive. Bulstrode, Lydgate, and Casaubon do not produce male offspring. Their kind of egotism condemns them to extinction. This passage from morals to "science" helps Eliot to bypass the total failure of her human community. She remains fundamentally ambivalent about whether this community can or cannot be made responsible for its failure.

The abdication and renunciation to science is also an abdication and renunciation of art and control. Eliot, for all her artistic devices and skills, her patterns, irony, and abundance of conceptual images, which made Henry James accuse her of excess reflection and of lacking the free aesthetic life, cannot herself master and dominate the proliferation and multiplicity that she has produced. In a sense, the excess of detail, bordering on the anarchic, makes her realism more real; on the other hand, it is a sign of art's defeat by the world. The very presence of the "Finale" reinforces the defeat because it is the sign of the impossibility of concluding this world.

Conclusions, as Eliot herself said, are by their nature "at best a negation," a denial, a withdrawal from concluding, which in its original sense would have to be an affirmation.[9] Thus Eliot also acknowledges that her own urge for aesthetic control is arrested in formal incompletion. Novelistic art is but a troubled self-affirmation, always leading to negations and always lacking solid substantiality. Eliot and Lukács do not feel that the novel, despite its technical, conceptual, and ethical achievements, produces a body, or that art and language themselves are a body. God's creation had substantiality; the novelist's lacks it. Yet, although Eliot strips the self fundamentally of its transcendental selfhood, confining it to the real and narrow conditions of its particularity, she does not strip the novel of its totalizing aim, though what this totality in its relation to the particular human may be becomes extremely problematic. Certainly the whole project of human history and development is no longer as clear and orderly as it appeared to be in Hegel, where an individual could submit to it as a way of being relieved from the anxiety of his own death, his own meaninglessness, and goallessness. The "development" is perceived by Eliot to be disjunct and alien from the human. Ultimately, it is an unknowable process of simultaneous growth and decay.

Eliot's novelistic irony is dazzlingly theoretical, and more objective than subjective. Its focus is on impermanence, change, and the annihilating effects of temporality. She is keenly aware of multiplicity, diversity, various points of view, and the variety of forms of explanation. But the nihilistic effect of her radical multiplicity and plurality is overcome by her faith in science and in a radical turning point in the self toward a positive. The self finds a turning point in its inability to deny the actuality of its own existence. All her major characters have experienced their servitude. Each has, as Hegel put it, experienced "this complete perturbation of its entire substance, this absolute dissolution of all its stability into fluid continuity." Each "has trembled throughout its every fibre, and all that was fixed and steadfast has quaked within it" (p. 237). The consequence of their experience is a sense of the truth of self-existence and of pure negativity. The balance of these two truths helps them to persist, but no longer to dream of becoming what they are not.

Tolstoy's *Anna Karenina*

The novel comes of age in the age of negativity. In order to encompass the pluralizations and multiplications produced by negativity, the novel's structure grows more complex, strained, and ironic. In Eliot, irony seeks to absorb, to organize, and to point to a genetic origin and to the aim of this multiplicity. In Austen, the authorial irony becomes a submission to a Socratic unknown knowable, while the form reaches a resolution of its ironic contradictions, and stasis. The novel does not abandon the goal of totality, though the totality to be achieved has to be projected into the future. The increased pressure and complexity both of the diachronic and synchronic dimensions makes a synthesis in the present unavailable. Whereas in these two novels, as in Hegel and Goethe, the logos becomes divided between the yes and the no, being and nothingness, without being finally sundered, in Tolstoy the logos is split. This sundering has profound consequences both for the form of the novel and the development of its characters. In *Anna Karenina* there is no projection of a totality into the future, because the logos is no longer remediable dialectically in a rational or symbolic way. The unity that Levin achieves is like a dream, momentary and fleeting, in a lived reality of chronic dissociation and perplexity.

As the affirmation of a totality in the present loses its ground and validity, the novel's sense of formlessness and insubstantiality increases, and both are viewed, at first, not as conditions of art, but of consciousness. For Hegel the insubstantiality was a consequence of self-consciousness. For him the negation of substance and the body was less an intentional than a necessary oblivion, brought about by the mind's concern with its own inwardness. Thus someone like Dorothea Brooke may mistake the denial of the body as a Protestant or puritanical demand, but for Eliot and Hegel it is a drive of consciousness which incorporates the body and then passes beyond it. Existent, objective bodies, even that of the self, are no longer felt to be adequate or objective correlatives for or expressions of the self's explosive inwardness. As far as content is concerned, the novel comes to be a bodiless work of art. As Hegel saw, it is not Christianity, but the development of our own consciousness that demands the denial of the body. But the price of this denial is that strange sense of insubstantiality, perplexity, and groundlessness that comes to haunt consciousness everywhere in the novel.

By contrast, in Tolstoy, consciousness in its spiritual striving appears to remain grounded in its body, in its bodily-affective unity, in its own objectivity, its knowledge of itself as an object. This perhaps above all gives Tolstoy's novels their singular Homeric quality, their sense of being epical. As in the Homeric epic, everything in Tolstoy is externalized, presented in its bodily objectivity and externality. Everything becomes fully visible and palpable, acquiring a body in space and time. For Tolstoy, as for his artist, Mikhaylov, the things in the world are already there: they have only to be perceived, recorded, and revealed. Mikhaylov speaks of creation as a process of "removing the wrappings," where one must take care not to spoil the thing that is already there as an existent.[10]

If Levin saves himself from nihilism, it is primarily because he can experience himself both as a consciousness and a body, as subject and object. Momentarily grounded in himself as an object, he can escape the anxiety that is time and consciousness, and experience stillness. Such a moment of stillness occurs to him when he is mowing. The body absorbs consciousness, giving him "moments of oblivion" and "unconscious intervals"—ultimately also of the body itself—so that "his arms no longer seemed to swing the scythe, but the scythe itself his whole body, so conscious and full of life; and as if by magic, regularly and definitely without a thought being given to it, the work accomplished itself of its own accord" (p. 230). The miracle of the body in its own pure reality is that it puts us in contact with other objects, energizing them and giving them an existence and power of their own, as happens here between Levin and the scythe.

A different kind of moment of unconsciousness occurs to Levin the morning when he is waiting to make his official proposal to Kitty. On this morning it is, in fact, a deep sense of detachment from all the conditions of material existence including dependence on his own body that brings him to gaze unthinkingly on the world. On that morning his body is there and not there. It is effortlessly there as an unreal power. "He was sure that he could fly upwards or knock down the corner of a house, were it necessary." It is in the body and not in his consciousness alone that his heightened state of existence is registered. When one lives unconsciously, it is the body that lives, and it is that unconscious, nonthinking bodily affirmation of life that makes us receptive to the objective. To be deeply immersed in the self is to come upon the reality or unreality of the body, its independent existence and support, and the gift of this bodily life is a perception of the objective world in its autonomy, completeness, and singularity. Tolstoy then writes what is no doubt one of the most beautiful passages of the book:

> And what he then saw he never saw again. Two children going to school, some pigeons that flew down from the roof, and a few loaves put outside a baker's window by an invisible hand touched him particularly. These loaves, the

pigeons, and the two boys seemed creatures not of this earth. It all happened at the same time; one of the boys ran after a pigeon and looked smilingly up at Levin; the pigeon flapped its wings and fluttered up, glittering in the sunshine amid the snow-dust that trembled in the air; from the window came the scent of fresh-baked bread and the loaves were put out. All these things were so unusually beautiful that Levin laughed and cried with joy.

(p. 367)

For a moment, Levin catches the perfect particularity of everything in the world. He sees the objects in their perfect objectivity. Everything is separate, individual, and autonomous, but complete and perfect in it-self—the two boys, the pigeons, the loaves. Perfect bodily subjectivity makes him capable of perfect objectivity. It allows him to perceive and receive the objects in the world with perfect perceptual clarity. But even in the midst of this experience of bodily reality, with Levin im-mersed in himself to the point of oblivion because what is about to be fulfilled has to do with his deepest fantasies, Tolstoy writes: "And what he then saw he never saw again." This moment in which he sees the perfection of the most ordinary things in life is a unique singular mo-ment, the gift of his stillness and suspendedness in an imminent satisfac-tion, the gift of his anxietylessness. The moment is swept away in tem-porality, unrecoverable: "never" reminds us that all these perfect particulars are awash in temporality and that temporality is the true god of this novel.

Levin's experience with objectivity is almost a model of how all rela-tions involuntarily occur and can be (a mutual letting be), but in the human sphere all relationships are those of anxiety, as they also are for Levin, with Kitty and his son. But Levin—even when he fails in his search for right relationships with which to comprehend his world either ethically, rationally, logically, or psychologically—can and always does maintain his relationship to himself as a body. The bodily–affective is the ground equally of his "senseless joy" and his "senseless grief," a ground of affirmation that enables him to withstand the meaninglessness and nihilism that he so clearly perceives with his consciousness. Levin's religious feelings are not an illusion for him because they are grounded, not in God, but in the unthinking life of himself as a body. Levin's body is for him the ground of a complex set of relations, of himself to his metaphysical moments, to his work, to others, and to his duty to others.

From the beginning Levin recognizes and acknowledges his need for another who will recognize him and his desires, another who will say, "All that interests him interests me" (p. 88). Levin is the "stranger" in the world of this novel, its greatest individualist, and yet he is the one who does not recognize his core as individual and singular. He experiences his need for Kitty and her presence in conjunction with his own existence. He is the paradox of the alienated and solitary man who yet feels that he is, at his core, two. He acts like the autonomous, singular, ontic individual, like the old "one," but he feels that he is coexistence. For him the old riddle of man has become not a riddle of the one but of two. Furthermore, his new riddle is mysterious because the sense of coexistence cannot be defined by reason. It can only be felt.

Levin believes what his nihilistic era teaches, that reason is nihil, nothing. It is nihil because it yields no meaning or purpose. It can establish neither God nor an ethic. Reason is no longer meaning-giving as it had been in Hegel. Reason only sees death and individual egos in a struggle for self-preservation. This perception drives Levin to despair and to the idea of suicide. He feels that his voided reason gnaws at him, making it impossible for him to live without knowing why he does. In his *Confessions*, Tolstoy acknowledges having felt the same dilemma: "No matter how often I may be told, 'You cannot understand the meaning of life, so do not think about it, but live,' I can no longer do it: I have already done it too long. I cannot now help seeing day and night going round and bringing me to death. That is all I see, for that alone is true. All else is false." [11] For both Tolstoy and Levin, reason has grown purely negative, but the need for reason, for a meaning persists.

Levin feels that the definition of the ego that the nihilists give is not the truth: mere self-preservation and self-love is not enough and not a reason for living and persisting. Levin knows that his love for others is undemonstrable but true. "But the law of loving others could not be discovered by reason, because it is unreasonable" (p. 722). Levin reaffirms "the meaning of goodness" and God after, and because he discovers that his soul is two and not one. This "objectivity" in the self prompts him to affirm his ethical relatedness to others and their coexistence with himself. And this relatedness to others feels like a meaning.

Levin curbs the demands of his questing and questioning reason by making them bend to the unreasonable and irrational law of loving others, of being in relationships of concrete love and obligation. He feels that his innate need for love and the benefits of love are tied to an ethics, an innate knowledge of good and evil that has been given to him. Yet we know that it was only by chance and accident, and thanks to Levin's own deep harmony with his bodily-affective life, that his negation of Kitty was overcome and that the pain of his rejected love was turned into the good of relatedness, which feels like a meaning. Furthermore, we know that what he calls his "innate" knowledge of good and evil is but the content of his inherited and traditional superego.

Levin feels that he must trust that his subjective need for meaning is a testament to something and not to nothing. Not reason, but intuitions, actions, and feelings overcome nihilism and are a constant demonstration of purposiveness. Levin is intuitively and "irrationally" willing to believe that the world picture is, ethically, rationally, and theologically as his forefathers had believed it to be. He accepts as valid the traditional-conventional world picture, knowing that it cannot be submitted to rational scrutiny. He reaffirms Hegel's vision of a purposive force and becoming without the aid of reason. He discovers that his "unconscious" or his inherited self and superego are positive and affirmative, and that his conscious mind is negative and nihilistic. He also knows that this gap between his consciousness and his unconscious can never be healed. A dissonance—the constant potential of a disjunction—will always remain part of his experience. He will again and again experience the negativity of his mind and have moments when his reason will question and torment the validity of what he believes. The Hegelian possibility of affirming the world and the self by reason is over for him, yet he holds on to the telos that is at the heart of this world, because subjectively he cannot do without a purpose or accept an irrational world picture such as that, for example, of Schopenhauer. What Levin comes to believe—that meaninglessness is a product of consciousness whereas the unconscious is meaningful, purposive, life-affirming, and antisuicidal—comes to be demonstrated in Anna, who in her final lucid moments submits to the evidence of her consciousness.

Levin's irrational self affirms that what Lukács called "totality" still exists. Levin projects the old metaphor with only a part of himself, metonymically. Hence he will forever reexperience the opposition and contradiction between his consciousness and unconscious, the fact that they were not designed for each other and not designed with the end of intrasubjective harmony in mind. Levin affirms God because he cannot stay in or endure the suspended state of irony and paradoxy of the

Lukácsian novelist. He needs to draw the old gods of the epic, as it were, into his present reality. For him, "the present, non-existent God" has to become present. The old customs function for him as the epic functioned for Luckács. It is in the old customs that "totality" lives. Like the Lukácsian novelist, Levin seeks God in the old forms into which He has retreated, but unlike the Lukácsian novelist, Levin also makes the leap of faith. He cannot live in a world abandoned by God, giving his complete assent to incompleteness and negativity. Yet, Levin also knows that even after having found God, he may lose Him again and again. His relationship to God is somewhat analogous to his relationship to Kitty, a relationship both of marriage and "divorce." For although Levin longs for God as he had longed for union with Kitty, his sense of disjunction from both is also always potentially present, his sense that he is alienated from her, that she is, at moments, a "stranger" for him.

For Levin the other is duty and work. He feels his coexistence ethically. Anna feels it primarily passionately, and comes to destroy the other whom she needs. Anna also knows that the self is two, but she "unethically" perverts love into mutual suffering. She affirms the need for coexistence in despair. In the world of this novel as a whole, the coexistence is silently felt, but not spoken about. And this sense of felt coexistence is also feared because it is coterminous with another perception that all the characters have, that the other who is needed is also a stranger. Thus Stiva feels like a "stranger" to Dolly, as Vronsky does to Anna, and even Kitty at moments to Levin. Each one suffers terribly when experiencing this strangeness of the other to the self or of the self to the other, but no one can fully overcome the experience. All come to see at times that the image of the other lies silently in their soul, but they do not and cannot speak to this other.

Individualism is criticized and negated in the novel, and yet it is the singular, autonomous, and monological individual who dominates this novel. Each one feels that he has to achieve and determine himself alone and in isolation, and yet all know that they are not alone and cannot determine themselves alone. The paradox of isolate being in a world of coexistence is one with which each character has to contend. Thereby the very problems and contradictions of isolate existence versus coexistence, and the ethics of each, achieve a far clearer delineation in Tolstoy than in Eliot. What determines the quality of each character's life is how each handles this dialectic of strangeness and coexistence. Anna insists on the lovelessness, strangeness, and isolation only to demonstrate that she and Vronsky are one. She destroys their lives to reveal the alienation in love, its pain and reality, and its untruth.

Anna also lives in the body, the bodily-affective, as does Levin and everything in the world of Tolstoy, but she lives in a very conscious and ethical relation to the body, coming increasingly to experience its potential for dread. The body becomes not an "opening" for her—as it does for Levin in birth, death, and marriage—into a sense of relatedness, but a source of disrelatedness, of lovelessness, solitude, and the ugly, meaningless particularity of things. That her disruption and distress begins in the body becomes particularly evident in Chapter Eleven of Part Two, where her first sexual union with Vronsky is described in terms of a complicity in the murder of a body, a complicity which fills Anna with disgust and horror. Anna feels that her body has been murdered, deprived of life. This feeling is a sign of her ethical complexity as well as of the fact that she fears genital sexuality and finds it difficult to accept. What is tragic for her is that her need for assurance that she is loved will always have to be sought in sexuality. Hereafter, she always deals in her dialectical relationship to herself with one part that is absent, condemned, and dead. Her ambivalent sense of her body becomes most obvious when she finally choses to die, not, for example, by taking morphium, but by being mutilated and destroyed by a murderous and punishing object like the train. The train punishes her declassed, mysterious, peasant-like body.

When Anna "destroys" her body, she destroys and warps her unconscious, for in Tolstoy unconsciousness, or as much of it as he knows, is almost synonymous with the body. The death of her body weighs on her from the beginning as a concrete, disorienting nothingness, a weight which no longer allows her to think clearly, even though she struggles with increasing obsession to maintain this body and its beauty artificially. When Vronsky grows irritated and weary of her domination of him by her beauty and calls her "unnatural," he wounds her deeply precisely because he confirms what she long knew and felt. It is in their first sexual encounter that Anna loses her ordinary self-feeling and abandons her libidinal investment in the most vital part of herself, her body. If Anna ultimately feels left alone in a world devoid of love, it is precisely because her intense unconscious guilt long ago produced in her a feeling of emptiness, a sense that she had destroyed part of her interiority by her badness. The relationship to the other depends on the internal subjective relationship to self grounded in the body, a relationship which is disrupted in Anna at the beginning.

The "human self," as Kierkegaard argued, is a synthesis of the soulish-bodily, grounded in Spirit. It is the unity of the body with the soul (with will, intellect, and imagination).[12] A disorder in the spiritual relationship will reveal itself in bodily and affective traces or, conversely, certain disorders in the latter are signs of the spiritual disrelationship. For Kierkegaard, there is dread in all erotic experience, and especially in childbirth because the suspension of spirit is felt as dread, and the erotic is the discovery of sensuousness that does temporarily break the self-relationship of the self to itself.[13] Anna comes to experience the break permanently as guilt and shame. She immediately feels disconnected both from her pleasure and from spirit, and struggles initially to recover from her spiritual alienation by guilt and shame. In a sense her spirit, as Kierkegaard describes it, looks back over its shoulder at itself in the body, which is not its proper abode, with dread. By her act, Anna confines herself to the perpetual reexperiencing of erotic dread. She must seek being—self-perpetuation and relationship—in the erotic nothing that she dreads; when she is no longer capable of seeking being in what has truly become a stale and empty experience of nothingness, she turns and comes to seek nothingness itself in a loss of faith in being. Thus Anna comes fully to experience what Kierkegaard called the "prodigious contradiction (*Wiederspruch*) that the immortal spirit is characterized as sex."[14] In Kierkegaard the sundering from spirit, its exclusion in the erotic, is felt more completely and spiritually in women precisely because they are more sensuous. Kierkegaard and Tolstoy recognize the body as the ground of the instincts, but they relate the instincts themselves, in different ways, to consciousness rather than the unconscious.

As soon as Anna meets Vronsky she feels both "frightened" and "happy" (p. 95). She feels the apprehension, alarm, adventure that Kierkegaard calls the approach of possibility, the sense of a new more complete and more animated synthesis of the human self. But this apprehension of becoming is always a feeling simultaneously of nothingness and something, of dread and being. Anna feels dread because on the one hand love is a risk, a recklessness, the possibility of loss, emptiness, and dependence; on the other hand, it is a possibility of fulfillment and union. But in the erotic union, the synthesis and linkage is always temporary, fragile, breaking. Furthermore, from the beginning Anna's own spiritual conscience rejects the linkage as a guilty one. She projects her guilt and, accompanying it, her need for punishment onto Vronsky as his desire to leave and abandon her. This is the source of her demon, her spurts of malevolence toward Vronsky. She blames herself for her desire and also blames him for arousing it. Her punishing dreams and perceptions of doubleness are her own divided perceptions of herself in ethical and erotic terms which she cannot make cohere. Her dissociation is the manifestation of her intrapsychic conflict and a primitive defense against it. She experiences what Hegel calls "the essential moment, viz. that of breaking up into extremes with opposite characteristics" (p. 234) as a permanent moment that she cannot overcome. She lives more and more in the relentless atmosphere of the self's negativity.

In her illness and close brush with death, she reasserts her ethical sense; as soon as she is well, she sees only how much Karenin's ears stick out. Her inalienable consciousness of the body dominates again. She feels that her wholeness depends on Vronsky's attraction to her, and thus all her possessive impulses are set in play: to keep him, attract him, test him, repossess him—and always by way of her physical beauty. The conflict narrows down to a mutual conflict of wills, of self-preservation, in which every departure of Vronsky becomes an occasion for a traumatic scene. Anna's urge to own and control turns into an urge to punish what she cannot control. Her suicide is an active mutual punishment, of him for his abandonment of her, of herself for her guilt, and also a way of putting an end to the terror, the suspense of being or not being loved. The suicide is a part of their mutual struggle for recognition, their mistrust, lack of communication, their fear of a crisis and their desire also to provoke a crisis in order to end the dilemma. Suicide has a terrible ambiguity here and the characteristics of a synthesis, a total solution to all the problems. Finally her inner, desperate sense of self-guilt, hatred, ugliness, and lovelessness become the characteristics of the objective world as a whole.

Is any kind—not of happiness even but of freedom from torture—possible? No! No! . . . 'It is impossible! Life is sundering us, and I am the cause of his unhappiness and he of mine, and neither he nor I can be made different. Every effort has been made, but the screws do not act . . . A beggar woman with a baby. She thinks I pity her. Are we not all flung into the world only to hate each other, and therefore to torment ourselves and others? There go schoolboys—they are laughing. Serezha?' she remembered. "I thought I loved him, too, and was touched at my own tenderness for him. Yet I live without him and exchanged his love for another's, and did not complain of the change as long as the other love satisfied me." And she thought with digust of what she called "the other love."

(p. 691)

Anna's relation to her erotic experience remains radically conscious, spiritual, and ethical. She cannot tolerate the idea of lovelessness that she anticipates in Vronsky and sees in herself in her relationship to her son. The fundamental fact of fickleness, infidelity, and disrelationship is at the core of her negative spiritual vision. "It's all untrue, all lies, all deception, all evil!" (p. 693). Anna caps the truth of her body by reason. "Reason has been given to man to enable him to escape from his troubles," she hears a lady saying, and Anna "reasons": "Why not put out the candle, if there is nothing more to look at?" (p. 693).

If we look back from Anna's and Levin's experience of their reason and their body to the scheme we derived from Ficino, we can see that we have come almost full circle. Reason apprehends not God but the nihil. Anna gives her assent to this apprehension, Levin does not. The body, however, which had been in Ficino a source of torment, contradiction, and unreason, is now the very ground for the apprehension of God. When the split logos *is* healable, albeit only momentarily, it is so only in a self grounded in the body, in a self that assents to the body and its unreason, its unreasonable law of two, of union and birth. For Anna, who has in a sense lost and "murdered" her body, this indispensable ground for the spiritual synthesis, the synthesis is no longer available.

What is so compelling in Tolstoy's novel is the equal spiritual strength of Levin's affirmation and Anna's negation. Both emerge from a deep and solitary need to create a synthesis in the self and for the self. Both emerge from a spiritual persistence to relate the self to a totality and to have a clear answer of yes or no to the experience of existence, a persistence which echoes the old hankering after a clear vision of being or nothingness, a hankering after the knowledge of the ground of existence. What is so frightening and powerful as well is exactly the fact that the answer of yes or no appears ultimately, as in Kierkegaard, like a choice in the self, rather than as an answer forced on us by objective conditions. The objective conditions, though very present and powerful, are ultimately not what tips the scale one way or the other. The self itself finally makes the choice: it can readily and easily be either a yes or a no. It is the very identities between Anna and Levin that make the difference in the ultimate choices so troubling and mysterious. By a miracle, Levin leaps out of spiritual dread into being, ethical existence, goodness, and a faith in relatedness. By an equal dread of spirit Anna leaps to nothingness, meaninglessness, disbelief. These are disjunct possibilities in fundamentally the same world and the same self.

It is this very disjunction of the stories of Anna and Levin which early critics immediately criticized as a "basic deficiency in construction," as "a lack of architectonics," and which Tolstoy answered by a series of somewhat vague rebuttals. He claimed that the architectonics was perfect because the links were precisely as indirect, as invisible as he had wished them to be. He claimed that the unity of the structure was an "inner continuity" based not on an idea but "on something else" which could not possibly be expressed directly in words (p. 751, 754). Yet Tolstoy also said that everything he wrote was "guided by the need to bring together ideas linked among themselves," which, however, became debased and meaningless when directly expressed. A close formal study of the novel, of course, reveals that not only Levin's and Anna's but everyone's experience in the novel is a repetition with variations.

This formal repetition is both more "indirect" and "invisible" than any plot coherence could be. It points to the "inner continuity" of isolation and self-disjunction experienced by each, and hidden by each from the other almost like a shame. This negative linkage—this continuity of discontinuity—brings together "ideas linked among themselves," and brings into relief the fundamental concept of character here: the idea that character is a consciousness alone, for all its social ties, acting on itself, concerned with its own spiritual synthesis (which cannot be achieved), ignorant of other consciousnesses. The architectonics emphasizes what the representation of more direct social and plot relations might obscure, self-consciousness in its solitude and self-disjunction.

Tolstoy's architectonics allows the fundamentally monological nature of the self to appear, its ontic, epistemic, emotional, and bodily solitude, and the immense perturbation that it suffers from coexistence. One revealing authorial phrase reinforces this effect of the architectonics, namely when Tolstoy comments that someone "did not know this" (p. 423). What each ultimately does not know is some crucial psychic fact about themselves and about others they love. It is the fact of the lack of self-knowledge that makes them both unable to see that they are making choices and to make these choices more consciously. Thus each character faces the dilemma of what to do, and puts off approaching the dilemma actively by saying "things will right themselves," by drifting and postponing (unaware that this too is a choice); or the characters feel that the choices are ultimately imposed on them.

The other aspect of their monological being has to do with the characters' lack of knowledge of the other and their lack of a drive to know the other. They live with each other, unaware that they do not really know each other, or they brush this awareness aside, repressing it as a kind of aberrant idea when it does come, as it does to Levin before he marries Kitty—a sense of panic that he does not know her, nor she him or herself: " 'But do I know her thoughts, wishes, or feelings?' a voice suddenly whispered. . . . 'Supposing she does not love me? . . . Supposing she does not herself know what she is doing?' " (p. 404). But failure to face the fact that not even love gives us insight into the other makes the characters fail to pursue the dialogue that is necessary for understanding. They act on assumptions about the other based on the self's monologue with itself, or its hopes and fears. Notable in Anna is her almost chronic inability to use and confront words. She fears words and yet takes wordlessness as an important sign for feeling. She does not know that the only way we can penetrate others is by dialogue, that dialogue alone turns us into subjects in relationship to each other. But imagination, with its objectifications and projections, keeps the other an object.

Thus the characters' perceptions of each other are fundamentally metonymic; they are based everywhere on a lack of full presence or being, a part substituting for the whole. It is this metonymic and projected relationship that is so clearly demonstrated in the tragic failure of communication between Anna and Vronsky. But it is also evident in lesser ways in Dolly's relationship to her children, whom she does not know when she fears at moments that they will become evil, or in Levin's final moment, when he decides to keep his vision a secret from Kitty, an act which echoes Varenka and Koznyshev's lost moment of speaking. It is this fundamental penchant of the characters to remain monologic, working things out in solitude, including their relationship to crucial and nearby others, and the metonymic, partial relationship of the characters to each other that constitute the troubling and overall effect of Tolstoy's architectonics. Tolstoy's clarity in representing this becomes the possiblity of a vision that criticizes this entire manner of self-existence and coexistence—one so characteristic of the nineteenth century, so inadequate, and so obviously based on an old religious model where the relationship to the self and to the spiritual other could not be anything but private, monologic, and partial.

In a world of coexistence, a subjectivity that asks primarily "What am I?" is not enough. An ethical self constituted in solitude with itself or even with God is not yet ethically adequate. There is a level at which the hidden linkage of Tolstoy becomes a form of ironic criticism of a certain kind of subjectivity which gives the novel a nontragic dimension despite its predominantly tragic form. Tolstoy's structuration demonstrates simultaneously the practice and truth of the Kierkegaardian notion of spiritual selfhood and self-development in the nineteenth-century world and the inadequacy of this notion of selfhood in a social world of coexistence. In Kierkegaard, man is by definition spiritual and the presence of spirit in him will either help him to find God or, undeveloped, will torment him and make him seek an identity against spirit, an identity in nothing. "God tempts no man" and "is not tempted by anyone," says Kierkegaard, but "every man is tempted by himself."[15] What Kierkegaard's spiritual self-dialectic omits is the self's relationship to the other human self. In Tolstoy's characters we find fundamentally the same omission. They come into a positive relationship to themselves and to others via the detour of God. Without the supportive and radiant transcendental moment, the self sinks into despair and disrelationships. The Tolstoian "human self," unlike the developed "theological self" of Kierkegaard, can only maintain its synthesis temporarily. Furthermore, the "human" self needs a dialectic, which must in essence be dialogical, with another "human" self. The clearest sign of the split logos of this artistic world on the level of coexistence is the absence or inadequacy of full, human dialogue. This absence or inadequacy, which is not acceptable, contradicts the tragic forms tendency to accept everything as inevitable. Eliot sought relief from the tragic vision of her novel by the projection of a non-tragic future, and sometimes, by the direct censure of the inadequacy of a particular moral will. In Tolstoy, there is neither the projection nor the censure, and yet there is an opening up of the tragic form by the critical representation. In both, despite the difference in degree, there is an ambiguity toward the tragic form that is in itself one of the most intriguing aspects of their novels.

The world is disjunct, so are the lives of the characters, and so is the self. In the self, the clearest sign of the split logos is the depths of the experience of the body-mind split. All these disjunctions are a truth of which the formal plot disjunction is but a small and necessary reflection.

In Tolstoy's novel the Hegelian conjunction of the self's negativity with Reason disintegrates. The self in its development through self-negativity has difficulty in overcoming the divisions, splits, oppositions, and antitheses that it itself produces. There is no longer any ultimate meaning-giving, rational force to help heal, synthesize, and reunite the perplexing consequences of negativity. Anna's absolute despair lives on in Levin's sense of disjunction at those moments when his reason will question his unreasonable persistence in living. Anna's life is but an absolute dramatization of what will continue to happen to Levin. In the actual, meaningless world of becoming, true despair is as little reversible into joyous synthesis as the logic of concrete bodily-affective experience is defiable. The novel leaves us finally with a double vision: a sense that on the one hand everything depends on the individual's monologue and dialectic with the synthesizing spirit, as in Kierkegaard, and on the other, that the crucial determining factors are, first dialogue, and then, respectively, Levin's positive and Anna's negative relationship to the body, the ground of human truth, spirit, and coexistence.

Excursus on Nietzsche

In Nietzsche's *The Birth of Tragedy*, there is one brief reference to the origin of the novel form, which summarizes in effect much of what I have been trying to say:

> Plato has furnished for all posterity the pattern of a new art form, the novel, viewed as the Aesopian fable raised to its highest power; a form in which poetry played the same subordinate role with regard to dialectic philosophy as that same philosophy was to play for many centuries with regard to theology. This, then, was the new status of poetry, and it was Plato who, under the pressure of daemonic Socrates, had brought it about.[16]

For the Nietzsche of *The Birth of Tragedy*, the greatest and the most authentic art is tragic. It is not the apprehension of a logos, but the apprehension of the split, tragic Will of Appollo and Dionysus, a Will divided fundamentally and irrationally between nature and art (objectification). The dialogue form, however, and by implication the novel form which derived from it, are exceptions. They *are* under the aegis of a logos, and therefore, again by implication, they are not authentic art.

In so far as Nietzsche ties the novel's origin to the birth of reason in Socrates, and the novel itself to a desire for the logos, he agrees with Lukács, though the logos of the one is Platonic and that of the other Hegelian, and though one finds it in the dialogue form, and the other in the epic.

By arguing that the Platonic dialogue provides the pattern for the novel, Nietzsche implies several things. First, that the novel, like the dialogue, must be dominated by conceptuality and optimism, the optimism inherent in dialectical philosophy, at the expense of art and truth. Second, that this form had somehow to hide, displace, repress, or annihilate the tragic truth before the form could come into being. And third, that this annihilation was accomplished by means of Socratic irony. Socrates annihilated the irrational and tragic truth, and substituted the pure logos in its stead. Perhaps Socrates was a nihilist, so Nietzsche dares to suggest, but one who tried to dodge the truth of pessimism by irony. "Most secretive of ironists, had *this* been your deepest irony?" (pp. 4–5). Irony and the dialectical search for the logos seem inevitably to go together. But all of this also means, finally, that dialectical philosophy as well as the dialogue and the novel hang, unbeknownst to themselves, over a void, a loss, the negation of irrational truth, nature, and art.

Plato burned his youthful tragic poetry, banishing unreason for the sake of reason, but unable to suppress his creative gifts, he created the form of the dialogue, and into this form he managed to draw all the available poetic styles and forms of his time. His dialogues assimilated, amalgamated, and thereby rescued, the arts of his day, which he himself had consciously repudiated. "By a detour," says Nietzsche, Plato the thinker rescued Plato the poet (p. 87). The dialogue is a new amalgam of the existent arts as tragedy had been, only now they are conjoined under the sign of reason rather than tragic unreason. The dialogue "saves" unreason only by negating it or only in so far as negation has also a power to preserve. And for Nietzsche, negation does have this power. His entire re-evaluation of the course of our history depends upon it— upon negation as the sign of a radical exclusion. In the *Birth* what is at stake for Nietzsche is nothing less than the exclusion of true art (unreason) by reason. Philosophy tried to kill simultaneously tragic truth, the

Will, and authentic art. Nietzsche's inditement of dialectical philosophy is complete.

It follows from Nietzsche's argument that to become authentic art once again, the novel and the dialogue will have to become tragic. They will have to repudiate the logos, sever their connection to it, and substitute in its stead the truth of the Will. They will have to reverse what was itself once a perverse reversal, and restore the dreaming and mythic nature of art. This restoration of art to its truth will involve a struggle, a struggle that pits the void against the mind, or irrational nature with its objectifications against rational, dialectical becoming.

Nietzsche suggests that such a struggle may even have begun in Socrates shortly before his death. He points to the voice in Socrates' dream which told him, "Practice music." The voice is an indication for Nietzsche that unconsciously Socrates recognized what he had denied and ignored all his life in his despotic logic. The voice indicates what he had excluded from his intelligible world. Nietzsche imagines the voice saying to him: " 'Have I been too ready to view what was unintelligible to me as devoid of meaning? Perhaps there is a realm of wisdom, after all, from which the logician is excluded? Perhaps art must be seen as the necessary complement of rational discourse?' " (p. 90). The one who would acknowledge the voice and the necessary complementation of rational discourse by art would be "a Socratic artist," a new kind of artist whose birth Nietzsche deems both necessary and possible.

The kind of confrontation between art and Socratism, between tragedy and logos, which Nietzsche here imagines, is precisely the point at issue in Lukács' vision of the novel and of novelistic irony. For Lukács the crucial question is whether irony will be both tragic *and* ethical, unreasonable *and* logical. Will it be able to reveal and maintain its paradoxy? Will it acknowledge insuperable dissonance? Or will irony be tempted to return back to its Socratic superiority, ignoring the negative ground on which its ironies are built? For Lukács the novel would be differentiated from the dialogue precisely by the fact that here art and Socratism cease to be diametrically opposed to one another. Instead, the novel, like Socrates after his dream, begins to "practice music," at first a music that is rather apollonian, and then a music that is more and more dionysiac. In the novel, Socratic logicality turns back into Socratic irony, dissolving meaning and order by skeptical doubt, and confronting the problem of the excluded, the negated, the ultimate possibility of nothingness, consequencelessness, of tragic unreason. The novel reverses the pattern of domination and submission of the dialogue.

The novel struggles for equalization and confrontation. In this struggle, the annihilating effect of irony has to pass over into tragic recognition, the recognition of the will to be and not to be, to recognize and not to recognize, to see and to be blind to the fact that the will may prefer to will nothing than not to will. The novel becomes a struggle in which the apollonian (in Lukács, the epical form impulse) has to yield to the formless impulse of tragedy. Logical and ethical individualism, which is one pole toward which Socratic irony pulls, falls back into the abyss of psychological dionysianism, the other pole of Socratic nihilating irony. The novel's strain and tension issue from this struggle, this revolutionizing of its old dialogic paradigm. Lukács' vision remains true to the old paradigm precisely in so far as he sees an ambivalent irony, not tragedy, as untimately dominating and controlling the novel. Socratic irony succeeds Socratic logicality in the novel, but it is the spirit of Socrates still that dominates the form. The unintelligible is acknowledged, but as a nothingness that has the power to unify art. Socratic irony displaces Socratic conceptualization in order to acknowledge the primacy of art over rational discourse but not at the expense of rational discourse. Lukács' novelist makes the nihilistic acknowledgment in his creation of a purely technical basis, the ultimate that he has to offer, which is a renunciation of all but art. Yet technique is a rational objectification and discourse, mastery and domination rather than nonmastery or madness, which would be the absence of production of the controlled work of art.

In Lukács' *Theory*, the novel is a form that displaces the logos of the epic world by its vision of the meaninglessness and absurdity of the objective present. The novel's form restores pessimistic truth, but ultimately only ironically. The Lukácsian novelist is always Socratic because he still believes in his formal guidance by the epical logos. He has, as it were, a double "logos," if I may use the world thus, a rational and a tragic one; yet, they are not equal because the tragic is the present and actual one, the other is available only formally. Thus, whereas Nietzsche calls for the total repudiation of the novel's origin and oneness with the logos, Lukács regrets the novel's disconnection from its origin, and hopes for a time when this dissonance may be healed. The Lukásian novel goes back from dialectical optimism to the moment of annihilating irony, out of which the former developed, but not all the way to the acceptance of tragedy.

Nietzsche's implied conception of what the novel could become is far more radical than Lukács' description of what the novel is. I think that both descriptions are correct for the novel at different moments in time. Austen and Eliot are certainly, to different degrees, "Socratic artists," mixing tragic perception with rational faith. Austen's irony was infused by a tinge of pessimism which did not bring any tragic destruction. George Eliot explicitly conceived of her fiction as a kind of novel-tragedy, a hybrid genre; part of her aim in fiction was to "urge the human sanctities through tragedy—through pity and terror."[17] In both, artistic technique emancipates itself from the logos, but it does not therefore perceive itself, though troubled in dim ways by a sense of its inadequacy or its multiplication of points of view, as fully tragic, as unreasonable or self-negating. In Tolstoy, we come closest to the submission of the novel to tragic form, yet even here there is an opening of the tragic, a criticism, that disrupts it. Something new happens in Dostoevsky and Dickens which tips irony and technique over into a tragic confrontation. The dialogue threatens to sever its connection to the logos altogether and to become a confrontation directly with unreason and death.

The reason for this reversal has first of all to do with the fact that the novel turns more seriously and consistently toward the dialogue itself as its model, to the discovery that true dialogue is arbitrary, open, and nonlogical. In a true dialogue with others one cannot plan what will be said. Dialogue feeds off itself, going in unexpected directions, controlled not by reason as the logical Platonic dialogue was, but by free association or the demands of the unconscious. At its core it is movement and interchange, without a logically apprehendable or definable goal. It is a speech demanding recognition by another, but one is not certain precisely of what. A true self-dialogue is equally open and nonlogical, as is indicated by the fact that it so often and so easily comes to an impasse. Both dialogues have in them the kind of displacement and repression that the dream does, seeking simultaneously to reveal and to disguise, coming to a halt in anxiety when there is inadequate disguise. Both by their displacement have invariably a demonic element to them, for the demonic is inherently the displaced, the other, for which metaphor or metonymy substitutes.

From its beginning the novel has been the place of dialogue; dialogic scenes have dominated it to a lesser or greater extent beginning with *Don Quixote*. In *Don Quixote* we see the Don's dialogue with Sancho modifying and contradicting his "dialogue" with the world. Sancho is in an inequal position and has to obey the authority of his master—a fact which always makes dialogue difficult; nonetheless, he is able to bring Don Quixote around to making certain (verbal) compromises with reality. By representing the reality which cannot speak for itself, Sancho forces Don Quixote to address it as he did not have to on his first solitary journey. For example, Sancho forces him from the position that it *is* Malbrino's golden helmet, to the acknowledgment that it is *like* a barber's basin. The simile acknowledges all that is missing, more than merely half the helmet, and allows that a substitution has occurred. Ironically, therefore, the ignorant squire and the master can speak to each other by reinventing the world of fiction, of simile, metaphor, and symbol. They come to understand each other by pertually making use of the fictional translation, with Sancho using literature to translate fiction back into reality and the Don acknowledging reality as a translation of his fiction. Sancho speaks the language of the particulars; the Don the language of essences, but each comes to know the other's language in the medium of fiction.

Via the mutual recognition of substitution, fiction, and translation, the Don's madness, his "no" to reality, becomes more malleable and less absolute. Because of his dialogue with Sancho, Don Quixote's monologue with the world also becomes more dialogical in the sense that he becomes freer from his model and more creative in relation to a reality that he now knows to be preeminently a world of substitutions. The Don learns to labor and to create, rather than to imitate. He learns how to use reality to give substance to his fictions as in the dream in the Cave of Montesinos. In this dream, he is also able to face the real other half of his idealized anima image. His need for Dulcinea encompasses now her need for him; he gives her four of the six reals that she needs. He comes to transmute reality rather than simply to negate and dominate it. The Don remakes his identity in order to negate the uninteresting old gentleman landowner who he was, and, for a time, reality, but given the dialogue with Sancho, he learns also to accept and "receive" reality. The irrational statements of his persona, wonderful and dangerous as they are, dictatorially create Don Quixote's own reality, laws, and system of communications to which others must yield; and everything does yield—except language, which finds in dialogue a way to acknowledge both the madness and the reality. But the language that can acknowledge both is fiction—a language in which words have become dissociated from substance and truth. This language is a site of absences, but it is in such a site alone that fictions can flower, and also errors, lies, and madness, as Sancho so clearly sees. The classical novel is born at the moment when language is dislodged from substance and truth.

In the novels after *Don Quixote*, the dialogic scenes most often function in imitation of the pattern set by this book: they work against the hero's monologic self-objectification and his insane attempt at a "dialogue" with a world that he does not perceive but has invented. In these novels it is the negation of the "real" self as well as of reality that is ironized. But it is also true of these novels that these dialogic scenes remain subservient to the hero's pursuit of his transcendental self, and do so even when the partners in the dialogue become less subservient to the hero than Sancho is to Don Quixote. The dialogue is rejected as a source of truth, or the speech of the other is accepted only partly so, as in *Don Quixote*, or much later in a solitary self-dialogue. The hero characteristically makes his recognition alone. The recognition never occurs in the dialogic moment or process itself, although the dialogue may precipitate it. This is true equally for Emma Woodhouse, Dorothea Brooke, and Anna Karenina. None of them profits adequately from dialogue or lives in dialogue. Dorothea Brooke, who comes closest to doing so, has her insight in perceiving the need for dialogue alone, but what occurs between her and Rosamond is in fact not a dialogue, but a particularly open and affective monologue made by Dorothea to a listening partner.

Most importantly, these are not yet true dialogues precisely because they are tied to recognition. They are not free, but have a function and a goal. The goal is not the Platonic but the subjective logos. In other words, the dialogue is not Platonic but Hegelian, oriented toward the individual and not the general. The dialogue is as if secretly planned to contribute to self-recognition, to self-enlargement, albeit a painful one. The dialogue still maintains its dialecticality, though this is now the Hegelian dialecticality of self-development.

Thus the novel's dialogue is not yet free of logicality, because the impasses, the tremblings, and the dissolution of his being that the hero may experience always lead to a further development and recognition of the self, to action and production, rather than madness. This is true even of Anna Karenina, not only because she becomes incapable of dialogic communication, but because her final self-dialogue is a "rational" recognition and her suicide an action and work which she intends as a recognition of herself, as a self-objectification.

It is because of the repression and unavailability of true dialogue, which must be a mixture of conscious and unconscious speech, that the novel—which was imminently to become force—remains form. It turns the force of becoming into the state of becoming, into the stasis of technique. By dialogic-dialectical self-objectification, the novel makes epical a subject that inherently lacks the substantiality and objectivity of the epic. The hero's self-objectification substitutes for the lacking epic substantiality just as the author's technique substitute for his. The substitutions of each act as a medium which deforms the speaker and their speech. And this deformation occurs precisely and paradoxically because their experiences are given form. The fundamentally monologic goal and function of these partly sham dialogues and self-dialogues become evident in the form of the novel. The great advantage of the monologic is that it allows or even naturally sinks into form. Thus it is the very achievement of form in these novels which points to something that these novels did not understand about subjectivity and intersubjectivity. And to investigate what they excluded about subjectivity we come invariably upon what they excluded from dialogue, its nonepistemic reality, its unreason, its goallessness, its inmixing of consciousness and unconsciousness, and its living speech of tragic nondemanding recognition, its despair and its unconscious, unknown dimension. It is via the transformation of dialogue, first of all, that the novel returns to tragic art, to a vision of blind will and unreason.

Dostoevsky's *The Brothers Karamazov*

A negative tragic recognition is forced upon Ivan in and after his third dialogue with Smerdyakov. He has first of all to absorb the shock of the permeability and openness of individual consciousnesses to each other. He has to learn that while we speak, an unconscious speech accompanies the conscious one, and that the former can dominate and negate the latter. The self is not like a fortress, autonomously closed in itself and for itself. Only in silence could we achieve such an autonomy. But speech communicates. It is heard and absorbed. It is the way individuals become intertwined in each others' consciousnesses. Speech, furthermore, is also not autonomous, not logically in and for itself. It also is permeable, open to the unconscious which seeps through it. Speech is inherently dialogic or double, invigorated or infected by the unconscious will. Smerdyakov only makes plain what he had understood, what part of Ivan's speech he had listened to, when he is convinced that Ivan truly did not know what he, Smerdyakov, was going to do or what he had done. Then, against Ivan's conscious denial of knowing, Smerdyakov elaborates the unconscious speech and will of which he made himself the agent and servant. Smerdyakov is profoundly disappointed and disgusted that so "clever" a man as Ivan knows really so little about the reality and cleverness of unconscious speech.[18]

Following this comes Ivan's self-dialogue, his shocking and only partial avowal of the cowardly, drab, accommodating, limited, conscious, and pettily critical "devil" he has been. Ivan's devil is a purely subjective devil. He knows nothing about God; he knows only Ivan. What is so dazzling about this devil compared to Goethe's Mephistopheles, who was also subjective, is that he has lost all the transcendental, sublime aspects of subjectivity. He is no longer the grand No issuing from a transcendental ego to match its sublime Yes. He is merely the ordinary Ivan, who Ivan does not want to be, and his least glamorous doubts and negations. He is so thoroughly reduced, subjectivized, and secularized that he cannot any longer understand his origins, the story of fallen angels and other such anecdotes about him. These origins have for him the meaning of a dead and now merely puzzling and senseless myth which had best be forgotten. The only devil to whom he refers and feels any relationship to is Mephistopheles, precisely because the latter was also the representative of a subjective dimension in Faust, but he refers to Mephistopheles only in order to negate thoroughly his identity with him. Mephistopheles is his antithesis. Thus he signifies the death and end of all grandiose, transcendental rebellion—the end of the transcendental No, of all negative aspirations and defiance. He is the aspersion cast on Ivan's own "root"—his nonacceptance of the world. He points to Ivan's negative idealism as mere sham, misplaced effort, romantic dreaming. He is the self's negation of all its own grander, more singleminded, and goal-oriented negations. He is negation reduced to mere negativism, to petty resistance. In his denials he represents not so much the reduced power of negation as its dispersal in triviality, stupidity, and egotism.

He is the possibility of Ivan at fifty, without his grand illusions and theatrical rebellions, a gentleman in reduced circumstances, faithless, domesticated, but still philosophizing. He is stupid, trivial, base, contemptible because he is so realistic and nonaspiring. He is so accommodating because he knows Ivan thoroughly and knows that he recognizes no intellectual equals. But it is precisely by his mere animal cunning and cleverness that he undermines Ivan and overcomes his disdainful intelligence. He torments Ivan with the very opposite of the noble intellect by proving, undeniably, that the base intellect is a match for it, a formidable power in its own way. Intellectually he is the caricature of Ivan's mind. He holds up the mirror of the base mind that avoids, escapes, and survives by committing no absurd, senseless, noble deeds. Ivan's devil is "a clever man"—too clever and base to be theoretically consequent. He loves life too much; he is too earthy and sensuous to deceive himself by theory. He can theorize but, given his debased existential attachments, he can also trivialize his theorizing. He is too sensuous to be a consequent nihilist. He has proposed not that the world be annihilated as Mephistopheles did, but that he be. Yet he is easily swayed from this extreme and willing to play his part of negator in the world's comedy for the sake of the pleasure of occasionally living, taking on human shape, suffering, going to the baths, catching a cold, getting rheumatism.

He reduces the transcendental Goethean drama of negation and affirmation to mere farce and comedy. It is a "tragedy" in the hands of men and ideologues, one that they blindly insist on perpetuating. He plays his intellectual part as a critic, creating contradictions and oppositions to keep the intellectual game going, but his real interests lie elsewhere, in the concrete, bodily life of men. He is amazed by the concreteness and substantiality of their real bodily pains and pleasures. His measuring rod for all things is existence. Life is not unarrestable Goethean striving, but suffering. That's given. But it is a suffering *in* existence. "But what about me? I suffer, but still, I don't live. I am x in an indeterminate equation. I am a sort of phantom in life who has lost all beginning and end, and who has even forgotten his own name" (p. 609). His aspiration, in so far as he has any, is precisely the opposite of Goethean infinite striving: he strives for the finite, the limited, the circumscribed—for all that man with his body represents. He tempts Ivan, too, to be purely human, stupid, and real. He tempts him cynically to forget his overreaching, his dreams of a new godless man, and his fictional impulses, in which he reorganizes the real and projects new possibilities and conditions of existence. He tries to show him that existence as it is in its most banal form is something that one can be content with. He tempts Ivan with contentment and with the reconciliation with trivial existence. The devil knows thoroughly the incongruity in Ivan's existence—the discrepancy between Ivan's existential love for life and his dreams of an existence for men other than this one that he loves—and he exploits it to the hilt. As a very clever man he knows what is out of tune and nonadapted in Ivan's thoughts, feelings, and conduct, and he knows that it is banal, brute existence that Ivan always ignores. Thus he brings it to the foreground, holding Ivan's attention by what his whole conscious being denies and rejects.

In appearance the devil is comic compared to other devils, who were awe-inspiring and admirable, and his procedure is comic. He knows what every brilliant comedian knows and Ivan does not: that the intellect can be caricatured because its values are arbitrary and not based on reality. Everything that has no final authenticity can be caricatured; for the devil, that is everything. The persistence of Ivan's refusal to accept banal existence as the foreground, with intellectual activity playing merely a part in the background, is dramatized in the dialogue as Ivan's acceptance or nonacceptance of the devil as a reality. Ivan's denial of the devil's reality is his denial of a part of himself. He cannot maintain this position with any kind of logical consistency because obviously the devil knows him and his thoughts, but knows and sees them in a way that is different from the way Ivan consciously knows and sees his thought. Yet the devil also knows more than his thought or knows how to extend it further into banality and stupidity. He knows that thought oscillates between the extremes of the trivial and the exalted, the base and the noble, and that Ivan has had in his thought processes to repress a whole series of less ripe, powerful, or convincing notions, which now the devil takes delight in retrieving as inalienably a part of thought itself. If the devil is real, and Ivan in desperation tries to make him so, his knowledge of hell and the other world, which is merely paltry and anecdotal, contradicts this. He knows no more about it than the common man. His "transcendental" conceptions echo precisely the changes in the human moral vision of sin and redemption. If the devil had at least some connection to the grand archrebel, Satan, Ivan's own grand negations would at least have a context, albeit spiritually merely a negative and demonic one. But this devil denies his connection to the grandeur of past evil and rebellion. He cannot be sublimated. And thus all that Ivan had struggled to be and thought that he was is reduced to petty, egotistic, and meaningless evil. The reduction of the demonic is what Ivan finds so painful and unacceptable, even as his mind forces him to recognize it.

Ivan's confused efforts to perceive the devil on a real objective level, and yet to deny *this* devil and this dreadful and drab demonic subjectivity, lead him into the logical trap of acknowledging together with the objectivity of evil the entire transcendental enterprise pinned on faith. "Confess that you have faith even to the ten-thousandth of a grain," says the devil (p. 612). Ivan violently denies that he has any such faith, seeking to escape his own trap. But this makes his only alternative accepting this part of his subjectivity. And this for him is so terrible, so equally nonacceptable, that he confesses both now and to Alyosha later that he should like to believe in the devil; he would prefer to. For Alyosha this is sufficient to be the beginning of a sign of conversion; for Ivan it is the beginning of madness. His madness lies in having to deny what he knows is himself. If subjectivity is all there is, his rebellion is reduced to confounded self-negation.

Ivan's grandiose refusal of faith is reduced by the devil to a refusal that hangs merely on common sense. He describes how he was with Christ at the cross and how he longed to be borne aloft on the bosom of Christ together with the thief who believed. But like the nonbeliever, the other thief, he remained where he was, fastened down by common sense.

> But common sense—oh, a most unhappy trait in my character—kept me in due bounds and I let the moment pass! For what would have happened, I reflected, what would have happened after my hosannah? Everything on earth would have been extinguished at once and no events could have occurred. And so, solely from a sense of duty and my social position, I was forced to suppress the good moment and to stick to my nasty task.
>
> (p. 614)

Atheism and disbelief need no elaborate intellection—the immense strain of reason that Ivan had put into them. Atheism has always existed and it is merely the consequence of the inertia, the stop, the "this is ridiculous," by which common sense prompts us to stay where we are and think before we act. Common sense—our inability for spontaneous self-abandon—"let[s] the moment pass." Faust had been able to seize every moment because he lacked this unhappy trait, because he was not concretely human but ideal. This devil, unlike all others, has the desire but not the ability for exaltation. Reason is but the rationalization of common sense; it issues from common sense to justify the arrest of emotion and action. Reason quite reasonably demonstrates the absurdity of Goethe's *Faust* and its hosannic conclusion. This conclusion signifies the end of everything, an apocalypse, and this is absurd and untrue because obviously everything has gone on and must go on. The devil undermines Ivan's faith in the freedom of his intellect. The old Socratic *daimon*, which said no and prevented Socrates from doing various things, was not reason but merely his common sense, telling him to think before he acted. Reason is but the inhibition of feeling and movement. It stops them and then proceeds to justify the arrest, sometimes elaborating them into grand negations and necessity. This devil, unlike all others, does not feel free, but determined.

Ivan's "Geological Cataclysm," so the devil demonstrates, was nothing but a rather paltry and noncommonsensical revision of Goethe's *Faust* in existential terms.

> Everyone will know that he is mortal and will accept death proudly and serenely like a God. His pride will teach him that it's useless for him to repine at life's being a moment. . . . Love will be sufficient only for a moment of life, but the very consciousness of its momentariness will intensify its fire . . . .
>
> (p. 616)

Ivan's vision stands in the shadow of Goethe's, sharing in its fire, ethicality, and idealism. That there is a reversal between existence and the beyond is merely superficial compared to all the optimistic baggage Ivan retains from Goethe. Ivan wanted to swindle, to commit a crime. But why, the devil asks him, does he have to justify a desire by moral and logical constructs? Why can he not swindle honestly out of irrational emotion or for the sake of common sense? To Smerdyakov it had made good common sense on all grounds that he wanted to murder his father. Emotionally he hated him; he was disgusting and useless and troublesome and he had the money that Ivan needed. Later at the trial, Ivan utters the irrational truth: "Who doesn't desire his father's death?" (p.

651). But he goes to the trial, unable to let the moment pass, unable to stop himself by common sense. It is the sheer irrationality of his conscience, which he knows or condemns reasonably—out of common sense—as being no more than a habit, a reflex acquired by a practice of seven thousand years to which he cannot reconcile himself. He breaks into madness not because he cannot rationally accept the fact of irrational, unconscious emotions, but because he cannot rationally accept acting on an irrational impulse, and thereby confirming the existence of an unconscious conscience.

The devil's appearance signifies the destruction of Ivan's intellect. The intellect is simultaneously enlarged and reduced. It acquires a dubious, shadowy, shabby side, an origin in base impulses. Ivan indicts his own intelligence as his Grand Inquisitor had Christ. He devalues it as banal, reactive, derivative, and unoriginal. If we cannot affirm and rely on the intellect, what then? Then we are tottering at the boundary of our mind, of our very being, toward madness and incoherence. The devil scene is Ivan's masochistic attack on his own grandest affirmations and negations, and the reversal of Goethe's *Faust,* with its ultimate triumph of affirmation, into the option of a reduced finite affirmation on the one hand, and an endless struggle of self-deception, self-evasion, and self-justification on the other. We can continue to negate until we grow mad and stupid or make the limited affirmation, the confirmation of another, that is possible.

Ivan is the author of "The Grand Inquisitor," which Dostoevsky called "so powerful a rejection of God" as has never yet been conceived (p. 769), and he was himself worried whether he could contradict the chapter. The Grand Inquisitor is Christ's antagonist, believing the devil's interpretation of mankind. His conscience obeys his intelligence, which received its illumination from the devil. The devil is for him the eternal intellect who revealed his comprehension of the human condition by the three questions he posed to Christ. It is the devil who understands man, and not Christ. "From those questions alone, from the miracle of their statement, we can see that we have here to do not with the fleeting human intelligence, but with the absolute and eternal" (p. 233). Men need material security; they put the self-preservation of their bodies foremost. They deeply desire immortality and fear a life aimed toward death which strikes them as meaningless and purposeless. They also crave authority and fear choice, disorder, and anarchy. They cannot fully believe without palpable proof or the presence provided by concrete, sensuous experience. Christ's demands demonstrate that he misinterpreted human nature, that he did not love man, and that he was mad. Christ condemned man to suffering by elevating him and giving him freedom. But man is by nature a slave to his own cravings and weaknesses. He is weak, vicious, worthless, and rebellious. There is madness in the Christ-ideal, which the Grand Inquisitor refuses to serve in order to reduce men's suffering. "I awakened and would not serve madness" (p. 240). The answering kiss of Christ "glows in his heart, but the old man adheres to his idea" (p. 243). The Grand Inquisitor adheres to the truth of the intellect revealed by the devil. He succumbs to the cunning of intellect, its power to maintain itself against all other truths.

Ivan's "Geological Cataclysm" is the optimistic parallel to that work, written by a Grand Inquisitor who joyously affirms that from the negation of God alone, man's transformation into another, higher creature will follow. "Geological Cataclysm" is a Feuerbachian work but, as the devil points out, the hitch in it is that men are inveterately stupid, and self-deluding as in fact the Grand Inquisitor had said, and that this vision of the new man is, therefore, Ivan's alone, giving only Ivan license to do anything he please.

In Ivan's nightmare the devil is not at all, as is the Grand Inquisitor, a negator of Christ. "Before time was, by some decree which I could never make out, I was predestined 'to deny' and yet I am genuinely goodhearted and not at all inclinced to negation" (pp. 608–9). When he negates, it is against his will and inclination. He cannot really negate because there is nothing he is sure of. Negation is for him a mystery; it presupposes certitude, and he is not certain of anything. He is an agnostic, he doesn't know whether God exists or not. He dreams only of what he does not have: a human body, of "becoming incarnate once for all and irrevocably in the form of some merchant's wife weighing two hundred fifty pounds, and of believing all she believes" (p. 605). He longs simply to be human, bodily and real, on any terms. The devil lacks the transcendental intellect that the Grand Inquisitor gave him credit for having. He is the Grand Inquisitor's definition of the human, only suffering from a lack of realism. He is a skeptical kind of Enlightenment intellectual, perpetually ironizing and banalizing his own thoughts; he is a Descartes split permanently and irrevocably from his body. He is the destruction of Ivan's intellectual beauty and pride, its leveling, trivialization, and reduction. He is Ivan's life-force, his existential will to persist, his "longing for life" and his will "to go on living in spite of logic," now made apparent as a contradiction to Ivan's intellectual aspirations and negations. The devil's intellect represents the one that is more coherent and in tune with Ivan's primitive, crude, unbridled, earthy love for life. The devil is Ivan as his father. The devil is, above all, irrational negation. Ivan has erred in thinking that his grand repudiations were rational.

This is the other half of the grandiose devil we have imagined, the negativism, the stubborn resistance to meaning, the trivial, the insignificant, and the shabby that Goethe had largely excluded from his vision of Mephistopheles. He is not intentional evil, but unintentional, ignorant, and undesigned evil, the evil that comes about unconsciously, as Ivan's evil does. His is the evil of the functionary, of the servant and sponger who does what he is told in order to be accepted, or who does what he thinks others want him to do in order to be amicable; he is accommodating so as to be able to remain comfortable and unperturbed. In that sense, he is even a debasement of Smerdyakov, who at least believed temporarily that his action was a truth. This devil knows no truth, nor does he believe it exists. He only knows existence *is*, and that this is what he lacks. He is less than a will to murder; he is the inertness of the self itself, its death, its sense of life as comedy and farce.

> We understand that comedy; I, for instance, simply and directly demand that I be annihilated. No, live, I am told, for there'd be nothing without you. . . . So against the grain I serve to produce events and do what's irrational because I am commanded to.
>
> (p. 609)

He is the death impulse pure and simple made to serve, against his will, other and complex purposes that he cannot comprehend. He has an obscure part in maintaining the diversity and plurality of this world. But he does not understand why this diversity and contradiction are necessary. He is the negation that comprehends neither its relation to death nor life. He is a wish for death too weak to refuse life, weak out of inertia, not desire. He tempts Ivan not into disbelief but belief. Thus he becomes the utter perversion of the satanic idea. His vision of paradise, of course, is utterly banal, conventional, and inert. It is like his dream of being human, two hundred fifty pounds of inactivity and utter lack of striving. He wants to prove to Ivan that what he claimed was "his root"—to refuse, not to accept the world as it is—is meaningless and absurd (p. 217). Further, the perfection of rebellion, never to be reconciled to what is, cannot logically be maintained.

The radical secularization of God's attributes that Feuerbach urged, attributes which were to be reabsorbed and rediscovered in man, have in Dostoevsky a counterpart in the radical secularization of the devil, who has also to be reappropriated as the stupid, inert, and contradictory self, the self incapable of otherness or the absolute, the self as Thanatos. Both God and the devil, however, have too vast a subjective significance to be readily appropriated. Dostoevsky portrays the shock of consciousness suffering under this excess and remainder, this need to absorb into the self what was thought to be objective and may still be so. Consciousness staggers as its definition of autonomous self-recognizing and self-recognizable selfhood is broken. How can the question "What am I?" be answered when the self is evidently another, an unconscious, something permeable and open both to itself and the other, doubly double, always speaking toward an inaccessible unknown both within and without? The negativity of the self becomes truly formidable when the essential pluralizing moment within the self breaks it into irremediable extremes with opposite characteristics.

Dostoevsky no doubt demanded to read Hegel, declaring "My whole future is bound up with this," because Hegel's vision of coexistence also entailed the vision of the self as another, the problem of recognition, and self-multiplication.[19] All the Karamazovs suffer and exhibit the force of fickle, fragmented selfhood. They are all the actors of the volatile, free, spontaneous spurts of energy in the self. Like Dimitri, they do not know which of their impulses possess true reality. Their prankish and theatrical self-presentation is an assertion of the self regardless of the other and regardless, too, of the self. Their freedom is a freedom from and not for anything. They are all driven naysayers. They are, to begin with, psychologically free of any social bonds, so that Dostoevsky can reveal how they might not be free as brothers. If and when they do become bound in their fantastic self-inventiveness, it is only by the limitations and possibilities and effects of each upon the other. Ivan is the last to recognize any bonds to himself and the last to recognize another as part of himself.

Dostoevsky knew that the recognition of coexistence had to be based on something other than either sympathetic imagination, the powers of identification, or conscious intellectual recognition. It had to be based on a necessity other than consciousness or imagination. He found this necessity in living speech, that act of selfhood which inherently declares "I am the other," a need to speak, to recognize and be recognized. Only speech entails the actuality of the other, even when the actuality of that other is denied in the very act of speaking. That actuality then reappears in the self as its own negated speech, as it does in Ivan when he has to come to accept his ties to Smerdyakov, his father, and the devil.

In the time of negation, in the slowness of impeded perception that is negation, he comes to acknowledge his cowardly, arrogant participation in the murder of his father and also in Smerdyakov's suicide. Negation in his nightmare functions as the agent of retardation, allowing him to glimpse the discrepancy between the simplicity of consciousness and the unsolvable complexity of an unconscious that accompanies it. What is important for Dostoevsky, however, is not primarily the mystery of the unconscious, but the extent to which it is clearer, more "intellectual," more dialogic than it had ever been before. Dostovsky is concerned with the extent to which the consciously negated points to a new definition of selfhood, to that which destroys Ivan's notions of identity. Dostoevsky searches for a basis, a ground from which individualism can be criticized and overcome. He establishes that the recognition of the other can occur only when consciousness breaks.

Until the idea of coexistence is felt as a reality, the master-slave reality in which the Grand Inquisitor believes cannot be overcome. It is a division that the conscious intellect inevitably sees in reality. Zosima's conversion occurs at the moment when the question of the validity of the master-slave relationship forces itself upon him. His ethical and affective denial of any basis in reality for the relationship produces in him instantaneous bliss. Zosima discovers that he has the power to say "I am and I love" (p. 301). "I am love" is the core of Christ's meaning, the meaning of his kiss, and the answer to the Grand Inquisitor's "I am intellect."

Zosima's conversion consists of four stages. First, he spontaneously discovers that he has done wrong: "What a crime!" (p. 277). The reality of conscience erupts in him inexplicably, suddenly. Suddenly he feels "something vile and shameful" and he knows that his feeling has to do with the fact that he beat his servant, Afanasy, the night before. Suddenly the servant who had been to him no more than an object becomes a full subject, a living real human being whom it is a crime to beat, to treat like an object. The miracle of conscience is that it makes others into subjects. Suddenly they acquire the same reality we have for ourselves. Conscience is the birth in the self of the other as a subject, the moment of the transformation of the other as object into subject. After Zosima spontaneously discovers that he is wrong, the model of what is right is provided for him by his brother. Suddenly he remembers the words of his brother Markel and his example of love. This memory completes Zosima's ethical awareness:

> Yes, am I worth it? flashed through my mind. After all what am I worth, that another man, a fellow creature, made in the likeness and image of God, should serve me? For the first time in my life this question forced itself upon me.
>
> (p. 277)

Full ethical awareness means that the other cannot be my servant or I a master. From this follows Zosima's act of going to his servant and asking for his forgiveness. Since the servant seems not to understand these words, Zosima feels impelled to reinforce them by a gesture: "I dropped at his feet and bowed my head to the ground." This bow becomes the great symbol of the overcoming of the master-slave dialectic in the novel, and it is repeated in various ways—inadequately, half-heartedly, or with conviction and joy—by others. Zosima, who had never thought ethically about his relationship to others, who had lived merely by social codes and conventions, such as those that told him to fight a duel and kill a man for his honor, comes for the first time and independently to question what this relationship to the other could and should be. He becomes an ethical man who acquires a sense of the absolute value of another man, another who cannot be beaten without this beating being felt to be a crime. He gives birth to the reality of the other in a deep unconscious conscience and then feels compelled to communicate this new feeling in a deed and an action. He resigns his singular, individual "human self" not, as in Kierkegaard, for a new "theological self" with God, but for a self of coexistence; only after that experience do the truth and reality of Christ come flooding back to him. The way to Christ is via the detour of coexistence, the recognition of the self and the other, the self as love ("I am and I am love"), via the bow that overcomes the Grand Inquisitor's master-slave reality. There is no other way to Christ or God in Dostoevsky. The leap of faith can only occur after the recognition of the other. "Active love" alone expels doubt (p. 48); the only way to God is the existential way of coexistence. Finally, after this act, Zosima feels ecstasy, bliss. He is in paradise.

> We don't understand that life is a paradise, for we have only to understand that and it will at once be fulfilled in all its beauty, we shall embrace each other and weep.
>   . . . there was such bliss in my heart as I had never known before in my life.
>
> (p. 279)

It is by this sense of bliss that never again leaves him that he truly triumphs over the Grand Inquisitor, who is forever unhappy, suffering, morose, and tragic. Zosima is converted not by dogma or by a sudden vision of Christ, but by having a new vision of man. He gives birth in himself to a man and then he gives birth in himself to Christ. Coexistence—the transformation of his servant and slave into a man—is established here by conscience and love and not, as in Hegel by reason. Faith is not reason, or paradoxy as in Kierkegaard, but active love. Faith follows from a spontaneous awakening to the other. Zosima says," I am two," "I am this vibration and resonance with another." As soon as one commits the act of love and recognizes the quality and freedom of the other in oneself, one believes in Christ, because then one has acted out the truth of His vision of humanity. We rediscover the eternal model of love only when we discover our own ability to say, "I am and I am love." This is the certitude of selfhood that Zosima opposes to the Grand Inquisitor's individualism, to his "I am I," "I am intellect," "I am autonomous reason." Zosima opposes the conscience of the heart to the rational conscience of the Grand Inquisitor and of Ivan, each of whom tries to adhere ethically to what merely his consciousness tells him.

Behind Zosima's conversion, and unimaginable without it, is the "unconscious" example of his brother. It is not Zosima but his brother who first had the vision of servantless brotherhood. It is his example, which Zosima had consciously denied and ignored, that now erupts as if from his unconscious into a vital, meaningful memory. This memory of a living example, and not the model of Christ, is crucial in his conversion. Zosima preaches his faith in the importance of the example because it is the concrete, living demonstration men need to persist in their faith and to believe that men can live together rather than in solitude: "Some-

times even if he has to do it alone, and his conduct seems to be crazy, a
man must set an example, and so draw men's souls out of their solitude,
and spur them to some act of brotherly love even if he seems crazy, so
that the great idea may not die" (p. 283). The memory of the model is
what, for example, Dimitri lacks at the moment when he bows to Katerina. He bows to her need; he discovers an ethical impulse in himself
that strikes him as utterly inexplicable and absurd. The impulse comes
neither to a full-fledged ethical awareness in him at that moment nor is
there the memory of a model to reinforce and make flower the impulse.
The model has to take us by surprise—it has to seem to erupt from the
unconscious. But actually we are not dealing here with the real unconscious but with an unconscious memory. Dostoevsky, unlike George
Eliot, does relegate the unknown to the self, but the unknown is not yet
the truly hidden unconscious. He is trying to say that the "thou" of the
"I" is born as if in a dream, out of some other, deeper level of selfhood
than consciousness (in Zosima's unconscious memory, in Ivan's unacknowledged dimension of speech and self-dialogue) but that this dimension still has the characteristics of consciousness. It can be objectified, it
is like what is known, and not yet radically different from and opposed
to the known. If for Zosima there had been no crucial living model, this
very absence may have prevented his conversion. The conscious
model tends to become a law; the unconscious model, when it becomes activated, strikes us as a free choice in the self. Love cannot be
compelled; it has to be freely chosen. Love is the free choice of non-
autonomy, a free rejection of the intellectual vision that posits autonomous egos. Love is the awareness of the other, a conscience that
testifies to them but that does not judge them.

The Grand Inquisitor's vision of man believes in inequality and by in-
stitutionalizing it, it perpetuates the separateness of men. Zosima's vision hopes to overcome this separateness by presupposing looser ego
boundaries and the possibility of men's discovery of each other. His
vision presupposes the need for communion and dialogue. Speech, confession, is for him the sign that the intellect itself is entwined in love,
exhibiting itself as the need to speak and to be heard. The devil's vision
criticizes and points to the madness in both visions. He acknowledges
his aesthetic and affective attraction to Zosima's ideal, but states that in
practice common sense and reason bar him from that bliss. He sees that
in man there is an unfortunate and inexplicable tendency not to leap or

an inability to leap out of consciousness, a tendency which turns into full-fledged atheism. He proves that when a man does leap, not to God, but to the side of another, the moral dimension of the leap is highly dubious. It may be a leap not only out of habit, but pride in being admired, both for the boldness of one's sins and for the generosity of renouncing oneself for one's brother. The seeming "ethical" aspect of Ivan's resolution may be nothing but a darker extension of his egotism. The overcoming of separateness here may be merely a sham way of perpetuating and exhibiting the domination of one by the other. One makes the given situation serve the aims of the self and turns others into functionaries and applauders of the self.

Ivan tortures himself with his need to be suspicious of any ethical, outflowing impulse. The devil is not allowed to comment on the figure of the suffering, noble Grand Inquisitor at all, but he comments on him indirectly by elaborating on the "Geological Cataclysm" and making evident its strength (the authority of the use of power and the domination of the exceptional over the nonexceptional) and its weakness (its need to justify the domination ethically, which in fact weakens the case for domination). For domination is just an irrational, inherent impulse, a kind of will to power that defies ethical justification because it simply is. So the devil argues for the existence of a different type of man, one who is readily an atheist and master, or even a murderer, even as he undermines his very argument by also proving the utter commonness of Ivan both as an intellectual and as a sensuous man. He is only a potential atheist, master, and murderer in the grand style because he doesn't have the power to maintain his own visions or the courage to commit any final acts in thought or practice. Ivan is a master who begot a lackey and servant without even knowing it. And when he is forced to acknowledge the servant by the servant himself, he does so with disbelief and disgust. He who recognizes the other because he is forced to do so by the other has not recognized him. Everything here is the reverse of Zosima's recognition of his servant, a discovery, a creation, ending in bliss.

Ivan doubts, he revises, he undoes himself, and secretly he suspects himself of commonness, desire for faith, and stupidity. He is afraid he has had grand visions of the elect, the masters, to counterbalance the fact that in his soul he feels himself to be a lackey, a brother only to fools like his father and Smerdyakov. (And more like the former precisely because he could never kill himself.) Thus the devil's argument on the whole maintains a distinction between men as types but forces Ivan to acknowledge his general negative likeness to a certain thoroughly negative type. He breaks Ivan's sense of autonomy, but not the autonomy of the type. The situation remains the same: those who can love love those who cannot love in return. There are those who escape madness by giving birth in themselves to the other, and those who never can.

At the trial Ivan is on the stand to test the possibility of breaking the type, but he ends in incoherence and a fit of screaming, having testified once again to his desire for faith and his nonpossession of it. "I would give a quadrillion quadrillions for two seconds of joy," he cries, but he is still the man lying on the road in protest (p. 652). Ivan's dialogic impulse opens up the self in a new dialogic way, but when he speaks to other men it is a monologue he presents, the content of which is his dialogue with himself. He can speak, but he no longer listens or communicates. His monologue is mad and incomprehensible to others, but he cannot control his madness and is dragged out of court as a disrupter. The most he can do is to present himself as he is to other men, to represent to them his self-recognition in an undisguised way. He is the old hero in a novel with new heroes—a Don Quixote who has corrected his self-deception and deluded self-objectifications to the point where he destroys himself. In his anxiety to be accurate, to establish the true nature of his consciousness, he has undermined all the possible bases of truth and accuracy and the very possibility of coherent speech.

Speech is negation and identification, self-objectification and self-loss in the objectification. Ivan's speech becomes sheer negation and self-loss. Negation, which was in Hegel and Goethe part of the force of reason, demonstrates now its unreasonable and wild activity in consciousness, turning the idea of the unity and wholeness of the self into mere delusion. Consciousness appears but as a proliferation of symbols or negation, conscious statements that have to be retracted, until the self is consumed in the activity of making negations and retracting them. Ivan's tragedy is the impossibility of making a definite and final negation, one that could define him without destroying him. His tragedy is being caught in a mad, irrational paradoxy of negations. Consciousness here loses itself in and through its conscious negations. Symbols of negations become the self's exasperating ex-centricity.

The logos of the novel's irony and dialogue, in so far as it concerned the self, passes now beyond self-recognition into a tragic, boundless un-known, a realm where self-recognition depends on the recognition of the other and by the other, or the recognition of an intention not to recognize the other in the self. But the self as an entity that cannot and does not wish to recognize itself as an ex-centricity, as a need for recognizing or being recognized by another, is so purely negative a notion of self-hood that it has to be refused. Yet it is the logical counterpart of the idea that the self is this recognition by and of another.

Ivan's speech does not share his being but declares it. He speaks to himself; still, does he not speak to be heard? Does not every utterance presuppose another who listens? And has he not by the very fact of speaking given "an onion," though he would no doubt withdraw it as does the old woman in the tale? Or perhaps his kind of speech cannot be counted as an onion to begin with? For Alyosha it can. It is the sign of a pre-form of conscience. It is no more than that because Ivan tes-tifies to a crime for which he feels no guilt. The feeling "What a crime!" which initiated Zosima's conversion is absent in him. Yet he "gives" the testimony, something extra that he does not have to give. And behind it stands his traumatic recognition of himself as a model for Smerdyakov, whom he continues to hate, of Dimitri in his innocence and need, whom he also hates, and, above all, of himself as the son of a father who can only be hated. His recognition is of those whom he cannot recognize. He hates himself for doing a stupid thing for stupid and dead people. "Why, why is everything so stupid?" (p. 652) is all he is able to feel and think at the trial. It is still a rational perception, but one which registers the total absence of the rational. The perception of reason's absence is one moment away from its ceasing to be, its nonexistence. His choice and commitment to the end is to a reason that has ceased to be.

In Ivan, European rational subjectivity and its effort to constitute the ego, to liberate it from the superego and to establish a rational, critical self, unfettered by inherited social and historical patterns, quickly comes to grief. The Hegelian notion of a consciousness modeled on the au-tonomy of the intellect proves to be weak, powerless, and potentially, the source of immense evil. In Anna Karenina's case, consciousness chose rationally to will nothing rather than not to will. In Ivan's case, ra-tional negation is no longer possible. The immense remainder—all that consciousness could not encompass—is no longer one that can be ra-tionally absorbed into another synthesis, not even into a negative one.

The negativity of the self, its power to sever and disassociate and thereby to proliferate and produce opposites and contradictory polarities, turns into an activity that can no longer be ordered into a rational process. The remainder becomes too vast for synthesis because consciousness turns out to be too deep, too continuous with an unconscious opposite. This madness of negativity, this double splitting that cannot be healed, is also felt in the form. This failure of the newly emergent ego to establish itself as a synthesis gives back to the novel the tragic dimension of art which the Platonic dialogue form had lost in its alliance with the logos.

To shore up the weakness of the emergent ego, Alyosha forms an alliance between the self and others. In his vision, that is the only way for subjectivity to avoid madness and despair. Alyosha's very manner of being in the world is as if based on an unconscious acknowledgment that the self is a reflection, given or received from another from the beginning. It bears from its inception, to borrow Lacan's formulation, the marks of another, and seeks throughout life confirmation in the recognition of the other.[20] There are marvelous moments in Dostoevsky where the self comes upon its recognition by another, such as the moment when Dimitri discovers that someone has put a pillow under his head while he was asleep. "Who put that pillow under my head? Who was so kind?" he exclaims in joy (p. 480). The great moment of bliss is always that of being recognized by the other or recognizing the other, and not as in Austen, Eliot, or Tolstoy the solitary moment of self-recognition.

In Dostoevsky these moments of the recognition of coexistence have a constitutive effect on the consciousness. The philosophic sense of wonder and mystery aroused by such moments has the power to convert the ego from self-absorption to an openness toward others. The heroes correct not merely a blindness in the self toward itself, but their whole orientation to others. They feel suddenly and completely estranged from themselves as they were, from their former autonomous egos in which they were closed off within themselves from others, those with whom they could only engage in a power struggle of domination and servitude, a struggle such as Katerina and Dimitri carry on throughout the novel. Instead of negating their particularity for a more open and spacious (but egotistic) generality, as occurs in the Hegelian system, they raise the struggle to another level altogether. For them the alienation in the self is not a self-alienation, a subjective otherness, but the concrete alienation from the actuality of the men who coexist with them. For them the recognition of the other ceases to be, as it always is for Katerina, a humiliation and displacement of the self, a self-loss.

No doubt there is as much madness and illusion in their sense of unity, wholeness, and continuity with others as there is in the autonomous ego's sense of its unity and wholeness. Both are based, in different ways, on the denial of difference, variety, multiplicity, fragmentation, and dispersal. At least this is why Alyosha appears to Lisa, and often to readers, as unreal, insubstantial, and unconvincing. "Alyosha, why is it I don't respect you?" asks Lisa. "I am very fond of you, but I don't respect you. If I respected you, I wouldn't talk to you without shame, would I?" (p. 549). Lisa disrespects him for his lack of borders, of determinate intellectual and moral judgments, of an autonomy that would prevent her saying everything to him and flowing into him. Alyosha has looser ego boundaries because he is not an "I am" but an "I am the other"; he is more like a mirror who reflects others, one in whom others find merely themselves, rather than his own "I." Alyosha has no self against which the other can struggle. It is as if he disappears, merely to listen, and the others go on speaking shamelessly because they are left free, undominated, unrepelled, and unabsorbed. Lisa cannot respect Alyosha because his "I am the other" means also "I am not myself," and if there is no self, there can be no self-pride, and therefore no respect from another. Here, in another sense, subjectivity is lost, for the self's becoming is absorbed and delayed in the becoming of others who fail to become, and who fail to become partly because they do not know how to become outside of a system of egos struggling for domination and servitude. What meaning can an asubjective subjectivity have? What can be its goal?

Its single meaning is affective. Its "truth" lies in the sense of joy with which it overcomes fear and despair. Nonetheless, some men consciously choose despair over joy, precisely because by that they salvage an ego, critical and detached from others, which strikes them as the truth. The major problem, however, with an ego like Ivan's is that it cannot recognize others as emotional wholes but only as part-objects. Alyosha is his openness recognizes others as complete persons, but runs into the same problem that Ivan runs into with himself, the incomplete and interminable aspect of the consciousness in the other. Thus madness and inexplicable rejections and repulsions also enter into all of Alyosha's relations with others.

What ultimately helps to organize the potentially explosive madness in the novel is Dostoevsky's parallelism of the new myths of subjectivity with the past myths of God. The religious fictions play the part of objective correlatives that partly illuminate and guide the significance of the purely existential experiences of coexistence even as they obscure and conceal them. Fundamentally, the book is an existential denial of the immanence of transcendence. Yet, subjectivity can by faith in coexistence leap the barrier and rediscover in itself a certain continuity with the old myths. The myths of selfhood come to be haunted by the old myths, even when the self, as is true in Ivan's case, wishes fundamentally to repudiate their existence. Ivan comes to apprehend that to repudiate their existence is to repudiate one's own existence. His dilemma is precisely that he does not wish to and therefore cannot resee and reconstitute the old myth of the devil. But if the shabby devil that he sees is all there is, then, he is shabby too and all *is* stupid. There is an imbalance in the book between the negative and positive characters' relationship to the past. Alyosha is at the marriage feast in Cana although he does not dare look on the face of Christ, but Ivan sits with *his* devil. Hell is nothing but "the suffering of no longer being able to love," as Zosima said (p. 301). Only to the positive heroes is objectivity given via the objectivity of the other. Only for these heroes do the old myths contribute to the self's stabilization in its objectifications. They are reintroduced boldly by Fyodor Karamazov near the beginning.

"Speak, all the same, is there a God, or not? Only, be serious. I want you to be serious now."
"No, there is no God."
"Alyoshka, is there a God?"
"There is."
"Ivan, and is there immortality of some sort, just a little, just a tiny bit?"
"There is no immortality either."
"None at all?"
"None at all."
"There's absolute nothingness then. Perhaps there is just something? Anything is better than nothing!"
"Absolute nothingness."
"Alyoshka, is there immortality?"
"There is."
"God and immortality?"
"God and immortality. In God is immortality."
"Hmmm! It's more likely Ivan's right. Good Lord! to think what faith, what force of all kinds, man has lavished for nothing, on that dream, and for how

many thousand years. Who is it laughing at man? Ivan! For the last time, once
for all, is there a God or not? I ask for the last time!"
"And for the last time there is not."
"Who is laughing at mankind, Ivan?"
"It must be the devil," said Ivan Fyodorovich, smiling.
"And the devil? Does he exist?"
"No, there's no devil either."
"It's a pity. Damn it all, what wouldn't I do to the man who first invented
God! Hanging on a bitter aspen three would be too good for him."

(p. 122)

The method is to raise a question and to demonstrate that any question inherently carries the possibility both of an answer of yes and no,
which is in fact no answer at all, but a demonstration of the ineluctable
presence of dualities, oppositions, and polar extremes. It is the ever-
repeated return of a maddening doubt and uncertainty.

It is axiomatic for the classical novel that what is represented in the
characters is repeated in the structure. The reason structural repetition
acquires a dimension in Dostoevsky and Dickens different from that
which it had in Austen, Eliot, and Tolstoy is that the self has acquired
another dimension. In the latter artists, the fundamental rationality of
self-development and self-recognition allowed the artists to construct an
artistic base of rational patterns of repetition guided preeminently by
the need to make a world formally palpable and sensuous. Even when
these artistic reinforcements of the world of the work included irony,
ironic reversal, or the multiplication of the point of view, they were free
of anxiety and compulsion. But in Dostoevsky and Dickens the need to
repeat grows less artistic and rational and more psychological, becoming
a need to repeat fundamentally because what has been represented has
not yet been understood or recognized and needs to be repeated because it demands to be recognized.

The repetitions, made in ironic composure in Austen, which produced
an orderly, layered series of new revelations and possibilities which
could be absorbed in spite and because of the negative shock of disjunction, turn now into an ironic anxiety over the impossibility of either adequate representation or recognition. Instead of the orderly temporal
ironic layering of Austen or even the additional spatial multiplication of
irony in various points of view in George Eliot, there is a sense of inadequacy and madness. The self-dissociation and doubling, signifying the
chronic intrapsychic conflict, is repeated in the doubling of the charac-

ters by parody, caricature, and repetition, and in the structure as the repetition of one small community in another. The radical parody and doubling leave no image sacrosanct.

"Negatively," the repetitions point to deep and unresolvable doubt. "Positively," the repetition points to a kind of negative, parodistic union of all opposites, where everyone doubled into their extremes do interact with everyone else on some level. But here, simultaneously, repetition becomes the correlate of the self's radical ex-centricity, its tragic and infuriating unknowableness, the very absence of the subjectivity on which the novel based itself.

In its new repetition-compulsion and anxiety, the technique that guaranteed the novel's form shows itself as unresolved and non-concludable, as tragic and self-negating. Technique, which was the guarantee of final clarity and control, comes itself to be invaded by an intention not to be understood, a demonic element of displacement, echoing that of the displaced and dispersed self. As in a dream, we reach the impasse of conscious negation, and perceive another speech, more terrible and more uncontrollable, of unconscious negation.

The self's negativity struggling with an unnegatable (because unknown) unconscious in the self, repeated in technique, signifies at once the limit and end of the novel's form as it has been and its return to tragedy. This return was made possible largely by the rediscovery of dialogue as an irrational manifestation and experience in life rather than a purely rational and controllable one. The breakthrough to free and open dialogue also breaks the rational dialectical model. What is characteristic of this new dialecticism is its tendency toward dispersal, its inability to be synthesized by reason or faith. Alyosha makes Ivan his hope. But what of Smerdyakov? Where is conscience to be found in his doubly conscienceless act toward the other in murder and toward himself in suicide? The all-consuming, maddening doubt which splits and dissociates everything into opposites, the doubt which is nothing but a figure for Dostoevsky's own doubt and ambivalence and which Dostoevsky would like to eliminate from the question of the existence of conscience in man, cannot be eliminated. The release of the mind's immense and productive capacity for negativity, its interacting conscious and unconscious negations, is no longer amenable to synthesis.

Irony is the novel's formal demonstration of its awareness of negativity. The irony is immense and extreme and there is no logos in the present to contain it. There is no answer in the present generation of the Karamazovs. Dostoevsky manages only to gather the present together by looking toward the logos of the past and by projecting a logos into the future: other fathers for other generations of sons. Dostoevsky's novel conforms to Lukács' idea of the novel's form as being capable only of the "affirmation of dissonance." Dissonance in Dostoevsky is the form, the only and tragic one available in a world, not merely split, but dispersed, and forsaken by God. If there is a truth or a consolation in this new, open dialogue, it has nothing to do with reason or unreason, but with feeling. The truth lies, if anywhere, in the sudden, unconscious pleasure and pain that this dialogue sometimes brings.

Dickens

There have been many attacks on Dickens' genius. Probably the most famous and devastating one came from Henry James in his review of *Our Mutual Friend:* "It were, in our opinion, an offense against humanity to place Mr. Dickens among the greatest novelists." As an answer to why this is so, James offers the argument that he failed at the central task of the novelist, the creation of character: "he has created nothing but figures. He has added nothing to our understanding of human character. . . . Every character here put before us is a mere bundle of eccentricites, animated by no principle of nature whatever." James goes on to say that "seldom . . . had we read a book so intensely *written,* so little seen, known, or felt. . . . It is one of the chief conditions of his genius not to see beneath the surface of things . . . we should, accordingly, call him the greatest of superficial novelists."[21]

F. R. Leavis did not think Dickens worthy of inclusion in *The Great Tradition* because his genius was but that of "a great entertainer." He lacked "sustained seriousness" and a profounder sense of artistic responsibility. Thus he offers no challenge for the adult mind. Furthermore, Dickens' structures lack "a unifying and organizing significance," except for *Hard Times* where he avoids his "usual repetitive overdoing and loose inclusiveness."[22]

Lord David Cecil cannot but agree that he is one of "the most brilliant" but "also one of the most imperfect" of English novelists. Dickens "had no sense of form. . . . His books have no organic unity; they are

full of detachable episodes, characters who serve no purpose in further-
ing the plot. . . . He does not tell us much of the inner life."[23]

One thing that all these criticisms have in common is a demand for a
more conscious intelligibility of structure and character. The objections
have all to do with what Dickens does or does not do for the conscious
mind. It is the mind that is disappointed here by a lack of organic structure, by a betrayal of the expectation of the unity of part and whole, of
an artistic organization proceeding according to some unitary plan that
is comprehensible.

These conscious expectations can be consciously refuted by drawing
on the long history of what constitutes genius, from Kant, Schiller, and
Schopenhauer to Nietzsche and Jung. For all of these thinkers genius is
an experience of being overwhelmed because in genius itself the unconscious overwhelms the conscious mind. By definition, in genius the intellect overcomes itself. Rational discourse is overcome by art. Thought
overcomes its own limitations, autonomy, and formalist demands, opening itself up to what is outside of thought: to nonsense, the illogical, contradictory, absurd, ridiculous, perverse, or meaningless. The great
works of genius, so the argument has always run, have a mysterious
power to include in their form the excluded, the remainder, the impossible, and formlessness itself. They present us with the miracle both of
form and its remainder.

This is certainly what Schiller felt the naïve artists, like Shakespeare
and Goethe in *Faust,* had achieved. For Schiller, their structures as if
defied the subjective mind by reuniting subjectivity and objectivity,
man and nature. For Jung, the miraculous unity is more specifically that
of consciousness with both the personal and impersonal unconscious.
The genius attains a "self" transcending his ego. For others more
linguistically oriented, the special power of genius is to make us realize
how it is nonsense which defines syntax or how syntax borders on nonsense, and how it is the excess or surplus of meaning which allows
meaning or the semantic. Thus making and creating meaninglessness
becomes the very ground and condition of meaning and the explanation
of the special charge and power meaning conveys in a work of genius.

Besides these traditional generalized explanations of the power of genius runs the somewhat more specific argument of two different kinds of
mental or artistic ways of structuring or systemizing. One produces a
structure of complex, dialectical, but organic relations, imitating the

organic possibilities of consciousness; the other produces a Gestalt form. In the latter case, the genius recreates in his form the mystery of perception: that we always see a whole, unity, a Gestalt, which is far more than the sum of its parts because the Gestalt overlooks the fragmented, varied, discrete, and dispersed. (For Lacan this making of unity out of the fragmented is not merely the power of perception, but the fundamental gift given with language: making the separate and disjunct one.) What the genius does in his form is to show us simultaneously the Gestalt, the unity, and the fragmentation that this whole has transcended. He shows us the sum of the parts in a Gestalt form or, let us call it, a system. And he shows the parts in a structure, which does not relate and resolve everything into pairs of relata, or complex relations, but allows them to lie in a relationship of precisely the kind of "loose inclusiveness" that Leavis condemns. In other words, the structure, paradoxically, does not structure or does not structure as much as it could. The parts, even if contradictory, lie together here in adjacency. The parts do remain, as Lord David Cecil accuses them of remaining, "detachable episodes" or appear as extra characters without an apparent function. Everything is not forced into a relationship with everything else on the structural level.

The parts of the system are not directly connected among themselves on the structural level, but are united in and by the whole, or on the level of the system. In this kind of Gestalt form or system, our structural urge is as if frustrated, and absolute structuration is denied, but system or the apprehension of totality is satisfied. We are not allowed to "comprehend," but finally we are allowed to "apprehend" a unity. The delay in satisfaction, the denial of comprehension, therefore makes the satisfaction and pleasure all the greater. Hence the common feeling before a great work of art that we both comprehend and do not comprehend, that we seem to comprehend more than we can explain. Thus the work of genius, by creating a delay in comprehension, or better by denying the possibility of comprehending, yields us only apprehension, a satisfaction that we cannot explain and that we therefore term mysterious.

Thus the sense of the miraculous in genius seems to depend on its creating a maximum time of slowness of comprehension, a time or dimension, in fact, of the negation of comprehension. Another way of putting this is to say with Shklovsky that "defamiliarization" and "estrangement" are a structural achievement which come about by way of negating structure.[24] This brings into the great work of art the sense that the familiar is irradiated by the unfamiliar, a sense of a dimension of the unreal and the unknown. Subjectively, we have that strange sense of having been on the border of or in touch with the new, the unknown, the unreal, the ineffable, the impalpable, the *je ne sais quoi*, madness, unreason, or whatever we choose to call it. The effect, however, is the specific consequence of the disjunction of system and structure, and of forcing into abeyance (or at least minimizing as much as possible) the structural function as such. Thus here the artist is in control on the ultimate perceptual-systematic level, like a God paring his fingernails, but on another, more intellectual–structural level he has abandoned control and has as if fallen asleep or become like the child of incoherent mind in *Our Mutual Friend* who would build the disordered, unstructured neighborhood where Bradley Headstone works.

> The schools were newly built, and there were so many like them all over the country, that one might have thought the whole were but one restless edifice with the locomotive gift of Aladdin's palace. They were in a neighbourhood which looked like a toy neighbourhood taken in blocks out of a box by a child of particularly incoherent mind, and set up anyhow; here, one side of a new street; there, a large solitary public-house facing nowhere; here, another unfinished street already in ruins; there, a church; here, an immense new warehouse; there, a dilapidated old country villa; then, a medley of black ditch, sparkling cucumber-frame, rank field, richly cultivated kitchen garden, brick viaduct, arch-spanned canal, and disorder of frowziness and fog. As if the child had given the table a kick, and gone to sleep.[25]

If we allow Dickens such a system or Gestalt form and draw him back into the circle of genius, the major accusations of his detractors immediately lose their ground. The formless in Dickens is to some extent, albeit not very precisely, immediately explained, and explained, it becomes acceptable. In fact, one can go further and say that Dickens' negation of structure or his intentional, genial, structural incoherence signifies the substitution or achievement of a dream-structure, for the dream is a system with a nonintellectual structure of "loose inclusiveness" and conjunctions, of mere adjacencies and lack of concrete relationships. The dream is primarily aware of identities rather than differences and able to put things together that the conscious mind never could. But this special relationship of Dickens to the unconscious and its dream-work heightens even more the mystery of genius and how it can consciously do what the unconscious does, make an artwork that is a dream. And no doubt such an argument would do little for his detractors who demand something of consciousness and comprehension from art before they allow it to be great art.

My argument is that in Dickens the unconscious is present not as a structureless dream but as a structure of unconscious negation, preeminently of repression. His novels register a point of transition in the novel from a predominantly conscious structure, making gestures toward the unconscious, to an unconscious structure struggling to achieve equal stature and importance with the conscious structure. What we can say is that even while Pip in *Great Expectations*, for example, is in the grips of a repression which surfaces in various and circuitous ways and finally breaks through (though it is neither consciously accepted or resolved), Dickens himself is struggling to overcome the fixation and primal repression of a new story of pain and unpleasure that he has to tell, one which obviously cannot be told very well in the inherited form of the novel, but which he still feels compelled to tell in this conscious form and to make fit this conscious form. An achieved form becomes itself like a fixation, a statue, a primal repression which an instinct seeking satisfaction must combat.

In this way, *Great Expectations* becomes a labor simultaneously against a psychic repression and a formal repression—a labor which advances very little because both repressions are upheld. But Dickens' structure is effective only insofar as it is structured, only insofar as the vague unknown unconscious has here become a more "precise unknown" which can be questioned or at least represented in the form of some kind of a coherent hypothesis. In Dickens it is not the dream that we confront but a structured unconscious, the mechanisms of unconscious intellection. In other words, only the structured is knowable; it is the fate of the unstructured always to remain a vague unknown, a kind of dreamlike thing, hovering at the edges of the whole and falling outside the denser areas of relationships. This does not mean that there cannot be an art that is insane (there is), but it means that insane art is structured because insanity is, and not because it has passed through consciousness and the ego in becoming art. Insane art has the structure of the insanity of the mind that produced it.[26] Equally, Dickens' art has in part the structure of the neurotic repression that underpins it.

In *Emma* we saw the subject matter of a repressed thought make its way into the heroine's consciousness by way of negation. The conscious negation "I will never marry" permitted the subject matter of marriage to proliferate in her mind and in the world of the novel. Probably, so Freud speculates in his article on repression, this kind of conscious negation would not even be possible if there were not a more primal, unconscious repression, ready to assimilate the conscious judgment.[27] And indeed, in *Emma* we saw finally that there was a more primal repression, namely her guilt, concern, and also unconscious discontent with her father, which could not surface at all until the problem of his future was solved, just as she could not consciously abandon all her arguments against immediate marriage, even after she had affectively and intellectually acknowledged her desire to marry, until this more primary and repressed need to resolve her relationship to her father could in fact be resolved, partly by passing on the burden and fear of it to another, to Knightley.

Dostoevsky's Ivan is similarly the possibility of a case where intellectual negation may be substituting for a repression, an ambivalence of love and hatred for a father (God) who has not made an acceptable world. In the Grand Inquisitor's tale, Ivan exhibits what Freud calls judgment's concern with the denial of a particular property of a thing. He asserts that Christ is bad, harmful, alien, and external to man. This kind of a repudiation still belongs to the pleasure-ego. Judgment's concern with the existence or nonexistence of an image in perception is a function of the reality ego.[28] Ivan's desperate attempt to establish the judgmental function of his reality-ego is defeated at the trial when the devil appears to him as externally real, or as more internally real than reality itself.

What Ivan cannot repress is the motile, active, unconscious hatred of his father (and hence God), a hatred that persists because it was once a desire for love. Ivan's is the example of what Freud calls the reversal of the content of an instinct into its opposite, a reversal for which the single example is the change of love into hate.[29] His hate-relationship to the world issues from a narcissism, for which "the relation of hate to objects is older than that of love" (p. 102); its aim is the ego's "self-preservation and self-maintenence" (p. 101). The world of objects is a source of pain and, hence, repudiated by the ego. Ivan cannot transcend the antithesis of love–hate. He cannot pass to the second antithesis of love: loving–being loved. He cannot transform narcissism either into the passive aim of being loved or into the active aim of loving, as Alyosha and Zosima do (p. 97). Instead he gets caught up in introjection and projection, and in the latter instance, with the development of hatred in himself, an aggressive desire to destroy this objective world of pain, a desire Ivan reveals in his fictions of a changed and transformed world, based in each instance on the negation and hatred of a once-loved object.

Ivan's experience of the reversal of the content of an instinct into its opposite is coterminous with another form of instinctual vicissitude which Freud calls the turning round of an instinct upon the subject's own ego. His attitude toward himself becomes one of sadism; his self-punishment and self-torture clearly arise from a desire to torture others (the existence of torture in the world is his neurotic obsession), but this desire becomes neither "passive" nor "masochistic." Ivan's self-tormenting hallucination of the devil is a clear example of the "reflexive middle voice" that for Freud characterizes the obsessional neurotic (p. 92).

In Dickens, what is new is the more elaborate and complex structural representation of the instincts and their vicissitudes. In *Great Expectations*, Dickens gives, as Freud himself does, a special place to the vicissitude of repression, one of the most complex and most circuitous of all. We can say that on the unconscious level, the story is one of an attempted repression which is not successful because the pain and anxiety that the repression attempted to avoid break through everywhere, turning the book into a chronicle of pain. What is also different here is that the focus is not primarily, as in Austen and Dostoevsky, upon an idea that is repressed, but upon "the charge of affect" detached from the idea which is repressed. Thus, besides the substitute-formations and symptom-formations left behind by ideational repression, we have here the three different ways of suppressing and recognizing affect: the possibility of a traceless suppression, the appearance of the affect in the guise of a particular qualitative tone, and its transformation into anxiety.[30]

Just as Hegel developed and employed the use of negation by the conscious mind, so Freud gave us a hypothesis of the activity of negation and the employment of negation by the unconscious mind. In its representation of the subject, the nineteenth-century classical novel of realism also moves increasingly from the representation of conscious negation to the representation of unconscious negation. What Freud calls the symbol of negation, the ideational negation of thought or intention, is the link between the two, and hence it is with the symbol of negation that the activity of negation announces itself in the novels of Austen and Eliot and with which it remains primarily concerned for a time.

For a long time the novel also elaborated this conscious ideational negation objectively into the struggle of the master-slave dialectic and sought to resolve it there. Dickens obviously does that, too, and is in fact so much a master of this kind of social plotting of necessary coexistence that his very facility in making these plots and presenting their resolutions (indifferently, negatively or positively, however the audience or editors wished) becomes a sign of a discontent with such conscious structures, so easily set up, varied, and resolved. Clearly the objective resolution could only climax in two ways, with neither very satisfactory. One could end with the demonstration of a need to change social classes, relations, laws and rules of exchange, both in the private and public sphere, a call for revolution and reform in the relationship of parent and child, master and servant, criminal and judge—all of which remained somehow vague, distant, unreal, and utopian, but allowed optimism and revolution. Or one could end with pessimism and tragedy, with the most willing, able, and potentially revolutionary subject exhausted by the very process of trying simultaneously to act and comprehend himself in such an unyielding hostile world. Thus revolution, impasse, or protective self-limitation were the only semirealistic possible endings, along with the unrealistic one of a conclusion in marriage or romance presented as happy coexistence or mutual comprehension.

The "real" ending of *Great Expectations* is neither version of Chapter Fifty-nine, neither the vision of physical union ("I saw no shadow of another parting from her") nor of sympathetic understanding ("a heart to understand what my heart used to be").[31] The only reason these conclusions can artistically stand at all is that each is a negation of Pip's declaration to Biddy that "that poor dream . . . has all gone by, Biddy, all gone by!" (p. 518). We know of course even as he states this, and without the concluding denial, that this is untrue because he has to admit that he remembers everything about his life ("I have forgotten nothing"). Thus the two conclusions are the fantasy conclusions possible for a sublimation that was itself never resolved, never understood, and never real. For various reasons, Pip must continue to believe that he really loved Estella, although he did not, and that either reality parted them or that they were united on some level. On the fantasy level he at least imagines being understood by the other whom he cannot understand. By passively being understood by her heart, he escapes the active need to understand his own pain, or that part of it which underwent idealization. Because this resolution was in itself purely imaginary and fantastic, Dickens felt no problem in pushing it further into a complete dream of romantic union, one which would be apprehended as so satisfying and real by his audience.

The real ending of the book comes in Chapter Fifty-eight with Pip's final disappointment even in his lowered expectations, with his humiliation by his "father" Joe, and his return to his masochistic vision of himself as "thankless," "ungenerous and unjust" (p. 514). It is a self-vision he can only undo by labor and by a final recognition of his contemporary, Herbert.

> We were not in a grand way of business, but we had a good name, and worked for our profits, and did very well. We owed so much to Herbert's ever cheerful industry and readiness that I often wondered how I had conceived the old idea of his inaptitude, until I was one day enlightened by the reflection that perhaps the inaptitude had never been in him at all, but had been in me.
>
> (pp. 515–16)

Pip's final reflection is a recognition of projection and of a failing in himself. He had projected his own inaptitude for success by labor onto Herbert and had mistaken his friend's far more realistically based fictions of great expectations to be similar in kind to his own, expectations which had not been based on active labor but passive fantasy.

Pip's final reflection is a demonstration both of the new self-reflective powers that he does have and of the fact that he still has no real "clue" to his "poor labyrinth." The generally masochistic and self-diminishing tenor of the reflection points to the continued absence in him of a positive sense of self-worth. In the last glimpse we have of the real Pip, he is still substituting moral self-criticism for real self-recognition. He has only learned protective self-limitation and self-skepticism. A reduced self with reduced expectations is the only kind of real self that consciousness can either propose or accept after the adventure of the unconscious has floundered, and this is all that the great conscious realists do offer us at the end with their heroes. These heroes do not become Hegelian philosophers on Freudian analysts and so their negations end in a conscious self-negation.

The difference between Hegel's vision of the activity of negation and Freud's is that the Hegelian consciousness knows its negations consciously and can articulate the theses and antitheses which the pluralizing force of negativity has opened up, whereas the Freudian consciousness does not know that it has or is negating anything. Because repression does not allow an instinct to come to consciousness, the negation produces something far more painful and complex than Hegel's conscious pluralization of contradictory theses and antitheses. Unconscious negation produces a ramification and unchecked multiplication that Freud compares to the growth of a fungus. Instead of a conscious pluralization that can be brought under control, we see something like a complete dispersal or a multiplication so devious and powerful that nothing seems capable of controlling it.

> It [psychoanalysis] shows us, for instance, that the instinct-presentation develops in a more unchecked and luxuriant fashion if it is withdrawn by repression from conscious influence. It ramifies like a fungus, so to speak, in the dark and takes on extreme forms of expression, which when translated and revealed to the neurotic are bound not merely to seem alien to him, but to terrify him by the way in which they reflect an extraordinary and dangerous strength of instinct. This illusory strength of instinct is the result of an uninhibited development of it in phantasy and of the damming-up consequent on lack of real satisfaction.[32]

Under these new conditions, negation is no longer used to apprehend the truth, as in Hegel, but to conceal it. In Hegel the mechanism of negation functioned to divide thought into parts which were known, and which could be synthesized on another level precisely when and because the new particulars were apprehended as particulars. In Freud, by contrast, negation produces an absence of consciousness, a blank, a void in self-knowledge, which, however, does not last and commences a new creation ex nihilo in consciousness of what the unconscious may be, of what may fill that new void.

Freud described four different ways in which consciousness voids the unconscious. In "Instincts and Their Vicissitudes" he listed these mechanisms of negation in the following order: reversal into its opposite, turning round upon the subject, repression, and sublimation. These are forms of negation, varying in strength, which alter the path of the instinct by blocking it and forcing it to undergo vicissitudes (p. 91). Repression is the strongest of these negations, producing the most complex vicissitude, and a mechanism that only comes into full play when the first two forms of negation prove inadequate and fail to master the instinctual impulses.[33]

When we meet Pip the reversal into its opposite of some kind of hostile, impermissible impulse has already occurred. The traumatic childhood encounter with the criminal Magwitch is, from the point of view of Pip's unconscious development, but a confirmation of the reversal of the active impulse into passive masochistic endurance. He is "mishandled, forced to obey unconditionally, defiled, degraded." He is treated in a way that makes terrifyingly clear to him that he is nothing but "a little, helpless, dependent child . . . a naughty child."[34] But it is exactly only this kind of experience that gives him certitude that the objective world is, that he is, and that he is someone who feels fear. The repetition of the verb "to be" tells us that the subjective and objective order come into focus together as an inalienable opposite of consciousness. The two other polarities that govern mental life are also established: pleasure-pain, active-passive (p. 97). On the subjective side he discovers his oneness with pain and passivity. He also discovers his instinct of self-preservation and his separation. He is a child, helpless and disconnected from a world that suddenly acquires solidity and ceases being the mythical dream-world on which he had imposed his fantasy of his parents.

> At such a time I found out for certain that this bleak place overgrown with nettles was the churchyard; and that Philip Pirrip, Late of this Parish, and Also Georgiana Wife of the Above, were dead and buried; and that Alexander, Bartholomew, Abraham, Tobias, and Roger, infant children of the aforesaid, were also dead and buried; and that the dark flat wilderness beyond the churchyard, intersected with dikes and mounds and gates, with scattered cattle feeding on it, was the marshes; and that the low leaden line beyond was the river; and that the distant savage lair from which the wind was rushing was the sea; and that the small bundle of shivers growing afraid of it all and beginning to cry was Pip.
>
> (p. 10)

The world acquires certitude at this moment in time because this experience is one he has had before; it is a repetition of the only thing he has ever known, as becomes clear when he goes home, promptly gets beaten, and finds himself on his stool, "crying and rubbing" himself (p. 16). But it is precisely only by repetition and a repetition with others than his sister and Joe that the experience could become clear to him and have the power to constitute the world, to separate the self from objective reality, and the man from the child, and to constitute the self as well, as something that is crying.

That the hostile impulse was felt toward his sadistic sister becomes amply clear later in his punishment by Orlick and by Orlick's insistence

THE NOVEL AND THE SELF'S NEGATIVITY

that it was Pip who did it, although her sadism toward the child can only be represented at the beginning through the screen and distortion of comedy. It is a rule in Dickens as well as Freud that the derivates of a repression, if they are remote or distorted enough, can pass into consciousness. This fact amply explains the many characters and episodes that consciously have only a distant relationship to Pip but that unconsciously testify to the proliferation of his repressed impulses.

That the encounter with Magwitch, the dark and extreme form of the strength and danger of this instinct, which has ramified like a fungus, has also to do with Joe may seem less apparent at first—but for good reason. It is truly dangerous to feel hostility toward a loved person, and in Pip's case, the only one who can be loved: "But I loved Joe—perhaps for no better reason in those early days than because the dear fellow let me love him" (p. 49). The hostile impulse must be repressed: I loved Joe. Yet we know that here is a source of deep ambivalence which becomes clear in his abandonment of Joe later, a ready abandonment which is, however, accompanied by a constant sense of guilt. The ambivalence derives from Joe's own helplessness, from his inability to protect Pip against Tickler, and his own massive masochism, which he offers, in fact, as a model for Pip to imitate. Pip wants to know why Joe cannot rebel. "Why don't I rise?" as Joe puts it, but his answer is inadequate. Joe's father, we learn, was a drunkard and sadist, but "good in his heart" so Joe insists to Pip's disbelief. Joe's marriage to Pip's sister is his recovery simultaneously of his father and of a woman, to whom it is better to submit than risk the chance of repeating his father's error with his mother. This fear of himself turns Joe into the masochist who allows himself to be governed without rebelling. "I hope you overlook shortcomings," asks Joe, and Pip does, "looking up to Joe" in his "heart," (pp. 56–59). But there is still Tickler, and the fact that Joe lives but the life of "a larger species of child" (p. 15). Scenes like this one confirm his dependent position:

> By this time, my sister was quite desperate, so she pounced on Joe, and, taking him by the two whiskers, knocked his head for a little while against the wall behind—while I sat in the corner, looking guiltily on.
>
> (p. 18)

Thus, although Pip thinks consciously that it is his sister's treatment which has made him morally sensitive, it is in fact his inevitable, repressed ambivalence toward Joe, who can only suffer with him and comfort him, but not protect him by rebelling against his sister, that has long ago initiated the reversal of the content of an impulse into its opposite and the alteration in his ego that Freud so aptly describes: "As a substitute-formation there arises an alteration in the ego, an increased sensitiveness of conscience, which can hardly be called a symptom." The final price Pip pays for the repression of his hostility toward Joe is also described by Freud: "The vanished affect is transformed, without any diminution, into dread of the community, pangs of conscience, or self-reproaches; the rejected idea is replaced by a *displacement-substitute.*"[35] The displacement-substitute for Pip comes to be the world of criminality, prisons, and judgments, from which he seems unable to separate himself, which engulfs him increasingly and with which he is deeply connected from the beginning because he has stolen from both Joe and his sister. But this is even more because he has felt hostility toward them both, and especially because he cannot confess to Joe, because Pip is afraid it would be equivalent to confessing his ambivalence and losing the only thing he can in a way love.

Thus Pip's story becomes the story of a moral masochism in which a good portion of his conscience is in fact devoured by this masochism, his need to be punished, to maintain a constant level of suffering. Freud calls this form of morality, an "unconscious morality." The sins and the guilt for which Pip punishes himself never become entirely clear. What does become clear are the punishments themselves and that Pip is heavily punished, ultimately as if by Fate.

> In order to provoke punishment from this last parent-substitute [Fate] the masochist must do something inexpedient, act against his own interests, ruin the prospects which the real world offers him, and possibly destroy his own existence in the world of reality.[36]

Pip's failure to master his instincts by the first two mechanisms of negation prepares the conscious attack on the instincts by the mechanism of repression. Satis House introduces the great drama of Pip's primal repression. It is a perfect symbolic representation of his interiority and the sign of a new reordering of his unconscious, a new vicissitude of the instincts, seeking active release in alteration and rearrangement. The dramatic sequence at Satis House is necessary because the unconscious seeks repetition and because the adolescent ego, in its development, makes a new effort to combine the instincts or parts of them into the new, larger ego. What cannot be combined is once again repressed, and "the remainder, just on account of its intimate association with the other [the repressed and abhorrent] undergoes idealization."[37] Thus Satis House also becomes the scene of the great instinctual self-splitting in Pip.

In Estella, Pip idealizes his own hostile and sadistic impulses. And in Miss Havisham's externalized hurt and sterile play of revenge he recognizes simultaneously his own immobilized instinctual capacity for satisfaction, his inability ever to have revenge, and an idealization of this dissatisfaction into gentility, into a fantasy of satisfaction: she will be his benefactress; she will rescue him from his pain because she alone knows it. Miss Havisham and Estella—each is an objects that satisfies several instincts in Pip simultaneously; they represent a confluence of instincts in him (p. 88). But, characteristically, all these parts of the instincts that do struggle through at this stage of his ego development by idealization and sublimation, bringing, so it would seem, the opportunity of pleasure, bring unpleasure instead. Satis House will not fulfill any of his ideal expectations from it, but will bring him the more severe pain of having to acknowledge his idealizations as empty self-deception. But Pip does not know this nor can he. He interprets his lack of pleasure as merely a postponement of pleasure, a delay in his desire to be avenged and to triumph. The imagined future pleasure is also idealized into a full-fledged romance of love in which he plays the noble part of the rescuer.

> She had adopted Estella, she had as good as adopted me, and it could not fail to be her intention to bring us together. She reserved it for me to restore the desolate house, admit the sunshine into the dark rooms, set the clocks a-going and the cold hearths a-blazing, tear down the cobwebs, destroy the vermin— in short, do all the shining deeds of the young knight of romance, and marry the princess. I had stopped to look at the house as I passed; and its seared red-brick walls, blocked windows, and strong green ivy clasping even the stacks of chimneys with its twigs and tendons, as if with sinewy old arms, had made up a rich attractive mystery, of which I was the hero. Estella was the inspiration of it, and the heart of it, of course.
>
> (p. 252)

The imperial and clichéd fantasy of mastery is an exact measure of the extent to which he has been deprived of his own humanity, his need for light, love, heroism, self-esteem, and recognition. His transcendental self has a negative origin in his unconscious. It is a sublimation of self based on a hostile need for revenge in a self that could never come into being either in hate or love, a self that has hopelessly introjected the scorn poured upon it for coming into existence at all, a self that only knows itself negatively as despicable, bad, and powerless.

Satis House is the very image of the form his project of repression will take throughout his adolescence and young adult life. And with Satis House he clearly establishes and "affirms" that his earlier efforts at negation were wholly inadequate and that he has begun a new project of repression which itself represses his older one. This is the primal repression. Thus it appears to him consciously that he must renounce his old self and its old ties, and he does. What continues, however, to haunt him most consciously from the past is that tie of ambivalence to Joe in which there had been unpleasure but also pleasure. But it is a memory of pleasure that haunts him only as unpleasure and guilt. Ironically, in the rearrangement of his instinctual life, he turns his only experience of pleasure into unpleasure as well, reversing and arresting his single, slender path to satisfaction and substantial ego development.

Satis House awes the boy because it is the perfect image of his own fixation, his unconscious knowledge of the nonsatisfaction of his own earliest instinctual life, his failure to have developed either the ability to love himself, unabashedly and narcissistically, or to love or hate others without ambivalence. Like Miss Havisham, by totally repressing his knowledge of the past once again, he also represses the one ray of daylight in his past into a darkness where it cannot grow and change, but where it festers as unchanging but proliferating guilt, needing ever new efforts of repression. Satis House arrests positive growth for all its inhabitants and fosters only the negative "growth" that fixation allows in a dark, Gothic, older, unreleased, and untransformed unconscious. This is Pip's transformation: the worsening of his condition and the fixation of his inner potentialities.

Miss Havisham's staging of the emotion of great disappointment ("I will never get over this") finds an unconscious echo in his own disappointed heart, which also speaks in the eternities of the affects: never–ever. Her arrestment is the sign of the negative eternity of emotional hurt. But though she has negated the world for the clearest delineation possible of the purely subjective self, she cannot deny any more than can Pip the activity and proliferation of the instincts. Because she is human and instinctual, she "creates" Estella out of her own dark nothingness. Estella is the "star" born out of the night of her unconscious, a fantastic stellar creation, symbolizing the indomitable life and activity of the instincts. In the dark, Miss Havisham endlessly stages and repeats the only drama she knows, that of her Broken Heart and its need for revenge. "Play, play, play," she commands so what has been done to her may be temporally reversed into its opposite, so that passivity may turn into active revenge and her self-inflicted masochism into sadism, a sadism created by herself to break her own heart once again and completely—unwittingly, she claims as far as her consciousness knows, but intentionally and wittingly by the laws of the unconscious. She creates sadism to incite and keep alive her own identity in masochism, and finally to confirm it in a self-inflicted death-blow, which for all we know may contain a "lust of pain," "a gratification of the libido," without which "even the destruction of anyone by himself cannot occur." [38]

The example of masochism set by Miss Havisham is of a far more dangerous type than what is offered by Joe. And it is well for Pip that he ultimately recognizes this and knows that the "vanity of sorrow," his own as well, can grow in the dark to a "master mania, like the vanity of penitence, the vanity of remorse, the vanity of unworthiness, and other monstrous vanities that have been curses in this world" (p. 428). It is, however, his own moral masochism that allows him this recognition, this intensely affective response which trails away and vanishes, repressed, into a pale echo of a Biblical lament. Pip's increasingly Christian orientation becomes a way for him both to mold, orient, practice, and contain the smoldering fire of his own considerable masochistic potential, and a way also to make his "unconscious morality" more masterable by bringing it into alliance with a consciously defined morality. It is but a meager step toward independent and conscious morality, if we measure it by the possible stages of moral development defined, for example, by Kohlberg, yet it is one of Pip's achievements.

The boy Pip makes a perfect third in the ambivalently masochistic-sadistic game played at Satis House because it is a game he knows so well as his own spellbinding and fascinating play at existence. Estella secures his masochistic development into adulthood because she is his pact with himself to love in an active way only what scorns, torments, and criticizes him—a creature who gives him no promise, peace, hope, or happiness, nor any encouragement or reason for loving her (p. 253). She gives him a new, totally senseless, and even nonsensical "reason" for loving; the mysterious senselessness, of which he is always aware, puzzles and pains him, and finally grows complete in an "ecstasy of unhappiness" (p. 391). But how else could this "visionary boy—or man" love, except in a way that is opaque to consciousness, this boy who has known no reason for loving, and who, in his turn to Estella, embarks precisely on the repression of the only poor reason he has known or that there is: to love in order to be loved?

His project of "love" guarantees the fixation of the second pole of love so that all he feels is his terrible, truly reasonless love for her. Thus, such "reasons" as he has for loving Estella are purely unconscious, obscure to him but "the clue to his poor labyrinth." It is an erotic project, but what has been eroticized is his masochism, the unconscious way in which he can relate to himself and therefore to others, when he can cancel his own hostile impulses. Estella "eroticizes" his masochism by her apparent sadism. Now he can and must abandon his old project of ambivalent love-hate with Joe. More importantly, he can abandon his incipient experience with Joe of the other polarity of love—to love/to be loved—especially "to be loved," which had entailed at least on one occasion such an intense sense of guilt, and which as a whole entailed gratitude and admiration for one who was after all dependent and a mere masochist himself. For what is the appeal of one masochism to another, when it seeks and can return to a more primary polarity of love-hate in an erotic exchange with a sadist who absolutely cannot love in return or even recognize him?

With Estella his masochism acquires new life, ardor, and reality. He can play out his very being to his heart's content in an active and seemingly vital way because she constantly feeds him with impulses of hostility which he must reverse into passive masochistic pain and crying. She gives him back his style of primal life and necessitates the activity of the ever-renewed repression of an old unsatisfied hate.

> I was so humiliated, hurt, spurned, offended, angry, sorry—I cannot hit upon the right name for the smart—God knows what its name was—that tears started to my eyes.
>   . . . I looked about me for a place to hide my face in, and got behind one of the gates in the brewery-lane, and leaned my sleeve against the wall there, and leaned my forehead on it and cried. As I cried, I kicked the wall, and took a hard twist at my hair; so bitter were my feelings, and so sharp was the smart without a name, that needed counteraction.

> (p. 72)

"The smart without a name" is the same old smart. Whether God does or does not know its name is no matter, for Pip knows its name, as his association with the name "sister" makes amply clear in the very next line. It is in response to his "sister's upbringing" that he had first, probably before he could speak, "kicked the wall" and twisted his own hair to find out which counteraction had the greater power to subdue the smart. Estella reactivates in him his sister's sadism and her loveless voice—that only voice of authority in his young life, for Joe had none, which attacked his existence relentlessly and mercilessly as valueless and abhorrent. His sister by her authority must have had a reason for hating him so (the child may have felt), an obscure reason which Estella now illuminates by revealing to him that he is coarse and common. He must change; he must become something other than he is. His sister's dissatisfaction with himself now becomes consciously his own. Estella provides him both with his old pattern of behavior and, seemingly, the clue by which he can escape this old pattern. She strikes him therefore as being nothing less than "the innermost life" of his life (p. 256).

This is why Pip cannot renounce her: "Never, Estella" (p. 391). Losing her means losing her sadism and therefore also the ardor of his own sense of being alive in his masochism. Far worse, losing her means losing the very reason for his existence in repression, his painful pact with himself to persist in the pains of a negated life, because it was to be no more than a delayed postponement of the satisfaction of his instinctual great expectations. Her loss signifies his loss of the "clue" to his poor labyrinth, which was finally to resolve his long-endured chronicle of pain, dissatisfaction, and lack of pleasure in himself.

But Estella, the star, turns to stone and then disappears altogether in the daylight of a factual reality. What he cannot believe is that there is nothing where she was and that there never was anything but the nothing of their real mutual indifference. Pip cannot really know anyone until he knows something about himself in the past, in his more primary, unfinished relationship to his sister and Joe. Estella's sadism turns into the indifference of stone because it too was largely his own imaginary projection and objectification which allowed him to initiate his identification with her. But she is indifference, the third and greatest polarity of love, the absence of both love and hate. To this self-annihilating indifference he pleads his "rhapsody," which "welled up within me, like blood from an inward wound, and gushed out."

"You are part of my existence, part of myself. . . . The stones of which the strongest London buildings are made are not more real, or more impossible to be displaced by your hands, than your presence and influence have been to me, there and everywhere, and will be. Estella, to the last hour of my life, you cannot choose but remain part of my character, part of the little good in me, part of the evil. But, in this separation, I associate you only with the good, and I will faithfully hold you to that always, for you must have done me far more good than harm, let me feel now what sharp distress I may. O God bless you, God forgive you!"

(p. 391)

She must be real because she came to his consciousness, but she came to his consciousness as a negation of his more primal effort both to love and hate, to love and be loved. It was he himself who wanted to become indifferent to these early, unsatisfactory efforts. And it is he himself who wants to be indifferent to her now, because her marriage to Drummle threatens him now with his own pure sadism, a sadism that is clearly in him and is no longer coming from her. And thus he knows that to win her back or even to have won her would have meant the triumph of sadism in him, which he must quickly repress by indifference, for no more is hate available to him to repress by hate the hate that he feels.

What he tries to salvage of Estella for himself, now that they are separate and she is about to vanish, is a moral notion of himself ("for you must have done me far more good than harm"), that the "clue" for which he searched was fundamentally for the release of a good impulse rather than a hostile one. That this is what he will "faithfully" hold on to indicates his uncertainty and ambivalence, but it is also a conscious choice, a positive intellectual judgment, albeit suffused in the semi-Christian unconscious morality that becomes now his characteristic note.

The insistence that a thoroughly disappointing, painful, and self-deluded experience is good for him is again a masochistic insistence, a way to prolong his pain in an "ecstasy of unhappiness" and also the only way to control his hate. Nearly destroyed, he reestablishes his sense of self and self-worth on the old familiar ground of suffering. To suffer is his only sign that he exists and that he is good. Shortly hereafter, however, he feels compelled to trace out the sense of a connection between what he idealizes and what he abhors, and he proves to himself that Estella is one with the criminal world he has dreaded. The chapter concludes, aptly enough, with Wemmick's (the man split, only partly—so differently from himself) sign, "DON'T GO HOME" (p. 392). Wemmick ought to know, but again Pip has not yet recognized him. The sign comes to be a "vast shadowy verb" (p. 394) which he has to conjugate first in his dreams and then in a reality where he does, unfortunately, have to go home in—as always—a somewhat circuitous manner. Pip goes home and becomes a split man himself, oscillating between his office and a borrowed warmth from Joe's life. He remains split because the repression of the hostility toward Joe has and never can be lifted, because it is in the shadow of Joe's love and masochistic manner of selfless being that Pip puts together his own destroyed identity. Thus the intellectual judgment of condemnation can come to substitute for his old repression of hatred of his sister. But no such condemnation can be applied to Joe; it can only be applied to himself. The "symbol of negation," as Freud argued, can enter consciousness as a judgment, but the concealed aspect of the symbol, repression, belongs to the unconscious.

Pip remains Pip, but an abridged version of human possibility. Both Pips at the end harkened back to the child at the beginning who named himself by negating and excluding what his tongue could not master. "My father's family name being Pirrip, and my Christian name Philip, my infant tongue could make of both names nothing longer or more explicit than Pip. So I called myself Pip, and came to be called Pip" (p. 9).

The epic's beginning was an important objective event; the novel's beginning, in its most intensely subjective, first person narrative form, is a subject event. Pip has to have a name to begin. He tries to imitate an existent sound that seems to belong to him or be associated with him, but he manages only to voice, to recreate a part of the sound of Philip or Pirrip. He deletes the more complicated consonants and the repeated vowels and abridges his name to Pip, creating what he can, absorbing and expressing all that he can master. He deletes the unmasterable excess. What is "longer" and "more explicit" cannot be mastered and has to be excluded. Thus he begins with and in an act of exclusion; he negates his true names and merely, accidentally, out of a lack, an inability to do more, he "creates" for himself a name. His small act of creation is a division and multiplication of a word into an utterable and an unutterable part. He affirms and utters one part and negates the other. His small achievement, based on negation, is a very paradigm for his own conscious life and the life of consciousness in the novel as a whole.

In a sense, the novelistic hero peeps or chirps (the intransitive verb "pip" means "to chirp or peep") his way into the world, or as he comes into the world, as he hatches (the transitive verb "pip" means "to break through a shell, to hatch"), he peeps. "Pip" as a noun, as a reference to a substantial thing, has varied, more and less substantial, more and less positive meanings: pippin, an admirable person or thing; a small seed; a disease, illness, or slight indisposition. All these varied definitions are applicable to Pip, who would like to be an admirable person, but who always rediscovers his smallness and his inclination to be indisposed and ill.

Pip wanted to imitate but he "created." His creation bears the marks of his smallness, his limitations, and his incapacity to complete and bring to a conclusion the project that he set for himself, to achieve his aim or goal. The project of every novel's hero and the structure of every novel is a similar "creation." All fail in some way to complete their goal, which at some crucial moment escapes them, because the goal itself is something too long, too complex, and too given over to turning the explicit into an implicit to be grasped. All conclude in producing a foregrounded "creation" against a background of failure. All these creations are determined by failure, inability, imperfection, misapprehension, and misinterpretation. Something flows through a subjectivity, the novelist's or the hero's, and in the course of this flow it is determined by the subject, becoming equal and adequate to the powers of this subject, to its power or absorption, or inclusion and exclusion.

But what is also important is that this inadequate "imitation" is recognized by others, if not as adequate, then in any case as his. "I called myself Pip, and came to be called Pip." Others are able to recognize us only by and to the extent of our own "creations." They seize upon the utterance as our identity, as our subjectivity. They grant the status of a full name to Pip's partial, metonymic articulation. They allow or are perhaps anxious for the part to be a whole. This recognition of the other is important and enables Pip to be. On the other hand, it is deceptive, distorting, and forgetful of the truth in that it superimposes wholeness on what was partial. And this too is paradigmatic for the way we read and perceive novelistic creations. We assume and superimpose wholeness and totality; we overlook the partiality, the negations, and the acts of division and multiplication on which the work stands; we interpret without including the necessary dimension of negation and exclusion. We have assumed that this dimension of negation is inaccessible, noninterpretable, an unknown. We call it the origin, the underived, the unconditioned, and ineffable with which we can have nothing to do—we who begin, who are derived and conditioned. But perhaps it is a "precise unknown"? And perhaps we have overlooked it because we are too anxious for the creation, for the affirmation, no matter what its price or precondition? Perhaps the very existence of the activity of negation still strikes us as dangerous, destructive, even as irreverent, unholy, and evil? Do we not still seek to read the artwork and the novel as if they were each imitations of the creation in Genesis, a whole that is awesomely affirmed, despite its patent divisions and negations? We say that language compels us to read in this way, by superimposing unity on perception, wholeness on the fragmented, and that this is the only way we do see or can speak.

All novelistic beginnings and creations are, like Pip's, but a poor parody of the creation in Genesis. They are imperfect creations, partly inadvertent and accidental. They are also imperfectly understood by others and the reader, who make their own inclusive and exclusive determinations, and impose their own conceptions of coherence. Yet we all continue to try to understand them, precisely because they have not been understood. There are haunting remainders and exclusions both in our own consciousness and in the "creations" of the novelists. The very life of the novel and our life of recreation and reinterpretation hinge upon these exclusions and remainders, the nonrecognized, nonabsorbed, the unknown, the excess which are there, which remain, and which will be repeated until they are recognized.

Excursus on Bachelard's *The Philosophy of No*

The classical realistic novel achieved all it could achieve in representing subjectivity in Tolstoy and Eliot where it basically followed the Hegelian model of rational self-development, of a successive creation of the self by negation and identification, self-division and resynthesis. It achieved all that it could achieve for subjectivity by following the Nietzschean model of tragic, dialogic self-development in Dickens and Dostoevsky. Here the novel shed its rational artistry as much as it was able in order to exhibit the tragedy of the unconscious will. Thus the logos of the novel, its aim to make the subject epical, shifts from an emphasis on

the self's potential for rational negation to the self's potential for irrational negation. In the one case, the negative movement of consciousness
is a consciously stated principle and belief, consciously negated; in the
other it is an unstated, unknown, and unconscious principle that surges
forth and is discovered. What, however, both these types of novels have
in common is the aim to represent the subjective processes as completely as possible and in an order of succession. Hence their long,
weighty, and epical structures and the use of repetition to insure that no
subjective possibilities have been excluded and that they have formally
been presented in a way that makes visible their contrary or contradictory relationships as much as possible.

These structures declare the poetics of the novel to be a poetics of
negation issuing out of the novelist's knowledge of the powers of the
self's negativity. The artistry and form of these novels have something in
common with Bachelard's vision of a "philosophy of no." Bachelard's
philosophy of no is a philosophy of affirmation based on the recognition
and absorption of all criticisms and negations of a primary model. In its
ardor to affirm all, Bachelard's notion is almost Piconian, but in its recognition that that which has to be affirmed is the power and productivity
of negation, it is modern.

The essence of Bachelard's philosophy of no and of his balanced, rational, and nonviolent approach to negation is given in this extraordinary
passage in which he characterizes the atom of modern physics as:

> exactly *the sum of the criticisms* to which its first representation has been sub-
> jected. Coherent knowledge is a product, not of architectonic reasoning, but
> of polemic reasoning. By means of dialectics and criticisms, surrationalism
> somehow determines a *super-object*. This super-object is the result of a critical
> objectification, of an objectivity which only retains that part of the object
> which it has criticized. As it appears in contemporary microphysics the atom is
> the absolute type of the super-object. In its relationships with images, the
> super-object is essentially the non-image. Intuitions are very useful: they
> serve to be destroyed. By destroying its original images, scientific thought dis-
> covers its organic laws. The noumenon is revealed by dialectizing one by one
> all the principles of the phenomenon. The diagram of the atom proposed by
> Bohr a quarter of a century ago has, in this sense, acted as a good image; there
> is nothing left of it. But it has suggested "no" often enough so that it keeps its
> indispensable role as initiatory pedagogy. These "no's" are happily coordi-
> nated; they are the real constituents of contemporary microphysics.

(p. 119)

Bachelard sees the superobject of modern microphysics as constituted of the coordinated negations and criticisms of the old model of the atom provided by Bohr. His vision takes cognizance of negation as a pluralizing and multiplicatory force, a power that destroys by splitting and doubling, producing contradictory divergence and ramification. But he also sees surrationalism as a power able "somehow" to turn the polemics into a new sum, a new coordinated superobject. Thus he can speak of the old, destroyed model without regret. Rather he sees Bohr's diagram of the atom as a good model precisely because it was totally negated and nothing is left of it. Negation thus becomes the mode or method underpinning the constitution and creation of new objects in modern science.

There is nothing destructive in Bachelard's view of negation. Unlike Feuerbach and Marx, he does not regard the old model as something false that deserves to be abolished, yet it is abolished and not preserved as it would have been in Hegel. Bachelard argues that a course of polemical negations has to be taken seriously because it is in essence creative.

Broadly, in the nineteenth century the old model which was criticized and destroyed by a varied course of polemical reasoning was a notion of subjectivity based in God. Feuerbach and Marx are only the most outstanding examples of a radical atheistic humanism which achieved the deconstruction and dismantling of this so basic model. Their criticisms, negations, and reductions of God became the models in turn for the criticism and negation of the autonomous self, which was modeled on God and had in a sense attempted to appropriate all of God's attributes and predicates. But what is most important is that the nineteenth-century novelists, who were engaged in the deconstruction and criticism of this old self, practiced an art which took account of all the negations, or which was itself the sum of all the available criticisms and negations. Their poetics of negation stressed and accentuated the negations. They felt their task to be the absorption or reintroduction into their art world of all excluded and mutually contradictory exclusions.

The classical novel's fundamental telos is the absorption of the negativity of its epoch, its doubly ironic and negative approach to God and the self. The novel's negative poetics was an effort to meet the challenges of the negative possibilities of the time. Their negative poetics was, like Bachelard's, an affirmation which accepted negation as a power and reality and which pursued it to try to discover its goal. In Dostovesky preeminently, the connection between the destruction of God (the father) and the self is clearly visible. In some ways, the contemporaneity of the two criticisms was unfortunate. It caused a confusion of the issues, a sense, as in Feuerbach, that the desymbolization of God would constitute man and social communion, or vice versa. On the other hand, the confusion itself pointed to the truth that man had indeed modeled himself on God and together with God for some time. Hence the intense dread of self-loss precipitated here and there by the sheer fact of atheism.

Another question becomes to what extent the novelists managed to create, out of the ironic polemics and dialectical criticisms of selfhood, a new superself. It becomes obvious here that Dorothea Brooke is a new self, engaged in realistic and concrete self-fulfillment with others, but that Eliot does not and cannot present her as a new superself because she has renounced too many aspirations simply to get in touch with herself and because the sphere of her influence is too narrow and insignificant. She is not a new superself because she cannot be represented as a new model. We remember that in her society she became in fact a negative exemplar.

Tolstoy's Levin is also a new self and presented as such, but what undermines his influence and value is that he reaches back to God to support his ego, and that without his irrational ethical faith he is not free from suicide. In Dostoevsky, besides Ivan's attempt at a new selfhood without God which Dostoevsky sees no way of bringing to realization, there is the somewhat unshapen selfhood of Alyosha. Alyosha, however, remains problematic because he is more like a catalyst for others than a self, a kind of prefiguration of the Freudian analyst with his "hovering attentiveness" and endless ability to listen to others. Also his selfhood is based on an existential practice modeled on Christ. The coordination of the criticisms into a new self is in fact not fully achieved until the birth of Nietzsche's superman, but we can see that all the novelists made efforts in this direction and that the more they succeeded the less they lamented over the old self that was lost or destroyed, over its disillusionment and negativity.

What is important in the novel's poetics of negation is that it manages to teach us to expect negation rather than affirmation. The novel's negative poetics is a break with the perpetual desire to be affirmed and reconfirmed; it alerts us constantly to expect difference. These novelists understood, as does Bachelard, that "above all we must recognize the fact that new experience says *no* to old experience, otherwise we are quite evidently not up against a new experience at all" (p. 9). The very signs of new experience are contradiction, negation, and the presence of the unknown. The philosophy of no is "the consciousness of a mind which constitutes itself by working upon the unknown, by seeking within reality that which contradicts anterior knowledge" (p. 9). The classical realists, for various reasons that will become clearer later, could not quite risk themselves in the unknown and in uncertainty, as is required by Bachelard's vision, but they all did approach the "zone where the mind thinks hesitantly, where it risks itself outside its own experience" (p. 79), and where it entertains negative possibilities. Or, in their risks, they returned in various ways to God precisely because the unknown, the other, had been defined as God.

Between the time of Johnson's *Rasselas* and *The Brothers Karamazov* the novel's tolerance for the unknown (which Johnson feared so absolutely) grew immensely, as is evidenced by its daring to be fundamentally more and more interrogatory. The interrogatory mode of "Why not?" is one the modern scientist must adapt so that despite the absence of an experimental interpretation of negative mass one might, for example, ask:

> Why can't mass be negative? What essential theoretical modifications could legitimatize to negative mass? What experimental prospect was there of discovering a *negative mass?* What characteristic is it which, in its propagation, would reveal itself as a negative mass? In short, theory stands its ground, it does not hesitate to seek the realization of an entirely new concept having no roots in common reality, at the cost of some basic modifications.
>
> (pp. 29–30)

Bachelard's point is that we have found a way of dealing with the *"totally unknown,"* the nonexistent, or nothingness. By our theoretically precise questions we turn the totally unknown into a "precise unknown." "This *precise unknown* thing is just the opposite of the *irrational vague* thing to which realism too often attributes a weight, or a function, or a reality" (p. 30). Bachelard's concept of the "precise unknown" as an intermediary concept between the totally unknown and the known is a radically new way of looking at the unknown as such. The approach is nonmystical, scientific, and rational, and yet, because it recognizes man's reason as noumenal, it is in fact "surrational," the term based upon surrealism which Bachelard chose to designate his new concept of the *cogito*. Surrationalism recognizes both the many negative concepts science has evolved and the fact that their discovery is intimately tied to our recognition of the unknown. A literary analogue to the probing of an unknown is, for example, the discovery of the formless and boundless sublime, the mystery of which was more and more turned into "a precise unknown," until it was coded as an exact experience. No doubt the systematization of this experience in the literature between the time of Kant and Hegel helped to provide a model, in turn, for the new unknown of the unconscious and its increased systematization into a more precise unknown.

Bachelard's surrationalism is an argument for a break with classical logic and "a conversion of the metaphysical values which have been postulated as fundamental" (p. 94). Classical logic, which was "the code for all the rules of normal thought" (p. 98), is no longer acceptable to Bachelard as an absolute logic because although it may work on one level of reality, it can, on another, lead to mere confusion. For example, the law of identity, "What is, is," must be reformulated when we are dealing with biology or the physics of the microobject into the postulate, "What is, becomes" (pp. 99–100). The new *cogito* must make itself mobile (pp. 91–92) and far more negatively dialectical to apprehend its object. The various formulas of classical logic and their cornerstone, the principle of contradiction, are mere postulates for Bachelard and no longer a priori forms of thought. Our task is to grasp the enlargement of rationalism or the mutation that has occurred in the *cogito* itself. This mutation was initiated by Hegel's addition to the *cogito* of negativity.

Bachelard's criticism of our unnecessary domination by classical logic is of course not new, but his particular way of presenting his argument and his vision of negative continuity between the old and the new is particularly applicable to the vision of the nineteenth-century novel. These novelists also avoided the broad error, made for example by Vico, of reading the pluralism and multiplications produced by rational negation as ultimately an inevitable decline and fall into chaos, darkness, and madness. They were aware of the possibility of such a vision—certainly Zosima's exhortation against modern radical individualism reads almost like a Viconian description of the age of man in its final phases—but they were artistically too enamored of and fascinated by the self's negativity to condemn or sum up its secular experience in a perpetual return to nothingness. They continued their explorations—although they knew that the first association with negation was always annihilation and death, and a near second, separation, the fear of being "cut off" or rejected—in order to make this fear and pain of destruction a more "precise unknown." They brought us face to face with the dilemma inherent in modern pluralism by representing it so completely. Their various technical resolutions show them as struggling with the very options which Bachelard defines. For Bachelard the options are

> either to preserve mental unity and regard divergent theories as contradictory (with confidence that the future will decide that at least one of the two theories was false) or else to unify the opposed theories, making appropriate modifications in those rules of elementary reasoning which seem to have become part and parcel of an invariant and fundamental structure of the mind.
> (p. 121)

In Eliot certainly, with her final turning to the laws of mutation and development and the consigning of the resolutions of the problems to nature, there is an effort to find and preserve mental unity. But then in Dostoevsky and Dickens we find the approach that Bachelard suggests of juxtaposition (rather than merely superimposition) and complementarity. These allow a veering from one insight to the next and not only contradiction; man, therefore, is not merely the passive subject of evolution but can to some extent influence it by his own awareness. But to do this, one cannot—and these novelists did not—step wholly over into the unknown, the incomprehensible area, or the area that was denied. They remained in touch with what had been, never believing as the negative ontology of Jean Wahl and others does that "negations speak to us of a plenitude of reality situated beyond all negations" (p. 117). Rather negation was for them a strenuously achieved metalanguage, a commentary upon affirmation, by which the ego liberated itself, in fear and anxiety, or first gave birth to itself as an ego. The self ceased living like Adam, in a superego that had to live in a life of affirmations. Conscious negation is as closely tied to the development of the ego and its separation from the superego as unconscious negation is to the life and the development of the id.

The self's negativity rests upon and is activated in the struggle with the three great polarities of life which govern it and which Freud summed up in these antitheses: Subject (ego)–Object (external world),

Pleasure–Pain, Active–Passive (p. 97). These antitheses form the background against which the activity of negation employs itself, becomes active and visible. The first is the most fundamental one and determines the other two, both in Hegel and Freud, but particularly in Hegel. The great question "What am I? and what is it?" governs all novelistic heroes, just as they discover the dreadful confusion possible between the subjective and objective order and particularly that projections and introjections are at the very heart of this subject-object confusion. The confused symbiotic relationships, false self-identifications with others, and misperceptions of others all issue out of a failure on the part of the ego to apprehend readily this antithesis. Hence the round of misunderstandings, the endless negations of self or of others, before the subject can even truly ask, "What am I?" Hence Emma's long detour to herself via Harriet, Dorothea's mistaken marriage to Casaubon, Pip's love of Estella, Anna's dreadful and self-destructive projections onto Vronsky, and Ivan's struggle with his hallucinated devil.

It is a round of struggles and negations in which pleasures and pains are externalized and apprehended intellectually. For the intellect remains ineluctably governed by this antithesis, which is, as Freud says, "sovereign" in all our intellectual activity (p. 98). This is the antithesis that governed Hegel in his description of the self's development and negativity and the antithesis that governed and guided the very development of the realistic novel. We can say that this is what allowed it to have a realistic pole or that this is what gave birth to its realistic pole. This is the antithesis that also allows a realistic reading, in which it always appears as if the struggle were between a subject and external forces, and in which the subject appears to be defeated by his inability to comprehend the external world and the external others. Such readings are "realistic" or conscious and intellectual because limited by and to the subject-object polarity.

This does not mean that the other two polarities are excluded or not acknowledged in a realistic-intellectual reading, but that they are also interpreted intellectually; for example, the subject failed because he was not active enough or at the right moment or in the right way, as Eliot and Tolstoy amply demonstrate. There was some failure of will or action, and therefore the objective events did not turn out right. The concern with the passive-active polarity gets deeper into the question of subjectivity and into a vision of choice and conscious self-determination, but it still remains ambivalent whether the choices are autonomous or whether they are merely opportunities provided or necessities imposed by the external world. And if choices are recognized as autonomous, why they are so different tends to remain a mystery.

Kierkegaard struggled with the active-passive polarity in the self, seeing that even the will to nonbeing was active, and he elaborated on this polarity as fundamental in self-development, loosening it from externality by making everything dependent on an autonomous choice guided by the awareness of dread or spirit. In Tolstoy, what the determinations of choice are remains ambivalent; his subject is still governed as a whole by a need to be in the right relationship on all levels with the external world. Levin derives his strength from his ability to be passive in relation to the external world and to bring what he perceives outside inside to still his troubled, active, and divided consciousness.

Dostoevsky is the one who drew the third antithesis (pleasure-pain) most firmly into his created world and who knew that for the subject this antithesis mattered more than all the rest, that it was the goal of subjectivity. He saw that the pleasure-pain polarity was paramount in determining our actions and will. He clearly defined and affirmed a state of pleasure—a state, in fact, of bliss. Active love is post-narcissistic, but dependent on the recognition of another. This very condition reveals the conception of pleasure here as one still dominated by the subject-object polarity, and by a desire in turn to bring this polarity into a coherent unity with the pleasure-pain polarity. What was so puzzling to Dostoevsky was why there were men like Ivan who persisted in unpleasure. The only explanation that he had to offer was that it was a defect, a consequence of narcissistic persistence in intellectual autonomy. However, Dostoevsky came closest to seeing, as Freud did later, that the pleasure-principle was not securely in dominance, and to seeking to know why unpleasure was so pervasive, and whether pleasure in fact did not serve the forces of unpleasure.

From the perspective of Freud and Dickens we have the privilege of looking back and seeing that the fundamental polarity which the classical novel itself represses and distorts is the most vital one of all: the pleasure-pain polarity. It is not a matter of these novels *not* being about unhappiness. Everyone saw that it was crucial not only to demonstrate its existence but to seek the solution to unpleasure. But in the very representation of unpleasure its deeper meaning or source is obscured by a conscious, objective approach, an approach that remains hopelessly inadequate to the problem. What remains fundamentally misapprehended is the basic need for pleasure or pain. The misapprehension turns into a kind of lament, a qualitative tone that is so characteristic of the novel and that we call its wisdom of disillusionment. It is, for example, this tone in Eliot:

> It is in these acts called trivialities that the seeds of joy are for ever wasted, until men and women look round with haggard faces at the devastation their own waste has made, and say, the earth bears no harvest of sweetness—calling their denial knowledge.
>
> (p. 462)

The approach is accusatory and condemnatory. The negative intellectual judgment reveals and hides the repression of the real quest in the novel after the source of pleasure and pain. The subject himself is at fault, but he is approached in an intellectual manner and probed for an answer to the question as an object in the world, rather than as a subject in himself. An exceptional moment, which perhaps defines the very limits to which the subjective probing of pleasure and pain could go in the classical novel, was given by Tolstoy in describing the sexual encounter between Anna and Vronsky, an encounter which immediately turns to unpleasure in the conscious mind and is linked by vital association to her subsequent development and death. For Anna, sexuality is a direct encounter with an instinctual force and its immediate repression. But this is largely an exceptional moment for the classical novel, governed so absolutely by the absence and disguise of a patent representation of the instinctual sexual forces. *Wuthering Heights* and *Clarissa*, though they manifestly do represent childhood and adolescent sexuality, the sexual force of the id, sadism, masochism, and perversions in love, are no exception to this view. For although this material does become available as content here, it is still encoded within and presented together with other ethical and mystical codes, and it is these codes that allow the elaboration of the material. Neither novel creates an unconscious structure which could directly represent this content and material.

One instinctual force that the novel does apprehend and elaborate from Defoe to Eliot is the instinct of self-preservation that Moll Flanders called the "authority" of necessity.[39] This instinct, given authority, flourishes like a fungus in Eliot, infecting everyone it can. It is dark, terrible, and persistently active enough in Bulstrode, Rosamond, Casaubon, and it also flashes its primeval head in Lydgate. But it is subdued and already surmounted in her heroine, unless we call her surmounting a sublimation, as we in fact must, but one that cannot appear as a sublimation because it is not fastened directly enough to what it abhors. Although the novel is nothing but the scene of psychic conflicts, it is a long time before it develops a structure adequate for the representation of purely unconscious conflict and negation. The oscillations in the novel between the subject in himself and the subject as an object in the world remain on a conscious plane to which the unconscious activity of negation is unknown. This itself is a "precise unknown" which does not negate the achievement of the novel but which defines its limits.

The novel could not establish the self as a new "superobject" until it discovered an unknown, an other that was not God but that belonged to the self. God had preempted the status of the absolute unknown for a long time, but gradually the novel gave birth to the id, the new unknown, by faithfully following the processes of the self's negativity. It discovered the new noumenon of the self "by dialectising one by one all the principles of the phenomenon." The basic phenomenon for the novelists was the ego, the self. This self was endlessly divided, split, and polarized into its affirmations and negations (into Anna and Levin, Ivan and Alyosha), but in all these novels, and not only in *Emma*, the fundamental protagonist is the one self, not the many seemingly separate and differentiated characters. What mattered was the totality of the criticisms and negations that would be derived from all these characters in their dialectical interaction for the idea of the one self. What we saw was that it was in fact this totality, this synthesis, of all the criticisms and negations which grew profoundly problematic and unapprehendable. In Dickens, however, the new, dark noumenon of the self is born. In *Great Expectations* it manifests itself as a particular unknown belonging to an individual. In *Our Mutual Friend* this unknown grows far grander, declaring its sway over everyone.

In Dickens there is, alongside the conscious structure, an unconscious structure which "realistically" conveys the unconscious material and content that do come to consciousness. It also realizes precisely the circuitous way in which instincts do come to consciousness and the very fact that they sometimes do not. It is from this perspective that the explosion of sexuality in Brontë is a kind of realistic allegory, a subjectively felt and imagined idea, but not a subjective experience of the unconscious supported by an achieved unconscious structure. The difference between all these novelists and Dickens is simply that they created their worlds, but that Dickens lets Pip create his. It is secreted out of him. And all the events and characters that may seem so random and dispersed find their coherence in him and in the work and labor of his repression. They are part of the very motility and activity of his repressed instincts, as, for example, that formidable figure, Jaggers, who points back to his first traumatic experience of needing to seek answers to questions that seemed to him a matter of life and death, and being refused by his sister the very right to ask questions (pp. 20–21).

Dickens' discovery bound his own earlier penchant to create by caricature and distortion insofar as these distortions had now to conform to unconscious plausibility, but it also freed him to distort even more, as becomes evident in *Our Mutual Friend*, which is Dickens' demonstration that all consciousness is in fact mere surface, mere theater, compared to the unconscious beneath. Here the novel loses its realism and Homeric substantiality to a further extent, becoming the jabber of voices of linguistic, fictionalizing beings who do not know themselves. The question becomes: If consciousness is surface, is not language also? To what extent is language a denial or distortion of inner impulses besides being a distortion or misrepresentation of exteriority? What is within, and do language and our fictions capture it?

No doubt it was the destiny of nineteenth-century realism to discover the structural and coding nature of fictions precisely because opposites discover each other. Writing displaces realism in both Flaubert and Dickens, and this is why *Our Mutual Friend* is "so intensely written," as James had observed. The very concept of a story, a narrative, is questioned, and "the story of the man from somewhere" lies within the work, dispersed and fragmented like the body of Osiris. Dickens asks to what extent fictions, besides providing us with a provisional identity that may only be partly true or a lie, help us to live by giving us pleasure. Fiction is a ghost, a nothing, built on an absence, a nonpresence. Like language itself it is always negative, yet it can say happiness "is," as Jenny Wren insists, rather than "happiness was" (p. 494). But is not the pleasure of aesthetic stasis allied to death, to the nirvana principle? Is art itself not an example of the fusion of pleasure and unpleasure, of Eros and death? But if art can erase the boundaries and conflict between the instincts of life and death in a way that is beneficial ultimately to life and pleasure, can this also happen in reality and how can this happen in a reality that is sheer mystification?

Our Mutual Friend is intensely interrogatory, a dialogue, like Freud's in *Beyond the Pleasure Principle,* about the basic instinctual forces of Eros and Thanatos that lie beneath the three great polarities of life, compelling the primary organism toward pleasure or pain. It is self-evident that Dostoevsky, facing the quest after pleasure and pain on the borders of consciousness, explored madness in a new way, and Dickens death. If Dickens seems to know less about madness it is only because he is already within it in his last complete work. The whole novel seeks to be a demonstration of the repression of death and seeks after the possibility of a fusion of the life and death instincts. All the methods of negation and reversal are applied to demonstrate the repression of death. Life begins as a negation of life, as its refusal. Life instinctively gravitates toward death.

And yet—like us all, when we swoon—like us all, every day of our lives when we wake—he is instinctively unwilling to be restored to the consciousness of this existence, and would be left dormant, if he could.

(p. 505)

Then how can the refusal of life or the nihilistic indifference toward it in a Eugene Wrayburn be turned into affirmation and desire?

Life at moments seems independent of the pleasure-principle, the erotic will to live, which Freud called the "the preserver of all things."[40] Like all the great novelists before him, Dickens reveals a paralysis in the pleasure-principle. But unlike the others, he does not simply accept or sublimate the evidence of this paralysis. To him, of all the great polarities of life, this failure of the pleasure-pain mechanism seems the most important. He knows that ultimately the question cannot be consciously answered. The failure of pleasure in life cannot be explained by externals or by an epistemological study of the subject. The failure can also not be accepted as fate or as a tragic flaw in some particular individual. It must have an unconscious answer; it must have to do with deeper, more inaccessible instinctual forces. The dilemma of indifference to or hate of Eros, life itself, cannot be solved consciously by a mere will or choice to turn it around. Yet this reversal strikes Dickens as the greatest challenge of life. Finally, Dickens shows that revitalization can only be

brought about on an unconscious level, by a reunification of the indifferent, disabled life-force in the individual with the death instinct itself.
Somehow, not always, from this submergence the pleasure-principle
reemerges dominant.

Somehow it is only the gap, the grave, the blankness of death that
"causes" everything in our consciousness to be there; everything is only
reborn from nothingness, including the love of life, as Pip discovered on
the event of his sister's death.

> It was the first time that a grave had opened in my road of life, and the gap it
> made in the smooth ground was wonderful. The figure of my sister in her
> chair by the kitchen fire haunted me night and day. That the place could pos-
> sibly be without her was something my mind seemed unable to compass, and
> whereas she had seldom or never been in my thoughts of late, I had now the
> strangest idea that she was coming towards me in the street, or that she would
> presently knock at the door. In my rooms, too, with which she had never
> been at all associated, there was at once the blankness of death and a perpet-
> ual suggestion of the sound of her voice or the turn of her face or figure, as if
> she were still alive and had been often there.
>
> (p. 301)

Eros, creation, and imagination are only possible against the background
of death. Death does more than haunt existence; existence is contingent
upon it. Thus Dickens bases his last great symbols on the instinct of
death and on no other absolute. What is concealed and hidden in all
symbolism is not transcendence, not God, but death. Death *and* God
are the unknown, the other. There are not one but two unknowns.
Dickens' symbolism becomes purely instinctual, concerned with the
unconscious resources of the mind. His novel is a representation of the
great oscillations of the mind between consciousness and the unconscious, surface and depth, and above all of the more primary rhythm of
life and death in the unconscious. Death, that great unknown, becomes
available and known to us as a force only when we ourselves bring it into
being by negation, destruction, and interrogation in a condition of extreme feeling that shakes and threatens the entire organism. But these
very activities of the mind presuppose a form of death in the very heart
of consciousness.

In its pursuit of the self's negativity, the great nineteenth-century
novel seemed increasingly to have lost its very grasp on affirmation and
pleasure, standing somewhat mystified before a fate that seemed like a

constant diminution and reduction of pleasure. These works discovered the complexity and riches of consciousness, but not how it could create pleasure purely from within without relying on the support of God, nature, ethics, or the saving love of others. In order to grasp pleasure and affirmation once again, Dickens seeks for their source in the instinctual life and finds that they are only to be had in a wrestle with death, that great source simultaneously of primal masochism, the unpleasure of life, and the pleasure of nirvanalike stasis.

Toward the end of his work, Dickens gives a great fictional demonstration of his concern with the fundamental rhythms of the unconscious and of consciousness by an almost implausible plot reversal from negative to positive, tragic to comic, in the Boffin sequence. What he no doubt hoped to effect in the reader was a final, striking experience of the motility and ambivalence of his own consciousness, ever poised between fiction and reality, possession and nonpossession, unconscious wish and conscious fact, between a Yes and a No, a negation and affirmation. Which impulse is stronger? Pleasure or disappointment and unpleasure? The choice of pleasure, when it can be a choice (as in fiction), is also one between the life and death instincts.

The point of the improbable reversal is to engage the reader in a free critical act in which the release from ambivalent feelings can only follow an act of belief and will. Pleasure comes if we can say what Bella says to John:

"I shouldn't like it [a carriage] for its own sake, half so well as such a wish for it. Dear John, your wishes are as real to me as the wishes in the Fairy story, that were all fulfilled as soon as spoken. Wish me everything that you can wish for the woman you dearly love, and I have as good as got it, John. I have better than got it, John!"

(p. 748)

All our "possessing" and "having" depends ultimately on our capacity for fiction. We can possess what we do not possess and never shall in the pleasure of fiction. Fiction is Eros, a human activity opposed to death.

Carroll's *Alice in Wonderland*

Alice in Wonderland is an epic of subjectivity focused on the subject's inherence and development in language. The novel's concern is with all that we repress, negate, and exclude about language in order to speak and communicate in the ordinary, conventional language world. Carroll's point is that together with this repression, we have also repressed a vast dimension both of pleasure and pain available to us only through language. So Alice's fall signifies, among other things, her release from this repression and her entry into a new, vaster, and more unconscious language world where language is both more perplexing and gratifying than it is in ordinary usage.

In this new world everything has to be rethought and reconstituted from the perspective of language: the body, the self, its identity and meaning; the relationship between dream and reality, work and play, meaning and nonsense, logic and illogic, rules and chance, words and things, nothingness and being, dialogue and solitude, life and death. The wedge between all these polarities is language, that fundamental source of misinterpretation, error, confusion, and noncommunication, but also of order, domination, play, fiction, Eros, and delight. Alice has to turn pain and frustration into pleasure; passivity into action, self-assertion, and mastery; and knowledge about the objective order of language into knowledge about her own powers, possibilities, and limitations as a linguistic subject. Language is a nothingness, a game, a dream, a fiction that is simultaneously our all.

Alice knows that the worst that could possibly happen to her is that she should go out altogether, "like a candle," leaving no trace of her existence.[41] This is unimaginable, because it is perhaps even more frightening than dying; it would mean being utterly reduced and consumed to an untraceable insubstantiality, leaving no remains, no reminder of existence at all. Tweedledum and Tweedledee tell her that she is "only a sort of thing" in the Red King's dream and that if he were to awake, she'd "go out—bang!—just like a candle!" (p. 145). To exist as another's dream is better than not to exist at all, but not as good as having everyone in one's own dream and existing still after one awakened.

> "Only I do hope it's *my* dream, and not the Red King's! I don't like belonging to another person's dream. . . . I've a great mind to go and wake him, and see what happens!"
>
> (p. 179)

What happens is similar to what happens in Dickens. After she experiences her lack of control over language in the unconscious, she becomes capable of controlling language and fictionalizing; she will be the one who will create the Red King in *her* dream.

Alice wonders if she is real or unreal, small or large, clever or stupid, sane or insane, dead or alive. Is the conventional language world she has known true or untrue, valid or invalid? Alice knows that she is fundamentally alone and must solve by herself the problem of her identity, a problem which others cannot solve for her. Time precipitates her identity crisis, but the absence of conventional language solidifies it.

"I wonder if I've changed in the night? Let me think: was I the same when I got up this morning? I almost think I can remember feeling a little different. But if I'm not the same, the next question, is 'Who in the world am I?' Ah, *that's* the great puzzle!" And she began thinking over all the children she knew that were of the same age as herself, to see if she could have been changed for any of them.

"I'm sure I'm not Ada," she said, "for her hair goes in such long ringlets, and mine doesn't go in ringlets at all; and I'm sure I ca'n't be Mabel, for I know all sorts of things, and she, oh, she knows such a very little! Besides, *she's* she, and *I'm* I, and—oh dear, how puzzling it all is! I'll try if I know all the things I used to know. Let me see, four times five is twelve, and four times six is thirteen, and four times seven is—oh dear! I shall never get to twenty at that rate! However, the Multiplication-Table doesn't signify: let's try Geography. London is the capital of Paris, and Paris is the Capital of Rome, and Rome—no, *that's* all wrong, I'm certain! I must have been changed for Mabel! I'll try and say 'How doth the little—,' and she crossed her hands on her lap as if she were saying lessons, and began to repeat it, but her voice sounded hoarse and strange, and the words did not come the same as they used to do:. . . .

(pp. 15–17)

Self-uncertainty is related to the problem of time and change. The self may depend on a contrast with others, the yes and no by which we identify others as not ourselves. The self is perhaps epistemological: it is what it knows. The self is language, but its sudden absence causes an identity crisis: she cannot remember how to recite the conventional verses that she had been taught. Alice tries different ways of apprehending her identity and is both determined to figure it out and tempted to wait passively to be rescued out of this difficulty and solitude. After she has accepted the scary realization that she does not know who she is because her self-definition has been provisional, inadequate, and external, she can learn from the caterpillar, the symbol of organic metamorphosis, who has no fear of bodily change and who refuses to comprehend

her anxiety, that bodily change is controlled by lack of fear and acceptance of change. Thus, when she meets the pigeon, she does not repeat
her mistake but makes an effort to explain herself, although not yet with
absolute certainty.

> "But I'm *not* a serpent, I tell you!" said Alice. "I'm a—I'm a—"
> "Well! *What* are you?" asked the Pigeon. "I can see you're trying to invent
> something!"
> "I—I'm a little girl," said Alice, rather doubtfully, as she remembered the
> number of changes she had gone through, that day.
> "A likely story indeed!" said the Pigeon, in a tone of the deepest contempt.
> "I've seen a good many little girls in my time, but never *one* with such a neck
> as that! No, no! You're a serpent; and there's no use denying it. I suppose
> you'll be telling me next that you never tasted an egg!"
> "I *have* tasted eggs, certainly," said Alice, who was a very truthful child;
> "but little girls eat eggs quite as much as serpents do, you know."
> "I don't believe it," said the Pigeon; "but if they do, why, then they're a
> kind of serpent: that's all I can say."
>
> (p. 43)

Alice tries to assert and ascertain what she is by declaring what she is
not. However, this merely negative self-definition is not yet adequate to
give her status in a world where she appears superfluous and dispen-
sable. She needs to find her place and her name, and to establish herself
as a center of definitions and rules so that she can rule the others who
insist on ruling her, and to prove to herself that she is not mad, as the
Cheshire-Cat insists she is (p. 51).

Alice acquires more certitude as soon as she is able to stop taking language literally ("Off with their heads") instead of as a sign for something,
and is able to call nonsense nonsense (p. 64) and negate the world that
does not fit her. She dares to become contradictory and to apply her
own logic to things. Language does exist as a set of rules, even though
the language of the mad violates these rules and even though we cannot
be certain that these rules are logical or that they bear any relation to reality. But these rules are all we have and nonsense language is characterized precisely by not existing and by not being recognized. She defines herself by defining them as irrelevant, meaningless, and mad. She
moves from deference and dependency ("O mouse") to triumphant self-
assertion ("I won't hold my tongue").

But Alice's acquired powers of subjectivity and its claim to be the
measure of all things prove illusory in *Through the Looking Glass*.

"Goodbye, till we meet again!" she said as cheerfully as she could.

"I shouldn't know you again if we *did* meet," Humpty Dumpty replied in a discontented tone, giving her one of his fingers to shake: "you're so exactly like other people."

"The face is what one goes by, generally," Alice remarked in a thoughtful tone.

"That's just what I complain of," said Humpty Dumpty, "Your face is the same as everybody has—the two eyes, so—" (marking their places in the air with his thumb) "nose in the middle, mouth under. It's always the same. Now if you had the two eyes on the same side of the nose, for instance—or the mouth at the top—that would be *some* help."

(p. 168)

From Humpty Dumpty's more radical, asubjective perspective, our prized individuation turns into nothing but sameness, an uninteresting repetition. It is only something other than the real subject that puts the subject in perspective. It is the nonhuman and the unreal that define the real in the episode with the unicorn.

He [the unicorn] was going on, when his eye happened to fall upon Alice: he turned round instantly, and stood for some time looking at her with an air of the deepest disgust.

"What—is—this?" he said at last.

"This is a child!" Haigha replied eagerly, coming in front of Alice to introduce her, and spreading out both his hands towards her in an Anglo-Saxon attitude. "We only found it to-day. It's as large as life, and twice as natural!"

"I always thought they were fabulous monsters!" said the Unicorn. "Is it alive?"

"It can talk," said Haigha solemnly.

The Unicorn looked dreamily at Alice, and said "Talk, child!"

Alice could not help her lips curling up into a smile as she began: "Do you know, I always thought Unicorns were fabulous monsters, too? I never saw one alive before!"

"Well, now that we *have* seen each other," said the Unicorn, "if you'll believe in me, I'll believe in you. Is that a bargain?"

(p. 175)

The pact echoes that of Sancho Panza and Don Quixote at the end of the episode of the dream in the Cave of Montesinos. Only by an agreement between the self and the nonself, the self's exclusions and remainders, can the self come to comprehend itself as something real against a background of the unreal. The surreal and fantastic novel alone puts the novel of realism in perspective, just as the basic, supportive, fictive game structure of the whole puts in perspective the latter's fictive narration.

Alice's journey is primarily a journey in language, an adventure in language. And at the heart of every encounter with the unreal is an encounter with the fabulous difficulties of language, its explosive contradictoriness, ambiguity, and opaqueness, its madness, nonsense, pathology, and genius. Every encounter turns into a problem of communication, a difference between what was said and what was understood, between what words say and what we mean to say, into an explication of the mysteries of syntax and semantics. The first things Alice finds in the Looking Glass World is the Jabberwocky poem, which makes no sense to her. Later Humpty Dumpty uses it to show her that the disturbances in the poem are compacted or condensed signs that can be elaborated and divided into various other more conventional signs, but that they are based in English. Thus he teaches her how, potentially, a surlanguage could be constructed upon existent language, as Joyce was to do with several languages in *Finnegans Wake*. He also teaches her how a potentially private, solipsistic, or schizophrenic language can be made by an entirely arbitrary use of words.

> "There's glory for you!"
> "I don't know what you mean by 'glory,' " Alice said.
> Humpty Dumpty smiled contemptuously. "Of course you don't—till I tell you. I meant 'there's a nice knock-down argument for you!' "
> "But 'glory' doesn't mean 'a nice knock down argument,' " Alice objected.
> "When I use a word," Humpty Dumpty said, in rather a scornful tone, "it means just what I choose it to mean—neither more nor less."
> "The question is," said Alice, "whether you *can* make words mean so many different things."
> "The question is," said Humpty Dumpty, "which is to be master—that's all."
>
> (p. 163)

Humpty Dumpty makes the all-important modern point: who is to be master? the speaking subject or language? Are we the victims of a language that we cannot change, that predates us, and that is primary and autonomous, constraining and predetermining the way we perceive and feel, or does language add a dimension of freedom to our existence by allowing us to reformulate our experience? Humpty Dumpty's way of assuming mastery is however one of the pathological possibilities of language within a subject.

Alice must become a master of language in some other way, but that master it she must she learns in the woods where things have no names. There she meets the fawn who asks her "What do you call yourself?"

"I wish I knew!" thought poor Alice. She answered rather sadly, "Nothing, just now."

"Think again," it said: "that wo'n't do."

Alice thought, but nothing came of it. "Please, would you tell me what *you* call yourself?" she said timidly. "I think that might help a little."

"I'll tell you, if you'll come a little further on," the Fawn said. "I ca'n't remember *here.*"

So they walked on together through the wood, Alice with her arms clasped lovingly round the soft neck of the Fawn, till they came out into another open field, and here the Fawn gave a sudden bound into the air, and shook itself free from Alice's arm. "I'm a Fawn!" it cried out in a voice of delight. "And, dear me! you're a human child!" A sudden look of alarm came into its beautiful brown eyes, and in another moment it had darted away at full speed.

(pp. 136–37)

We depend on language to be. Without it we are "nothing just now." Language is a loss and gain; it gives us everything and takes everything away. It is a contradictory rushing of presence into absence and absence into presence. Language, as a system of words, definitions, and distinctions, separates us from nature. It is purely negative in relation to nature, substituting words for things, or it adds, as Kenneth Burke has said, the negative to nature.[42] Thus the fawn rushes away, threatened by the return of language, for language is nature's negation or death. Alice recovers her oneness with language only to be shown thereafter that she is not, therefore, one with its signs. She comes, to borrow Lacan's formulation, to identify herself in language only to lose herself in it like an object.[43] When the fawn rushes away, he is also saying to Alice that as language she is no longer mere presence, as she had been in her namelessness, but a power, a value, threatening to him. Namelessness, for Carroll, is a condition of paradise, a sensuous union of bodies, an undifferentiated accord. It is satisfaction, pleasure, Eden. By contrast, namelessness in Beckett's *The Unnamable* produces no such unity, and for Lacan, it is not wholeness that lies beneath language but fragmentation, dismemberment, and death. Carroll's namelessness is the sign of his proximity to the romantic era.

From the beginning, what frustrates Alice above all is what the Looking Glass World itself is out to demonstrate: language is a mirror, not a window to the outside world. Its concern is not primarily external reference and reflection, but its own self-reflexive, autonomous nature, its inner adjacencies and differences, its determination of meaning and non-meaning by inner relationships between words. This autoreferential nature of words is demonstrated most simply in puns and that is why Alice is told she must learn how to pun.

Punning is a way of blocking and disturbing the referential potential of language. It is one way language can negate the world and affirm itself, as Mallarmé came to demonstrate so grandly in his own poetics of negation, and as Flaubert, with his almost sadistic hatred of reality and of what seemed to him the subject's poverty, wanted to demonstrated in a new novel that would be "about nothing."[44] For language does not give us the world or substance; it gives us itself and a set of relations. This frustrates Alice; puns are against logic, reality, and substance. But in mastering puns Alice also learns that language is indeed a system beyond logic, a metalogical system.

Alice has to learn how to take language both more and less seriously. She has also to be able to learn how to pun—" 'You might make a joke on that—something about 'horse' and 'hoarse,' you know,' says the Gnat" (p. 131)—in order to be able to joke and play with language, and invent fictions. Language games, as she learns in both books, are not merely for winning but for playing. Rules exist to be broken and this is why all the games in the novel are circular, nonconclusive, seemingly rule-less, and frequently narcissistic situations where everyone does as they like. This too is why the riddles have no answers and the battles merely arbitrary beginnings and ends.

When she has comprehended and stops denying the strangeness, complexity, and playful potentialities of language, she can escape this unconscious language world: "I can't stand this any longer!" (p. 204) she cries, and shakes the Red Queen back into reality, substance, logic— into her kitten. But then we see that she has indeed left the world of namelessness. She is a human being who desires to speak and to be spoken to, to engage in dialogue and communication. "It is a very inconvenient habit of kittens . . . ," she says, "that, whatever you say to them, they *always* purr."

> "If they would only purr for 'yes,' and mew for 'no,' or any rule of that sort," she had said, "so that one could keep up a conversation! But how *can* you talk with a person if they *always* say the same thing?"

On this occasion the kitten only purred: and it was impossible to guess whether it meant 'yes' or 'no.'

(p. 207)

In the subjective human world there is a Yes and a No. Alice understands this. This is why she gets the golden crown.

Alice in Wonderland is a seminal novel because it prefigures the novels that were to come, novels which never come back to the "kitten," which established themselves in language and outside the "grace" of realism, and whose very function was to prove, as Nabokov said, that "the novel in general does not exist."[45] These novels create, as *Alice in Wonderland* does, a new world of linguistic impossibilities—"Why sometimes I've believed as many as six impossible things before breakfast," says the Queen (p. 153)—as well as possibilities, and they reveal what the fate of negation and affirmation is in an artwork that has displaced the nineteenth-century centrality of the subject and its negativity in favor of language and its negativity. However, the displacement of the subject is only temporary in *Alice,* for the novel shows not only that language is more than logic, but more significantly, that meaning is more than truth. And at the center of meaning and the meaning-making operation is still the subject.

Modernism: Negation versus Deletion

But let your communication be, Yea, yea; Nay, nay; for whatsoever is more than these cometh of evil.

Matthew 5:37

In allen Korrelationen von Ja und Nein, von Vorziehen und Abweisen, Lieben und Hassen drückt sich nur eine Perspektive, ein Interesse bestimmter Typen des Lebens aus: an sich redet alles, was ist, das Ja.

Nietzsche

For Chomsky, negation is not part of what he calls the "underlying strings" or the deep structure of language, which is tautological, simple, separate, and repetitious. Negation is one of many possible surface transformations—into the interrogative, passive, and so on. Chomsky calls negation an insertion transformation, one of four elementary transformational operations, and one which adds something to or inserts something into the deep structure.[1]

Deletion is a transformation distinguished from negation by the fact that it is an operation of erasure. Deletion is a minus action; it omits, effaces, erases, and cancels. Deletion acts upon the deep structure, effacing the repetitiousness of the short "underlying strings" to produce a more compact, economic, and elegant surface sentence. Deletion in a sense releases the surface sentence by its striking power to subtract and reduce. By unburdening the deep structure of its excess, deletion extricates or makes way for the surface sentence. Negation, by contrast, is a plus action. Negation does not delete; it adds, multiplies, preserves, and separates. In a certain respect, the transformational operations of negation and deletion are not only distinct operations but opposites.

The linguistic operation of negation, as described by Chomsky, is in many ways similar to Freud's description of conscious negation. Both are surface structures, surface additions or augmentations—external, even superficial. In both, the simple negative insertion transformation is a way to unsay what one is saying. Negation is addition because it has to include the positive statement it seeks to deny in its assertion. Negation superimposes itself on an assertion. "It is not my mother," is, in Chomsky's view, a negative added to a positive. In this sense, negation is always tantalizing, provocative, and ambiguous, a positive descriptive force which implies and promotes the very idea or thing that it seeks to deny. It is an absence yoked to a presence, or a presence-evoking absence.

Deletion undermines repetition. For Chomsky, repetition is our most basic expectation. We expect the same; sameness, not difference, is what governs the deep structure. Deletion thwarts, circumvents, and overrides this expectation. It is at the basis of the surprise produced, for example, by the asymmetrical and by metonymy. Like negation, it is an absence (which presupposes a presence), but here the absent term is not yoked to the present term. They are not given together; rather the absent term is, comparatively, far more absent, more distant, more separate from the present term. Both transformation operations separate, but deletion is the stronger power of separation. Deletion is in a sense the true No. Negation tries to "create" absence, but fails, managing only to indicate it. Deletion, on the other hand, "creates" it. By its power of erasure, deletion cuts its ties to what is and what was, as negation cannot.

Freud

There is no No either in Freud's vision of the unconscious or in Chomsky's vision of language's deep structure. But hereafter the two part company, for there is never any possibility of deletion or erasure in Freud's notion either of unconscious or conscious negation. Unconscious negation creates, by repression or by other alterations of the paths of the instincts, merely a semblance of deletion in consciousness. Consciousness deletes or forgets even to the point of psychosis, but the unconscious always remembers and seeks to circumvent, incapacitate, disqualify, shatter, and unhinge consciousness and its sham deletions and amnesia. By comparison, the deletions in Chomsky's surface structure are not sham. Conscious linguistic structuration is not bound by anamnesis, by the insistent memory of the deep structure, nor is the latter constantly and deviously present in the former. Deletion separates the deep and surface structures by an erasure that prevents the former from incessantly infecting, disturbing, and distorting the latter in some way or other. Deletion is a true forgetting, an oblivion that appears, paradoxically, to belong to language but not to the mind governed by it. Language can delete and forget. Consciousness appears only to be able to negate and remember, or to repress and be haunted by the repressed.

Hegel

Hegel's description of the development of consciousness, like Freud's, recognizes and depends on negations, but makes impossible the very idea of deletion. In both systems, negation separates, doubles, splits, and disjoins, but the result of this activity is an addition, a substitution. For Hegel, thought is characterized by negativity, the miraculous ability to see the nonidentity in identity. This makes mind the archenemy of all positivity, unity, being, wholeness. The mind breaks the circle, the primordial image of the unity of all being. It is a negative activity that opposes the empty positivity of merely recognizing and receiving the what is, which for it is inherently not. By defining nonidentity, the unreconciled state, as negativity, Hegel reached the borderline of dialectical thought, but at this very moment his negative dialecticism turns back into positive, speculative, idealistic thought. The subjective mind, like Absolute Mind, separates to proliferate and produce, and to select from this proliferation what characterizes itself more precisely, or in other words, what identifies it more precisely. Its negative activity results in a union and new identification. The selective action of thought has to do with substitution, not deletion. This is why Hegel can say that the mind's negativity is a cancellation which preserves, because real cancellation or deletion is not the goal here or the essential activity, nor is it even the accidental by-product of the mind's drive for substitutions. Rather we can say that deletion does not occur because it is a goal that is intentionally abandoned. The mind negates to make available to itself its possibilities, alternatives, and options. Its cancellation "preserves" because it foregrounds a new synthesis and totality, and backgrounds the other. The other is neither destroyed or erased; although Hegel speaks of death to evoke the urgency and indomitable force of negation, the other is merely left behind, abandoned, suppressed. It is not forgotten because Absolute Mind or becoming, like the unconscious, never forgets; it is all that ever was, is, or will be.

The Classical Novel

The classical novel's aesthetics was one of negation, inspired by the processes of division, separation, multiplication, and addition. Increasingly, the classical novel paid more attention than had Hegel to the negative moment in dialectics, recognizing that there is truly no identity without nonidentity. Yet it yearned for identity and totality in the midst of its dissonances and dispersion. Its subject unfolded in relation to that which it is not by an affirmation, ever more troubled, of the way it is. For both Hegel and the novel, the subject was not merely itself, but more than it was.

The very process of negation in the novel dictated the acknowledgment of that which is negated and excluded. Negation keeps the excluded ever present even in the midst of denial. Negation attempts to dissociate and build barriers, but inevitably the axis of dissociation is also one of association, the royal road back to synthesis, conjunction, and identity. Thus, the very process of negation itself also dictated that the process be oriented toward some affirmation. The classical novel, like Hegel, evolved a complex, ironic structure of foregrounding and backgrounding that like the compound or complex sentence coordinated or subordinated without deleting.

Negation excludes, temporarily, this and that about Emma or Dorothea to find the truth that can be affirmed about the subject. In the course of negation's exclusions, everything excluded reappears under the sign or symbol of negation. Finally the subject is reunited with some part of what has been excluded, or the subject stands as the opposite of all that has been excluded. Emma is reunited with her conscious negations; Pip, in a way that is more complex, with part of his unconscious repressions. Ivan can only escape reunification and affirmation by madness. He attempts to stand in opposition to affirmation, within the negation that had tried to eliminate it. The very goal of negation, the reunification with something positive that can be affirmed, becomes more and more elusive, and the path to affirmation becomes more and more difficult and circuitous. The path leads through despair, death, madness, misinterpretation, self-deception, annihilation, verbal chaos, and nonsense, but always somehow, some affirmative is found, even if the self ends up reduced. Thus, Levin found intuition; Pip his labor; Alyosha a conscious Eros; and Eugene Wrayburn the force of the unconscious Eros. At the beginning, the process of negation, with its goal of affirmation, flows in one hero. In Tolstoy and Dostoevsky, the process is split, flowing to completion and affirmation in one hero, and being short-circuited and disrupted in another. It is only by an unconscious passage through death and madness that Eugene Wrayburn escapes the conscious death of Anna Karenina and the conscious madness of Ivan.

It is the very play of negation—its inherent antitheticality and pluralizing force, and its inevitably devious and circuitous route to affirmation and reconciliation via exclusions and substitutions—that also dictated the development of the novel and its expansions, its proliferation of ever vaster systems and structures in Proust, Joyce, and Mann. The genre developed on the ground of negation and elaborated the possibilities of the negativity of consciousness. Its context was a historico-philosophic climate that acknowledged no deletions or forgetting, only affirmations and negations.

Mann's *Doctor Faustus*

In *Doctor Faustus* the novel's negative poetics reach an impasse in a crisis of negative ambiguities. Here every opposite reveals another opposite in a radical antitheticality of nightmarish mutual negations. The world becomes a chain of substitutions, a musical score without transcendence which makes sense only because it draws upon itself and is self-referential. It is a world of too many meanings and consequently of none, because no meaning is without ambiguity. Leverkühn's "Lamentation" is therefore an endless repetition, but never an exact repetition because there never can be an exact repetition. But insofar as all absence is the absence of an expected repetition and as the repetitive principle is the very source of musical art, even when the repetition itself is not there at all, perhaps Leverkühn's "Lamentation" is still somehow a testimony to affirmation, or at least to the need for the yes and repetition that underlies all negation, as well as perhaps all deletion.

Doctor Faustus reveals the limits of negation to be affirmation, even when affirmation is no longer possible, available, or valid. The novel exhausts itself in scanning both the diachronic and synchronic orders in which the subject stands for the place and moment in which an affirmation can still be sought, but finds no point of arrest for its negativity. The diachronic orders of historical or genealogical development yield no illumination because, in the course of development, origins are necessarily obscured and obliterated, and because the beginning leads back to chaos, loss, and nothingness.

Secondly, the historical and genealogical approaches are of no avail because they have become invalidated by the complexity of the synchronic relationships and interactions. History and genealogy are not the wrong approach; rather, as Marx understood, they simply cease to be valid at a certain moment in history when negation by its power of pluralization has produced so complex a world of adjacent and parallel processes, interactions, and alienations that the explanation of these synchronic, spatial phenomena comes to absorb all our attention. The multiplicity of interacting synchronic factors cancels the hope of deriving the present from a past moment. The synchronic triumphs over the diachronic, a process initiated by Hegel's discovery of negativity. But the wild disorder, ambiguity, and contradictoriness of the multiple, adjacent, synchronic orders also offer no hope or ground for affirmation. In the midst of elaborating its perplexity over this immense and unyielding multiplicity, *Doctor Faustus* announces a yearning for simplicity and innocence, from which it is absolutely debarred, and which, when they do appear, announce a return to sheer barbarism.

At first the ambiguities produced by negation in the novel were beautiful because, as in *Emma,* they provided more than one way of seeing the surface of things and of consciousness. Even when the pluralizing force of negation grew threatening in its richness and complexity, the novel managed always to find something affirmative, pleasurable, or playful. It is these affirmations that allowed the closure of the work, or at least some kind of ending, even though the ending appeared also to take on the characteristics of a mere negation. It is the joyous affirmation, the pure assent that is simultaneously both emotional and rational, that the novel seemed unable to achieve. The emotional assents given by Levin, Alyosha, and Eugene lacked the support of consciousness, the demonstration by the reality-testing ego that the truth found within was also there in reality. The joyful assent is at best partial, momentary, radically subjective, and noncommunicable. As Dorothea says to Celia, who wants to hear the story of her marriage, it is not a wonderful story at all.

> "Can't you tell me?" said Celia, settling her arms cozily.
> "No, dear, you would have to feel with me, else you would never know."
>
> (p. 880)

The novel cannot fulfill Celia's expectations to hear a wonderful story because it cannot attain a deep or closed form (pleasurable, harmonious, whole, fundamentally affirmative and assonant), the form that was in traditional aesthetics the form of the beautiful. The novel's process of negation produces a surface or open form—more dissonant, painful, and uncertain, pointing to disparities, disjunctions, and incommensurabilities—which reveals "the wonderful story" to have been but the repression of all these experiences, and of all that is inconclusive, negative, ambivalent, divergent, ugly, and nonidentical.

The closed form, embedded in the open form, as here merely by Celia's yearning, acts nonetheless to reflect the tension between negation and affirmation that the novel's dialectic is everywhere about. Here the tension flashes forth once again as the novel's inability to resolve its incongruities, or to transform its suffering, or to fulfill our basic expectation of the repetition of an affirmation. We can say that the novel's negativity released and freed us from conscious denial or unconscious repression of fears, doubts, and incertitudes, but that it was finally unable to bind these up in affirmation. We can also say that the novel freed us, on the aesthetic level, from our narcissistic pleasure-ego by making us renounce the pleasurable aesthetic form of the beautiful for a more sublime, dissonant, and unpleasurable form felt as an incompletable negative force.

We can say that the fundamental dialectic of the novel is a positive dialectic, echoing Hegel's, insofar as it either achieves a partial reconciliation or affirmation, or hopes to, or is related to reconciliation by some form of desire, even if this desire is, as in *Doctor Faustus*, no more than the regret at its absence. But we can also say that the novel's dialectic increasingly becomes a negative dialectic, arrested in the very movement that Hegel had bid us to observe, the moment when a notion moves to become nonidentical with itself and self-autonomous, a moment Hegel, but not the novel, cancels. Negative dialectics becomes absorbed in these antinomies, these nonidentities, this irreconcilable negation, dispersal, and disintegration. In *Doctor Faustus*, the novel's negativity comes closest to climaxing in the dialectic that is purely negation's own, a dialectic in which it is only tied by a memory that is pure regret, loss, and absence to the positive dialectic that was once negation's goal. *Doctor Faustus* announces the end of a development and a new era that Foucault describes as the closure both of dialectics and the search for totality.[2]

Nietzsche

Doctor Faustus' final "Lamentation" is in certain ways a commentary on and negative answer to Nietzsche's vision of the Eternal Return —that vision of a pure Yes, undefiled by any no that Nietzsche evolved from his analysis of Western history, a history which he more than anyone understood to have been dominated by negations. In his deconstructions, he exposed the various affirmations of philosophy, religion, ethics, and science as weaknesses, as negations of the positive Will to Power, as triumphs only of a negative, perverted, insane Will not to be which was incapable of willing to be. Nietzsche revealed the fundamentally negative, reactive, and defensive nature of all our purportedly positive systems. He reincluded in our systems what they had suppressed: the nonidealistic ground of their birth. Consciousness was for him only a surface phenomenon dictated by unconscious forces and drives which consciousness had never dared to face. Logic and grammar were but equally superficial and false surface phenomena that simply aided and abetted us in our delusions, lending a semblance of reasonableness and substantiality to our self-imposed lies.

Nietzsche became intentionally and explicitly the greatest naysayer the West has known in order to scatter, destroy, and volatilize the affirmations we have known. He even insisted that there is no will, because what we have called will has nothing to do with the multiplicity, variety, and difference of the force that he called Will to Power. He saw the Will to Power in a crisis, the world and life slandered by their domination by the will not to be, by the accession of nihilism, a weak and joyless willing. He proposed the destruction and annihilation of this nihilistic, partial world of the will in order to recover the true Will to Power. To do this he had first of all to abolish all oppositions, all antitheticality, all divisions of the world into truth and untruth, appearance and reality, and show that the aim of all these polarities had been the avoidance of non-being by a fiction of being. By division, man escaped the totality of the Will to Power, condemning part of existence itself as nonbeing. Man perverted the very possibility of knowledge by grounding it in logic, in the principles of identity and contradiction. These were but rules for escaping contradiction, nonidentity, and a dispersed totality. As man ascribed unity to his knowledge, so he did to his identity and to his body. But the body is a flow of forces, a mobile, contradictory, multiple flow, coming to expression in a scattering, dispersal, and fragmentation. The changing body is the clearest analogue of the Will to Power that Nietzsche can think of, and of course it is the body, as Nietzsche is delighted to point out, that all philosophizing has ignored.

Consciousness itself is nothing but the special strange fruit of this body, of the Will to Power. Unrestrained by logic and systematization, this body will speak, as Nietzsche does, in fragments, aphorisms, and exclamations that aim to be demonstrations of the very spirit of this will. Consciousness, as we have known it, developed in fact as a consequence of the inhibitions and checks put upon this body. It developed as the interiorization of stalemated impulses; impulses that could not flow outward turned inward and created the negative consciousness that we have known. This consciousness had its genesis in a will to be that was impotent to be; it was born of the negation of the Will to Power, and in the course of history it has amply demonstrated the character of its origin by evolving first an ethics of hatred of the strong, then the bad conscience of self-hatred, and finally self-destruction because the self can no longer tolerate itself. Each of these mutations developed rationalizations, world views; the ideal of each is only a more exasperated demonstration of its knowledge that the only meaning and goal of life is pain, death, nihilism, and destruction. But this for Nietzsche is a lie, the false accession to truth of only part of the Will to Power. The self's no has become defiled and rancorous; it is reactive rather than active, outwardly oriented. The pure yes and no emerge from within; they are active and self-affirming.

What the West has called man must itself be negated. Overman is Nietzsche's effort to derive an idea of man not from men as they have hitherto existed but from the Will to Power directly. (Overman's origin is not man, but the Will to Power.) Once all our values have been devalued, Overman and the Will to Power will only say yes. Nietzsche's goal is the elimination of all negation, paradoxically, by allowing it to be, as it never has been, free. He wants to extirpate it as the source and cause of all our misspent and distorted lives so long as we aimed consciously and rationally to control it. Overman's yes is a yes to all that the Will to Power is—and it is everything.

For Nietzsche, consciousness can never achieve harmony with the Will to Power; only unconsciousness can. And unconsciousness knows no judgments about affirmations and negations; it only experiences their presence as dream, transformation, creation, and being. Man lives and expends himself in being the living work of art and objectification that he is, a flow of dispersed becomings, unmastered and unmasterable creations. It is to being in this flow of dispersion, negativity, and creation that man must say yes. For there is no truth. There is only nature and art. Art is the Will, the Will is art.

The Will to Power, however, is a temporal becoming. How can the negation that the temporal model of time carries ineluctably within it be overcome? Nietzsche's answer to this dialectic is the Eternal Return, which is an affirmation of time, even backwards, its synchronization, so that becoming is a re-coming. Overman, in the strength of his joy and affirmation, can will that what came once should come again. The Eternal Return is the very test and proof of Overman in the strength of his affirmation of the Will to Power. Only the Eternal Return guarantees that there is not an iota of negativity or rancor left in the Will to Power or in how it exhibits itself in Overman.

Nietzsche's Eternal Return is his effort to defy the fact with which this study began. For Nietzsche, negation and affirmation are not ineluctably linked. They are not inevitable polar opposites. This is an illusion by which we have allowed ourselves to be dominated. They simply are. Nietzsche's goal was to accomplish the seemingly impossible, to describe a vision of life in which man arrogates the perfect yes for himself and makes it the basis of his being. Like God, Overman says "it is good" to everything, but unlike God he commits no acts of separation or division. Overman is an artist and creator, like God, but unlike God he reaffirms his creations only *as* appearances, as art, as innocent, endless, explosive becomings in himself.

Overman's new "narcissism," which is unsullied by any self-negations, is a selfless love of life, an *amor fati*, the will to love what is. Overman is solitary, autonomous, affirmative, joyous, creative, and noble. But unlike the first noble men who exercised their Will to Power over others, Overman is not a master of others; he does not engage in the struggle of domination, though he will by his very presence indirectly "master" and govern the slaves, the rancorous and negative, who will also inevitably return in the Eternal Return.

Nietzsche's Overman is, like Dostoevsky's Ivan, cleared of his conscience and therefore of his need to fantasize having to play Grand Inquisitor to the weak, anarchic, and rebellious who need illusions. Overman is detached and separate from the weak. He has abandoned them guiltlessly. For Nietzsche, Hegel's master-slave dialectic is a waste of time. The slave will never free himself. Only the master can free himself of the temptation and futility of domination and mastership. The master and slave types will always exist, and Nietzsche's point is that they are to be kept apart so that the slave will not again "free" himself and in fact "dominate" the master. The master frees himself of mastership by separation and detachment, not as in Dostoevsky by freely turning about and abolishing the slave and recognizing him as an equal in love. Overman is also freed, as Ivan needed to be and Nietzsche himself, of his need to say no, to refuse the world as it has been. That terrible war of negation that both Ivan and Nietzsche needed to carry on against history and reality brought on Ivan's madness. One thing is certain—that Nietzsche broke into madness at some point beyond Ivan because his Overman rescues Ivan from this crushing need ever to refuse in a Yes in which Ivan can finally spend himself in that *amor fati*, that senseless joy in existence that was always his. Therefore, if Nietzsche heard voices in his madness, they were not those of Ivan's disembodied devil.

Nietzsche's madness occurs somewhere in that transition he made beyond Ivan, the transition from the latter's terrible and maddening hold on a No to a Yes. Somehow, in that transition there was more than joy or pleasure for Nietzsche; there was bliss. For bliss is that seam or edge where old values are destroyed and where the new comes into being. Bliss is therefore annihilation, loss, disturbance; it is brutal, unmediated, and immediate. Bliss is precisely beyond pleasure because it is more than reconciliation or culture. Bliss disfigures and breaks up what we have known as pleasure for the sake of the new. Bliss is also more than the tragic, a pleasure felt in pain itself. Nietzsche's madness

has precisely to do with the inadequacy of all that has been called pleasure or the tragic and with the new that is their conjunction, bliss.[3] But
it is impossible to know to what extent his madness was a final statement
to our inadequacy and to what extent it was in bliss.

No doubt Nietzsche's work and his madness are the most profound
and complete arraignment and negation of Western culture that has ever
been made—far more complete than Dostoevsky's negation of God in
the Grand Inquisitor's tale. Nietzsche made clearer than it ever had
been before that our life lacks authentic affirmation or bliss. He overturned and devalued the very idea to which the West has always clung,
that our origin and genesis were good, positive, and affirmative, free of
negation and nonbeing. It is an idea that is still frequently reiterated,
especially in comparisons of the West to other civilizations. Octavio
Paz's statement is typical of this stance:

> In the West, what is basic is affirmation: we view Non-Being from the point of
> view of Being. In India what is basic is negation: they see relation—the
> human world and the divine world—from the point of view of an Absolute that
> is defined negatively or *is* negation itself. The Non-Being of the West is subor-
> dinate to Being; it is *lack* of reality.[4]

Nietzsche certainly had no patience with the nihilism that masked itself
in the tranquillity of Buddha or the stasis of the nirvana principle, but
insofar as this statement arrogates affirmation for the West, Nietzsche
would consider it an outrageous lie and a grand illusion. For Nietzsche,
the West had never known complete affirmation; it had never even tried
to imagine what that would be, what its possibilities were. It had never
dared to approach affirmation directly. What we had developed were
the possibilities of negation in the guise of affirmation. We only knew a
partial affirmation, dependent on and defined by exclusions and negations. Hegel was his predecessor insofar as he had also inserted negativity and opposition into the very first principle and ground of being.
But Hegel's Absolute Spirit, though it was one with the spirit of negativity and nothingness, also contained and dominated its own activity of
negation by subsuming it under reason. Nietzsche's irrational becoming,
unlike Hegel's rational becoming, has only the "reasonability" of art.
The Will to Power creates and destroys art, not reason. Yet, when
Nietzsche posits the new Overman together with man (who has always

been a slave), even in the Eternal Return, his affirmation appears inherently incomplete, partial, and still dialectical. The master-slave dialectic is the one antithesis that is not shattered and dispersed in his new totality where all else is explosively scattered. Unlike any other major thinker of his century—Hegel, Marx, Dostoevsky—he considered the antithesis of these two types natural, given, and immutable. The antithesis was no longer evil, and it was not intended to provoke a dialectical struggle, because the presence of Overman makes the other type merely irrelevant. Nonetheless, the very acceptance of the split, the division, the bifurcation, connotes the presence of the old activity of negation. It would seem that Nietzsche, despite his vision of a new, nondialectical bliss utterly transcending the old model of negation and affirmation, has not in fact deleted the presence of the latter. He ends up with a model of subordination, foregrounding affirmation (Overman) and backgrounding negation (man).

Adorno

Nietzsche reevaluated the polarity of negation and affirmation, and seeing that our life had been dominated by their inauthenticity and partiality, he attempted to tear the polarity apart, to displace it by a qualitatively new and different dionysiac affirmation. Given the polarity, it is almost inevitable that someone else should try to subvert the polarity in the other direction. Among these many attempts, Adorno's negative dialectics is one of the most coherent and consistent. Like Nietzsche, Adorno's thought is concerned with the affirmation-negation polarity because it is fundamentally underpinned by an attention to and the recognition of the pleasure-pain polarity in man. Self-conscious ego-formation is no longer primary and sovereign, as it was in Hegel, but in the foreground stands man's essentially affective and creative nature. The quality of life and the power of selfhood is measured by affectivity and creative possibility rather than by the autonomy of self-consciousness. Adorno's fundamental demand, like Nietzsche's, is for happiness and freedom in creativity, and he too repudiates and exposes our renunciation of this demand in what Horkheimer called mockingly our "affirmative culture."[5] Like Nietzsche, he exposes such affirmations as we have produced as sham, but his sociologically oriented thought prevents him from displacing the rather dire vision of reality that his analysis yields by a vision of a new, cleansed, dionysiac affirmation.

The human subject is for Adorno but "the late form of the myth" of the absolute, yet he does not wish to create a new myth of the subject to replace the old one.[6] Like Nietzsche, he feels that what we have called man or "person" is a being that should not be perpetuated, but he also knows that what "the concept of the right human being" may be is not something that we can anticipate (p. 277). Adorno's concern is a philosophical criticism, which as far as he can see can never end or be completed, as Nietzsche hoped to complete his, and therefore the Nietzschean leap to bliss is also for him inaccessible and utopian. All that Adorno can say is that "without exception, men have yet to become themselves," and that "by the concept of the self we should properly mean their potential," a potential that "stands in polemical opposition to the reality of the self" (p. 278).

In his analysis of selfhood, Adorno returns to Ivan's root position of refusal, facing squarely the fact of suffering and pain. Against all the forces that praise "the power of positive thinking" he holds on to "the seriousness of unswerving negation" which "lies in its refusal to lend itself to sanctioning things as they are" (p. 159). Although he rejects the naïve attitude of naturalism toward the somatic pleasure-pain principle, he insists that it is the survival of *this* element in knowledge that creates the "unrest" of thought and not, as Hegel argued, Spirit. Pain, suffering, and negativity are the moving forces of dialectical thinking (p. 202) and the condition of all truth (pp. 17–18).

It is the somatic element's survival, in knowledge, as the unrest that makes knowledge move, the unassuaged unrest that reproduces itself in the advancement of knowledge. Conscious unhappiness is not a delusion of the mind's vanity but something inherent in the mind, the one authentic dignity it has received in its separation from the body. This dignity is the mind's negative reminder of its physical aspect; its capability of that aspect is the only source of whatever hope the mind can have. The smallest trace of senseless suffering in the empirical world belies all the identitarian philosophy that would talk us out of that suffering. . . .

The physical moment tells our knowledge that suffering ought not to be, that things should be different.

(p. 203)

All our ideas of the new, the different—hope, change, and transformation—derive from a suffering actualized in the body, and actualized and reinforced there thanks to the body-mind split. Hegel blithely passes over pain in his demonstrations of ever-new syntheses, but pain and suffering are for Adorno concrete sources of truth. The ability to remain attentive to this truth and, therefore, also to the horrors of history is, as Adorno says, our only hope, and an urgency because although there is no universal history that "leads from savagery to humanitarianism," "there is one leading from the slingshot to the megaton bomb."

> It is the horror that verifies Hegel and stands him on his head. If he transfigured the totality of historic suffering into the positivity of the self-realizing absolute, the One and All that keeps rolling on to this day—with occasional breathing spells—would teleologically be the absolute of suffering.
>
> (p. 320)

There is no telos in history, as Vico and Hegel believed, and if there were, it would not be the telos of a plan for a better world, but a telos of suffering and destruction. Rather man must overcome the illusion of a manifest telos in history, abdicate his passivity and idealistic illusions, and become critically and actively engaged in his own hitherto unconscious or merely semiconscious construction of theory and praxis, so that at last Vico's insight into man's ability to understand history because he has made it may be realized. For Adorno it has never yet been realized, because men do not understand themselves or their history and in the current era they do not make or control the latter.

Adorno's negative dialectics returns to the negative moment in Hegel's dialecticism as a new point of departure. It is the moment when Hegel discovered the nonidentity in identity, the vital contradiction, which he again lost when he overturned his own negative dialectics into a positive, speculative idealism in which identity always triumphs. From Hegel's new synthesis and identities there issued, among other things, the pure falsehood and fantasy that we call human subjectivity. Hegel saw the nonidentity between the subject and the object but ignored it turning the object (cat) into the subject (the subject's idea of cat). What disappears in this analysis first of all is the particular. The particular is subsumed under the universal and becomes a function of the universal, as it always has been in philosophy (p. 313). But only if the particular is granted the same right as the universal (p. 329) can the universal be changed (p. 313), and what Adorno calls the futile, Sisyphus-like labor of

our thinking away the negative side of the univeral be ended (p. 327).
We have made unity the measure of heterogeneity, and by this we have
impoverished our experience and have lost not only particularity, but by
extension all true sense of difference, diversity, divergence, and dissonance.

Thus negative dialectics, which is the consistent sense of nonidentity,
rescues the remainder, the particular, the nonconceptual that the concept dominates—in other words, all that Hegel called insignificant and
transitory (p. 8). What is of supreme importance to Adorno is the very
fact that the concept does reach the nonconceptual, otherwise our
thought by its autarky would be condemned to emptiness, stupidity, and
primitivity—as in fact it has been because we have failed to see that the
disappearance of the object is thought's own work (p. 149).

For Adorno, nonconceptuality is "inalienable from the concept," and
it "disavows the concept's being-in-itself" (p. 137). Thus, although
"thinking without concepts is not thinking at all," (p. 98) thought must
abdicate its idea of hegemony and autarky, and practice a disenchant-
ment of the concept, its transcendence. Thought must admit that it is
not only cogency but play, that it is random and can go astray, and can
only go forward because it can go astray (p. 14). Thought has an un-
shielded and open aspect, which is unsystematic, and which traditional
philosophy has repressed for fear of chaos (p. 20) and for purposes of
self-preservation. This "freedom" of thought is like the freedom of the
object which was lost in Hegel, vertiginous, inconclusive, unframed,
and unlocalized (pp. 32–33). To do this means to think "something," but
always to know that that something is not identical at all with thinking
(p. 33). Thus negative dialectics is by definition thinking against thought
without abandoning it (p. 141); it is a way to counteract the tyranny and
coercion of thought, a way to know and measure rationally when rationality becomes irrational (pp. 148–49).

Negative dialectics attempts to reverse the reduction of objectivity to
subjectivity, to end the fantastic and irrational idea of the subject's pure
inwardness and apriority, and what idealism has been drilling into us for
thousands of years: the idea that the object is a subject (p. 179). For
Adorno, idealism's presumption in taking mind as a totality is nonsense
(p. 199). Adorno's critique of identity aims to show "the preponderance
of the object" in the very subject itself (p. 183). He rethinks the mediation of the subject-object polarity, which is basic to thought and without

which "cognition would deteriorate into tautology" (p. 184), to point to the inequality inherent in the mediation:

> The subject enters into the object altogether differently from the way the object enters into the subject. An object can be conceived only by a subject but always remains something other than the subject, whereas a subject by its very nature is from the outset an object as well. Not even as an idea can we conceive a subject that is not an object; but we can conceive an object that is not a subject. To be an object also is part of the meaning of subjectivity; but it is not equally part of the meaning of objectivity to be a subject.
>
> (p. 183)

The ruthless repression of objectivity, particularly in ourselves, has not only devitalized subjectivity, but in a kind of return of the repressed perpetuates this negated nonidentity "in suppressed and damaged form" (p. 318). What we call reification and lament over is, for Adorno, but "the reflexive form of false objectivity" (p. 190). We cannot comprehend or cope with what we have repressed, and therefore it returns to negate us (p. 344), like a "spell" or poison. "Spell" and ideology are for Adorno "one and the same." And ideology dates back to biology: self-preservation (p. 349). What we currently call our new "pluralism" may signify the breaking of the "spell," but since the pluralism comes from disintegration, Adorno is not certain whether it signifies liberation or disaster (p. 346). For the sake of its unconditioned rule, subjectivity has paid a heavy price, part of which for Adorno is Auschwitz. For if the subject denies the objective conditions dwelling in its core, "if the nature in reason itself is forgotten," reason will be self-preservation, running wild, regressing to nature (p. 289). Therefore, after Auschwitz there is no word, for Adorno, "that has any right unless it underwent a transformation" (p. 367). There can also be no systematic philosophy nor any validity in a thinking that is unaware that "deep down, the mind feels that its stable dominance is no mental rule at all, that its *ultima ratio* lies in the physical force at its disposal" (p. 177).

Critical thinking is negative because it does not achieve something positive by its negation. Its achievement lies only in "the consistency of its performance" and "the density of its texture" (p. 35). Also critical thought does not really "discover" anything or generate ideas or provide answers; it unfolds the answers given in questions, allowing thought to catch up with experience (p. 63). Therefore critical thought has no use for any thought that preserves itself as an origin (p. 63) or that is "fascinated by the chimera that anything is absolutely 'first' " (p. 103). For Adorno the very "category of the root, the origin, is a category of domination" (p. 155), that domination which the mind is always fearfully and self-defensively seeking. "A new beginning at an alleged zero point is the mask of strenuous forgetfulness—an effort to which sympathy with barbarism is not extraneous" (p. 71).

Critical thought also has no use for causality, a notion made obsolete by the fact that "every state of things is horizontally and vertically tied to all others" (p. 267). Its concepts denote a function, not a substance (p. 65). A total, systematic philosophy can no longer be hoped for (p. 136), but philosophy cannot simply be obviated and realized in revolutionary praxis and change, as Marx had proposed. The primacy of "praxis itself was an eminently theoretical concept" (p. 144). Philosophy can only disappear into philosophizing, a continual thinking that restricts the mind to the real, and thereby escapes the imprisoning circle of identitarian thought.

Both Adorno and Nietzsche see what was once our substantial ontology as a construct of consciousness. For Nietzsche, behind this construct lies a radical ontological dispersion, the truth of the Will to Power, which we have negated but to which Overman will be able to commit himself by a free affirmation. For Adorno, what lies behind the construct is not readily apprehendable. The dispersal that we now appear to see is not the natural and the true, but a condition that has evolved historically because the mind segregated itself long ago from the object. The present condition includes deformation because it was shaped by processes of deformation and suppression, but these processes are neither readily analyzable nor reversible. It is, in a sense, an objective reality of particulars gone insane under the pressure of the mind's universal. "The universal that compresses the particular until it splinters, like a torture instrument, is working against itself, for its substance is the life of the particular" (p. 346). It is this deformation of the life of the particulars, their splintering and dissociation, that now appears to put life beyond the pale of human control. Perhaps we no longer have the potential to change it or our relationship to it (p. 345). We have abused consciousness too long precisely by elevating it and ignored the context in which it exists. For Adorno, it is, paradoxically, the principle of totality and not that of negativity which has produced our sundered reality. We discovered negativity, but were unwilling to submit outselves or our thought to its truth. The consequence of our fear and evasion, our anxiety to pre-dominate as subjects, is a distorted and maddened world, a world which accurately reflects our conscious misinterpretation and abuse of the truth of negation.

Certainly, given Adorno's analysis of the inauthenticity of this dispersal, it is not something he can affirm. For Adorno, there are no affirmations past, present, or future that can be made or remade; there is only the possibility of criticism. And at the heart of this criticism stands Adorno's conviction that we must rethink negation and negativity because we have never understood them or the nonthought, the unthinkable, the truly different and other that they imply. We have never dared to think to the limit for fear of confronting an undefiable negation. Such self-criticisms as we have made have never moved far beyond Odysseus' ruse of "No-man"; they were self-renunications made for the sake of self-preservation. Our aversion to the preponderance of the object is institutionalized because we have always been "afraid that heteronomy may be mightier than [subjective] autonomy" (p. 189). This is the "secret" of our affirmations: simultaneously the evasion and abuse of negation. We have fundamentally misunderstood the play of one polarity against the other. Serious negation begins with the affirmation of the immanent subject and object, and is the critical recognition of their power to tyrannize. Our history is the demonstration of this tyranny which can be neither escaped or affirmed.

Adorno's and Nietzsche's divergent though equally critical and radical interpretations of the historical pattern of our negations and affirmations take place within this obsessive polarity and point to their possession by it. Hence their visions of a violent and violated history, dominated by one part of the polarity or the other, and their need ultimately to disengage and clarify the true nature of the other part of the polarity. Both Nietzsche's vision of pure affirmation and Adorno's of serious negation are the direct product of their respective interpretations of inauthentic affirmation and negation.

Beckett's *The Unnamable*

Beckett's Unnamable, that disembodied voice of a dispossessed and voided language, also emerges from this polarity and the possibilities of an aporia.

What am I to do, what shall I do, what should I do, in my situation, how proceed? By aporia pure and simple? Or by affirmations and negations invalidated as uttered, or sooner or later? Generally speaking. There must be other shifts. Otherwise it would be quite hopeless. But it is quite hopeless. I should mention before going any further, any further on, that I say aporia without knowing what it means. Can one be ephectic otherwise than unawares? I don't know. With the yesses and noes it is different, they will come back to me as I go along and how, like a bird, to shit on them all without exception. The fact would seem to be, if in my situation one may speak of facts, not only that I shall have to speak of things of which I cannot speak, but also, which is even more interesting, but also that I, which is if possible even more interesting, that I shall have to, I forget, no matter. And at the same time I am obliged to speak. I shall never be silent. Never.[7]

Unanswerable questions, defeated negations and affirmations, aporias— these are what keep the text going. The *Unnamable* records the life of a voice. Beckett's hero spends his existence affirming what is not but can never manage to affirm it. The "body" of language remains, a signifier without a signified. The limit of language is found in the limits of affirmation, i.e., affirmation cannot affirm what is not, or these limits lie in negation. Negation is the restless, productive activity in language that says "never," exhibiting an operation in time.

Beckett's central protagonist is language. Language attempts to explore itself, to discover what it is, or was, or could be. But language does not know and cannot possess itself; it does not know and cannot find its own beginning or end. Language fails to place itself, to establish itself. It fails to say something. The Unnamable "feel[s] nothing, know[s] nothing"; he is a voice that speaks,

knowing that it lies, indifferent to what it says, too old perhaps and too abased ever to succeed in saying the words that would be its last, knowing itself useless and its uselessness in vain, not listening to itself but to the silence that it breaks and whence perhaps one day will come stealing the long clear sigh of advent and farewell, is it one? I'll ask no more questions, there are no more questions, I know none anymore. . . . I have no voice and must speak, that is all I know. . . . No, I am speechless. Talking of speaking, what if I went silent? What would happen to me then? Worse than what is happening? But fie these are questions again. That is typical. I know no more questions and they keep on pouring out of my mouth. . . . I shall not answer them anymore.

(p. 307)

Discourse is futile because it has lost faith in itself as containing anything, or as giving anything, or as possessing anything. Words have no connection to the things they indicate or signify. Words connect to words of necessity. That is all. That is what keeps the Unnamable going, even beyond the aporias, the interstices and gaps in thought. For language is not identical with thought. This is why we cannot know it, and why the Unnamable does not *know* what he is saying.

> I don't know who it's all about, that's all I know, no, I must know something else, they must have taught me something, it's about him who knows nothing, wants nothing, can do nothing, if it's possible you can do nothing when you want nothing, who cannot hear, cannot speak, who is I, who cannot be I, of whom I can't speak, of whom I must speak.
>
> (p. 404)

If thought does exist, it exists because of language. Beckett's Unnamable speaks, and therefore, perhaps, thinks a little (p. 301). But it is an old language that has reduced him to his condition of speaking, a language that asks "that he should first behave as if he were not, then as if he were, before being admitted to that peace where he neither is, nor is not, and where the language dies that permits of such expressions" (pp. 334–35).

It is within this old language of inclusion and exclusion that the Unnamable cannot name or find himself. He has intuitions of a new, unknown language that might emerge from this one, or he has intuitions that this language may grow silent or die, but none of these things happen, so in his "life" there have only been three things: "The inability to speak, the inability to be silent, and solitude" (p. 396).

The Unnamable, speaking from the perspective of language, discovers his need to speak and to negate the spoken because it no longer has any meaning for him or rather because the content, the images and objectifications that it always produced and brought into being with itself are for Beckett a falsification, an illusion.

Language writing itself, expressing itself, needs to become like an "impoverished painting, 'authentically fruitless, incapable of any image whatsoever'." In *Three Dialogues*, Beckett states that art has been primarily concerned with the possible, the feasible, the expressive, and a denial of what it inherently is: a medium, a failure.

> All that should concern us is the acute and increasing anxiety of the relation [between the artist and the occasion of expression] itself, as though shadowed more and more darkly by *a sense of invalidity, of inadequacy, of existence at the expense of all that it excludes*, all that it blinds to. *The history of painting*

. . . *is the history of its attempts to escape from this sense of failure.* . . . My case . . . is that van Velde is the first to desist from this estheticized automatism, *the first to submit wholly to the incoercible absence of relation, in the absence of terms, or,* if you like, *in the presence of unavailable terms, the first to admit that to be an artist is to fail,* as no other dare fail, that failure is his world and the shrink from it desertion. . . . I know that all that is required now . . . is to make of this submission, this admission, *this fidelity to failure,* a new occasion, a new term of relation, and of the act which, unable to act, obliged to act, he makes, an expressive act, even if only of itself, of its impossibility, of its obligation. (italics mine)[8]

Art lives in a world mediated purely by language, which means that art is a world of pure nonpossession. But we have always applied our formal resourcefulness to conceal rather than to reveal the absence, the true nonpresence of a world in the work of art. We use art to lie and to make formally present a merely phenomenal and evanescent image, an image that is to begin with absent. The aim of Beckett's negation is to demonstrate this absence.

But what happens to words dispossessed of absent images, to "nameless images," to "imageless names?" (p. 407) Words lose their boundaries, their limits, becoming unarrestable. The word proliferates erratically in pleasure and pain, a new realm of language that no one has dared as yet to explore as fully as Beckett, its great master:

If only there were a thing, but there it is, there is not, they took away things when they departed, they took away nature, there never was anyone, anyone but me, anything but me, talking to me of me, impossible to stop, impossible to go on, but I must go on, I'll go on, without anyone, without anything, but me, but my voice, that is to say I'll stop, I'll end, it's the end already, short-lived. . . . It's the end that is the worst, no, it's the beginning that is the worst, then the middle, then the end, in the end it's the end that is the worst, this voice that, I don't know, it's every second that is the worst . . .

(pp. 394–95)

The word becomes merely a voice, at times merely an acoustical murmur. The voice stops and starts. It is not even certain whether it is speaking or listening. It is the source of the voice that cannot be named or located. Language released from its illusions, forming and constructing what is not there, is an unending, undefinable, acoustical dialectic of voicing or being voiced where neither the center, the source, nor the direction of the voice can be determined. The word tells its story of what it is like to be the word: "that is to say, I don't know, you musn't believe what I am saying, I don't know what I'm saying, I'm doing as I always did, I'm going on as best I can" (p. 397). The "plot" of *The Unnamable* is language's war against itself, the truth of its poverty against the myth of its riches, its realizable and realistic potential. The voice speaks not knowing what it wants to say or what it has said. The "plot" is simultaneously the history of Western civilization seen, however, from the perspective purely of language. In *The Unnamable* we see, miraculously, all that we thought was, once again, but only as an illusion, an impossibility, as mere words:

> It goes on by itself, it drags on by itself, from word to word, a laboring whirl, you are in it somewhere, everywhere. . . . Strange, these phrases that die for no reason, strange what's strange about it, here all is strange, all is strange when you come to think of it, no. . . . Sometimes I act as if it were, but at length, was I ever there at length, a long stay, I understand nothing about duration, I can't speak of it, oh I know I speak of it, I say never and ever.

> (pp. 402, 407)

The "laboring whirl," a reference to the great oration (consisting mainly of rhetorical questions) addressed by God to Job "out of the whirlwind" (Job 38–41), has never been more than this inconclusive verbal whirl in which the Unnamable finds himself with his desubstantialized language.

Beckett's Unnamable is disembodied language "without" anything, trying to achieve Beckett's "dream": "an art unresentful of its insuperable indigence and too proud for the farce of giving and receiving."[9]

> That's all words, never wake, all words, there's nothing else . . . you must say words, as long as there are any, until they find me, until they say me, strange pain, strange sin, you must go on, perhaps it's done already, perhaps They have said me already . . . I'll never know, in the silence you don't know, you must go on, I can't go on, I'll go on.

> (p. 414)

This indigence can only be actualized by negation, by the constant reiteration of what language is not. This not, however, that he is constantly writing about—as absence, emptiness, negation, denial, destruction, silence, futility, impotence, impossibility—is not to be confused with the unnamable nature or essence of language. What language is not, was not, never will be, is not yet its essence. Beckett's denials break upon this elusive, not yet confirmable, not yet definable affirmation of a metalanguage. Metalanguage is a commentary upon the language of affir-

mation and negation that we have known. It is language talking about itself, saying "no" to what it has been.

What is common to Nietzsche, Adorno, and Beckett is the search for
the new—a new yes, a new no, a metalanguage—transcending the old
negation-affirmation polarity we have known. Nietzsche wants a purer
affirmation beyond the divided negations and affirmations of consciousness and the unconscious that have produced such distortion; Adorno, a
more negative negation that might make contact with the object, the
nonconceptual, with something beyond our subjectivity; Beckett, a new
language that would allow other possibilities than those now permitted
by our sentences, with their adjacency of clauses and phrases, their subordinations, coordinations, modifications, declarations, and negations.
They are all aware and tired of the limitation and tyranny of the old polarity and its dialectical processes.

Each of these texts begins with negation, not with affirmations that
have first of all to be eliminated or criticized. The negative is no longer a
shock or a discovery; it is there before the text begins. Above all, these
texts no longer wish to preserve what they have cancelled. The pluralizing, productive activity of negation is preserved neither in a new synthesis, nor a structure of subordinations, nor in a layered irony. Negation
renounces the hoarding of contradictions that is characteristic of irony.
The goal of this negation is deletion, the forgetting of what has been.
Negation seeks to counteract the operation of addition that is part of its
process and to become an operation of subtraction. Like the child, as
Piaget has found, who learns reversibility only belatedly and who understands only after knowing addition and subtraction that subtraction reverses the process of addition, so negation comes belatedly to seek
its possibility of reversing the operation of addition into subtraction,
deletion.[10] Then, by the deletion born out of negation, it seeks to
transcend the very condition of exclusion and inclusion, of negation
and affirmation in which it perceives itself to have been bound.
Negation has in this sense become not only more self-concerned or self-
centered, more content to abide by itself and less afraid of itself, but also
more practical or revolutionary in Marx's sense. It is this revolutionary
element of deletion and destruction that stands behind Nietzsche's no,
making possible the very idea of a new yes. It is the new will to subtraction and deletion that purges Beckett's text so that we may hear
only this clear voided voice or apprehend what such a voided voice may

be. It is by this same commitment to the reversibility of the operation of negation that Adorno seeks to decenter the very idea of an autonomous centered subject to which we have clung.

In all these texts negation's relationship to an unknown, a new, is far more clearly delineated and more consequently explored. Negation, by stressing its subtracting power, refuses to return to a single, immobile center from which all its activity will appear as but the distortion or repression of some primal truth. Negation now shifts, unfixes, and de-centers the very idea of such a center while aiming to become deletion, which would make the center disappear altogether.

If we look back from Adorno, Nietzsche, and Beckett to Montaigne, for example, and recall his complaint about the lack of a language of negation, we can see that these authors have established modes of radical negation and, in Beckett, a language of negation that no doubt far exceeds Montaigne's desire for a more definite way of expressing skepticism, hesitation, and doubt. They have created a serious language of negation which not only doubts but tries to sweep away a tradition that it believes to be at root inadequate. Negation tries to negate what negation has produced. Subtraction vies with division, addition, and multiplication.

In these texts negation faces its own exigency and crisis, but it is this very exigency of negation's desire to become deletion that prevents it from being deletion, and it is also the very exigency of these negations that keeps them bound to the possibilities of an affirmation. These are therefore transitional texts, still yoked in divergent ways to the past they resist. In a sense they are kept from the new that would erupt with deletion by negation. This is most obviously true of Adorno for whom the present is historical and always will be though history is no longer analyzable by traditional historical approaches, by concepts such as causality, or indeed by any concept that has not revitalized and revolutionized itself by the category of nonconceptuality. This is also true of Nietzsche, who feels the need to sum up the past in a negation and by a negation before he can begin again and forget. And this is also true of Beckett, at least up to the time of The Unnamable, whose very need to ascertain absence is so provocative and tantalizing. All these works still stand under the shadow of the symbol of negation, although they are not primarily concerned with revealing the concealed, but with forgetting what is not worth remembering. As such they are still subject to interpretation and the procedure of hermeneutics. In various ways, they still evoke, as did *Doctor Faustus*, the Biblical affirmative form, which may be literature's "deep" structure, or deep form, and the basis of all form. Unlike *Doctor Faustus*, however, they evoke this form without regret at its absence, in order to negate, to disperse, and, if possible, to delete it.

Barthelme, Robbe-Grillet

Deletion, unlike negation, is a permanent, nonretrievable erasure. What is well erased is no longer present, visible, or recoverable. The palimpsest effect of negation is no longer operative. A text dominated by deletions would no longer be subject to a process of hermeneutics; there would be nothing to recover, for there is nothing that has merely been negated, suppressed, displaced, or repressed. Deletion acts on the deep structure itself, leaving behind only a surface structure.

A text such as Barthelme's "The Indian Uprising" *begins* in a formal dispersal, matching Nietzsche's ontological dispersal, which the latter found only at the end. It is a text in which every sentence is de-centered, veering away equally from conclusions, order, meaning, co-herence, negation, or affirmation. A sentence is but an opportunity to make chance contacts between wholly unrelated and distant categories and words. The effect of such a sentence is to make it appear as if chance and not choice had put this sentence together. And with the apparent absence of human choice, the subject in the guise of an author making choices also appears to be absent. Technique appears free at last, truly metasubjective in a way that Lukács could not yet apprehend.

Chance, by freeing the text from the subject, also frees the elements of the text. They appear as particulars, unframed, unsystematized, unlo-calized, in the way that Adorno's negative dialectics would have them ap-pear. They appear as a randomness, in unstable constellations which easily dissolve. These particulars fail to become objects because they are bound only in perishable verbal relationships and not in those imagina-tive, emotional, cognitive relationships where they could be recognized as constituted objects. These particulars are themselves merely process, part of that sense of process which pervades the text, an inconclusive process conducted on a ground of emptiness. In such a text, realized as the shifting and the mobile, the simplicity of realism vanishes. There is no continuity of being or of becoming. Everything that appears is but a moment in a shifting, uncertain, and perishable verbal structure. Because nothingness is the ground of the text, it can stop and rebegin in its process of making new chance sentences. Chance, the aleatory, is art's new way to economy and elegance. A sentence is thrown like a set of dice, and the possibilities of its permutations and chance connections are recorded and transcribed. What appears is neither negated nor affirmed; it is merely written. Chance also excludes and includes, but by its very existence it denies the idea of intentional choice, the idea that there are radical alternatives, opposites between which we must choose.

Consciousness, giving way to language, giving priority to language, gains by this submission language's ability to delete. Deletion governs those texts where thinking submits to writing. Deletion is a gift foremost of language and not of consciousness. Deletion, like negation, can be an act of will, but it is an act made possible only in language and executable only there. Deletion puts negation in its service to forget the subject, meaning, temporality, and communication. Deletion is a praxis that allows a wholly new, clear, slender, and economic form; its own violence displaces the violence of negation. Texts such as Barthelme's and Robbe-Grillet's are truly surface texts in the sense that their concern is the possibilities of the surface sentence structure and not the consciousness that stands behind this surface structure. In their texts the play of negation is still evident, but it is backgrounded as consciousness is, part of a random content.

Robbe-Grillet's fidelity to linguistic construction and invention becomes evident in the small anecdote that he tells us about what happened to him while he was writing *The Voyeur*.

At the period when I was writing *The Voyeur*, for example, while I was trying to describe exactly the flight of sea gulls or the movement of waves, I had occasion to make a brief trip in winter to the coast of Brittany. On the way, I told myself: here is a good opportunity to observe things "from life" and to "refresh my memory." But from the first gull I saw, I understood my error: on the one hand, the gulls I now saw had only very confused relations with those I was describing in my book, and on the other it couldn't have mattered less to me whether they did or not. The only gulls that mattered to me at that moment were those which were inside my head. Probably they came there, one way or another, from the external world, and perhaps from Brittany; but they had been transformed, becoming at the same time somehow more real *because* they were now imaginary.[11]

The image of a thing favors its own existence over the existence of the real object. But the image in turn is given with or allowed by the word, which is neither the image nor the real object. Thus, by attending to the word, the writer can obliterate both the image and the real thing, or at least indicate the nonidentity between them. Robbe-Grillet's novels are concerned with this negative dialectics of nonidentity between the word, the image, and the real thing. Robbe-Grillet had started to construct his own imaginary-linguistic seagulls, ones having only so distant a relation to external seagulls that their reality no longer concerned him at all. His seagulls are based in the word, not modeled on the real object. Language has no need for the model; it invents "without a model" (p. 32). Robbe-Grillet's novels explore the possibilities of purely linguistic description and the reactions and interactions of these descriptions with the less innocent and neutral imaginings of an active consciousness.

In *Jealousy*, for example, we are made aware of a few neutral objects, standing in measured spatial relationships to each other, and of the efforts of consciousness to order them, to make them yield some meaning or communication. But purely descriptive objects are tied neither to value judgment nor to communication. Only consciousness demands an answer of yes or no, and appropriates objects for its emotional and cognitive ends, binding them up into its associations and fears, its jealousies and impulses to murder. Consciousness is always making what Robbe-Grillet calls *the* "humanist affirmation: the world is man" (p. 70). But the truth is that "things are things, and man is only man" (p. 52). Consciousness, however, is self-centered, eccentric, and determined to "perceive" the slippery and unharnessable object, to order and ingest it into itself by perception. Consciousness, in Robbe-Grillet's novels, is therefore represented as "*always* engaged . . . in an emotional adventure of the most obsessive kind, to the point of often distorting his vision and of producing imaginings close to delirium" (p. 138).

Robbe-Grillet's content is the "story" of the isolable existence of subject and objects. Its philosophical correlate is Adorno's analysis of nonidentities, an analysis which destroys the myth of the constitutive subject. In Robbe-Grillet both this myth and that of the realistic novel are destroyed.

> To record the distance between the object and myself, and the distances of the object itself (its *exterior* distances, i.e. its measurements), and the distances of objects among themselves, and to insist further on the fact that these

are *only distances* (and not divisions), this comes down to establishing that things are here and that they are nothing but things, each limited to itself. The problem is no longer to choose between a happy correspondence and a painful solidarity. There is henceforth a rejection of all complicity.

(p. 72)

Robbe-Grillet never tires of pointing out that this myth depended on the assumption of a hidden union and communication between the subject and the world. The subject sought to dominate and assimilate the world so that the latter would appear less alien. Tragedy is but the obverse of this desire for solidarity and domination. It laments the divorce, the gap between men and things, and turns the separation into nausea or the absurd. But neither posture is more than the demand of a subject that seeks first of all its own priority.

A common nature, once again, must be the eternal answer to the *single question* of our Greco-Christian civilization; the Sphinx is before me, questions me, I need not even try to understand the terms of the riddle being asked, there is only one answer possible, only one answer to everything: man.

This will not do.

(p. 58)

The novelist can reveal in his content his rejection and criticism of our habitual urge to relate, dominate, and appropriate, but in his form he escapes even this mere "presence" of a world that is always there by concerning himself primarily with style and construction. A new, less anthropocentric vision of men and things (or at least an interrogation about the relationship between men, their imagination, and things) may be born in the novel as well. But this is, as it were, only a by-product, made possible to begin with by the novelist's exclusive concern with language and writing. The work of art "must seem necessary, but necessary *for nothing*" (p. 46).

When he thinks of a future novel, it is always a *way of writing* which first of all occupies his mind, and demands his hand. He has in mind certain rhythms of sentences, certain architectures, a vocabulary, certain grammatical constructions, exactly as a painter has in mind certain lines and colors. What will happen in the book comes afterward, as though secreted by the style itself.

(p. 44)

Robbe-Grillet's only concern is to keep these linguistic elements from presenting and secreting what they had in the traditional novel. He avoids representation, as he tells us, by beginning with a tiny fragment, an insignificant phrase, or one that he tries to make insignificant. This prevents any sense of spaciousness and revelation, any "general view" like that of the realistic novel. Furthermore, these minutiae are not allowed to be "seen"; they are destroyed or their contours blurred, or they are made incomprehensible or made to disappear altogether.

> It is not rare, as a matter of fact, in these modern novels, to encounter a description that starts from nothing; it does not afford, first of all, a general view, it seems to derive from a tiny fragment without importance—what most resembles a *point*—starting from which it invents lines, planes, an architecture; and such description particularly seems to be inventing its object when it suddenly contradicts, repeats, corrects itself, bifurcates, etc. Yet we begin to glimpse something, and we suppose that this something will now become clearer. But the lines of the drawing accumulate, grow heavier, cancel one another out, shift, so that the image is jeopardized as it is created. A few paragraphs more and, when the description comes to an end, we realize that it has left nothing behind it: it has instituted a double movement of creation and destruction which, moreover, we also find in the book on all levels and in particular in its total structure—whence the *disappointment* inherent in many works of today.

> (pp. 147–48)

Robbe-Grillet is fundamentally not concerned with images but with ways in which phrases and clauses can be composed, cut, repeated, spliced, contradicted, omitted, obliterated, dissolved. He decomposes his incipient images or partial images or scenes by revealing that they are dominated and composed to begin with by a composition that is verbal and stylistic. Stylistic construction triumphs over imaginative construction by deletion, the force that condenses writing into style.

Robbe-Grillet's accent lies on erasures and deletions. He is content with the smallest particular, with the elaboration of even minutiae in writing and therefore, he has no need to concern himself with imagination's larger fantasies, its totalizations and systems. His only concern is precision and exactitude in construction and destruction. He is willing to disappoint because there is no subject in his work who possesses the world with his consciousness; there are only moments of subjectivity, moments interrupted, furthermore, by the space given to the description of linguistically constructed objects or partial objects. Consequently, no time passes in his novels; there is only movement, a movement that knows nothing about temporality. Construction and deconstruction comment on each other, but neither gives the satisfaction of a significance. The movement, moreover, knows nothing about dialectical thought. The grammatical subject-verb-object sequence is not explored for its development as it had been in Hegel. The dialectical processes inherent in the grammatical movement of subject into predicate are not elaborated; the movement is not granted the status of consciousness. It is not apprehended as a real and meaningful development of the thought processes. Grammar remains grammar, an autonomous activity separated from dialectical thought.

Robbe-Grillet's novels generate neither being nor nonbeing; they neither affirm nor negate. There is no echo here, as there still is in Beckett, of the novel in its heyday when it participated boldly in the creation and destruction of meaning, transforming affirmation and negation into comedy and tragedy, interiority and absent transcendence.

Robbe-Grillet writes in a new time of deletion, a time of the surface sentence. The surface sentence, liberated from dialectical thought, has forgotten its need for knowledge and its relation to the real subject and object. It has also forgotten what was once the deeper significance of repetition (sameness) and difference—the need for affirmation, synthesis, gathering together, and the need as well for negation, division, tearing asunder. The surface sentence is separated from the deep structure or form of affirmation by a deletion that is a radicalized no, a will only for stylistic elegance and simplicity. Deletion by-passes the corruption both of our yesses and noes. It no longer knows anything about that negation which was sin, the pain of separation, or the triumph of a weak Will to Power. It also knows nothing about affirmation or virtue, faith, and the access to bliss. It knows nothing about either because it emerges not from consciousness as such but from the activity and possibilities of writing. Upon the written, deletion acts with as absolute and as total a force as negativity had upon what is thought, but its consequences are disappointing: a surface form of meaningless, albeit exciting, dispersions and condensations. This surface form brings to a closure the classical novel of consciousness, dominated by the aesthetics of negation. In the postmodern novel inspired by deletion, negation and affirmation must submit to being merely momentary content in a form governed by an aesthetics of deletion.

CHAPTER 4

Negation
and the Tragic

His theory of tragedy is connected with his view of the function of negation in the universe.
A. C. Bradley, "Hegel's Theory of Tragedy"

To study the tragic theater from the perspective of negation, we must first imagine or hypothetically posit a moment when tragedy and negation did not or could not exist. Second, we must establish a moment or phase that could be called pretragic and prenegative. This moment, furthermore, is one of which we should find traces in the tragic form itself. Tragic form at its commencement may in fact be expected to be in contention with or a commentary upon the pretragic and prenegative.

Freud

In *Beyond the Pleasure Principle*, Freud speculates on whether the goal of life may not at all times be death. Perhaps the first and most fundamental reaction to life was unpleasure. Thus the first instinctual impulse may have been an impulse to return to death. Life seeks not change and the new, but a return to the initial, old state. At first, it was easy to die; now the route to death is more circuitous, devious, and complex, but it is still death that life seeks.[1]

Freud's speculation provides a pattern for an immutably tragic view of life. It also suggests that the tragic genre must inevitably be linked to the death impulse, the unpleasure at life, and a conservative, antilife urge toward stasis, simplicity, quietude, and origins. Freud's view suggests that tragic complications are but the barriers life and the pleasure principle put up against death, barriers the tragic hero must seek to dissolve and undo. For the lust for life, the pleasure-principle, is a secondary, later development, the ascendancy of which over death is ever precarious and, from the point of view of the primary, nonlife state, untrue.

The static quietude of nonlife, which Freud describes, could be called an atragic state, the pull of primal nondifferentiation, sameness, and lack of self-awareness. The pretragic is born together with and in the pleasure-pain polarity, the first yes and no. But here the pleasure-pain polarity, its direction and goal, is the obverse of what we commonly assume it to be. The first no is addressed to life, not death. It is not a fear of death, but an innate agreement with, even an eagerness for death because life is unpleasure. The first yes, if we can call it that, is addressed to death, to the initial nonlife state, for the charge against life of unpleasure makes this state, by contrast, pleasurable. The first yes and no are barely divergent or opposed; they exist only because the pleasure-pain polarity has come into being.

The strange and obverse direction of the initial pleasure-pain polarity is perfectly conveyed by what I would call the pretragic wisdom of the wise Silenus.

"Ephemeral wretch, begotten by accident and toil, why do you force me to tell you what it would be your greatest boon not to hear? What would be best for you is quite beyond your reach: not to have been born, not to be, to be nothing. But the second best is to die soon."[2]

Pretragic wisdom states that it is best to die soon and better not to be, because it knows life as unpleasure and nonlife as "pleasure." But though this pretragic wisdom is urged upon the first tragic heroes and though it continues to be felt perhaps in all tragedy, tragedy proper is born at a point beyond this wisdom where a further differentiation of pleasure, pain, and other possibilities of feeling occurs.

Among these new modalities of pleasure and pain at least three possibilities can be singled out. For one, the unpleasure at life could be transformed into pleasure. Perhaps the transition itself would be an experience of bliss, that strange inmixture of pleasure and pain, experienced at a point of radical turning. This transformation would guarantee the dominance of the pleasure-principle. Tragedy proper would itself then signify the struggle for the ascendancy of the pleasure-principle, of Eros, the triumph of the secondary principle of life over death. This transformation, in which a special pleasure comes to be attached to life and growth, could itself initiate a yet further mutation: the transformation of the agreement with death into a fear or dread of death. Death would no longer appear as a "natural" resignation of life. Tragedy proper, then, would also signify the coming to consciousness of death, and perhaps a new evaluation of the possibilities of the avoidance and deterrence of death.

A less radical transformation of the pleasure-pain polarity, but still a new awareness of the very existence of the polarity, could come about if the unpleasure of life is recognized for what it is and accepted as it is. Life is unpleasure and it is willed on its own terms, despite the fact that it can never be turned to pleasure. This would be the basis of a kind of stoical, rational tragedy, one which would short-circuit a development in the affective pole of life, and which would, in seeking for justifications, initiate a development of the cognitive pole of consciousness. Death here may still appear as "natural," but the processes of life and death are viewed as quite separate.

The third possibility is one in which tragedy proper would itself remain turned toward the pretragic vision, obsessed, fixated, and fascinated by it, confused by the turning itself of the pleasure-pain polarity, mystified by the possibilities of choice it opens up. Confused, hesitant, and ambivalent, tragedy would ask: Which is more true, life or death? which is better? to which impulse shall I listen? what are pleasure and pain? Here life could be arrested between the fear of living and the fear of dying. Both become unpleasurable, and if we are equally afraid to live or to die, we become caught, furthermore, in a paradox. To avoid death, we must seek life, but to be secure from pain, danger, and death we should also not seek life, or seek to live at all. Pretragic wisdom is recovered without the possibility of agreeing with it because death and nothing have become fearsome. Both life and death have become the unknown. Pretragic wisdom now appears naïve, but it does not cease to haunt tragedy because its very primacy gives it the status of possibly being the truth.

What is common to all these modifications and differentiations in the pleasure-pain polarity is the recognition, even the "affirmation," of unpleasure as an unavoidable state. Tragic consciousness seems inevitably to begin with this heightening of the charge of unpleasure. What is also common to the first and third of these mutations is the reversal of the address of the primal no to death. In the second variant this no is maintained at least long enough for the separate process of the development of life and its unpleasure to run its course. What is uncertain in all these modalities is whether unpleasure can be transformed into pleasure, and what the consequence of prolonged unpleasure may be.

Furthermore, if there is an evolution or differentiation of consciousness in tragedy, these changes find their point of departure in heightened unpleasure and in the reversal of the no. For unpleasure impels change, whereas achieved pleasure ceases to be impelling. Unpleasure, like the unfinished task, induces memory and aggressive action, whereas the completed task is forgotten. Unpleasure in the tragic hero is the source also of his turn from passivity to action. And it is the ground, no doubt also, for his perception of the subject-object polarity. This polarity is born in him out of his experience of the pleasure-pain dialectic. Thus, the very processes of ego development should themselves be visible in tragedy proper, for it is a development given together with the tragic sense of life.

Nietzsche and Lacan

Nietzsche's theory of tragedy has a deep affinity for Freud's speculations or for the kinds of speculations about tragedy that his thought allows. Nietzsche does not posit an atragic moment, for the moment of original Oneness or Will to Power that he posits at the origin is already a coexistent and simultaneous desire for unity and individuation, for non-differentiation and differentiation, for creation and destruction. Nietzsche's thought commences in the pretragic perception and in the pleasure-pain polarity. The reversals and re-reversals within the pleasure-pain polarity constitute for him the essence of the tragic myth. This myth never evolves; it can only be deformed or repressed. Tragic truth is ever one and the same: the transformation of the primal no to life into a yes, and the retransformation and reversal of this yes back into a no. As in Freud, the fundamental structure of tragic myth has reference to an immutable structure of nature, to the facts of birth and death, and to sexuality.

Music is the closest that we can come to an apprehension of tragic truth, and we always know only as much about this truth (Dionysus) as Apollo (art, objectification) can absorb and clarify. The evolution of the representation of tragic myth begins in music, in a pure, imageless manner. The evolution of tragedy is, for Nietzsche, music made more and more visible. The Dionysiac artist becomes "wholly identified with the original Oneness, its pain and contradiction, and produces a replica of that Oneness as music" (p. 38). Tragedy begins with the advent of music upon a bare stage, which itself here represents the desire for increased clarity and individuation. The stage gives birth to the chorus of chanting and dancing satyrs, who evoke the imagined god, his birth and death, at the height of their frenzy. The chorus itself is dionysiac, only barely apollonian. Then the god himself appears, but in the mask of his myths. Finally, these myths are clarified in the tragic life and actions of heroes such as Oedipus and Philoctetes. But each of these heroes is only a mask of the original god, Dionysus, who in turn is but one of a possible series of objective correlatives for the primordial Will to which oneness and individuation are equally necesary. In Nietzsche the unconscious pain of separation, of life and death, is reinforced and doubled by the consciousness of this pain in the hero; yet consciousness itself is born for no other purpose but to give testimony and recognition to this pain.

Nietzsche's descriptions of the interaction between Dionysus and Apollo have a kinship with what Lacan calls the relationship between the symbolic and imaginary axes of the self. Dionysus is at once the phallus, the signifier, the fragmented truth and body, "the other" that can never be known, to which the imaginary self nonetheless addresses itself. Apollo is perception, self-objectification, and identification. For Lacan it is the mirror stage, in which the self displaces the fragmented truth by borrowed and illusionary images of wholeness, oneness, and unity, which initiates the self into the imaginary process of self-objectification and identification. In Nietzsche the stage itself functions as a mirror initiating the series of apollonian objectifications. Apollo in Nietzsche plays the role of the imaginary axis. And for this reason, although tragic truth can never be changed, and although, in the strict sense, it cannot evolve, it can be more and more clearly articulated and objectified in ever-new images or illusions. For Lacan, these self-objectifications are a mirage, a *méconnaissance*, a misconstruction of selfhood. The imaginary axis is forever opposed by the symbolic axis, which speaks to it of "the other," the displaced. The self must turn from its empty, conscious dialogue with the imaginary back to an unconscious dialogue with the symbolic.

In Nietzsche, the apollonian objectification must also remain addressed to Dionysus. It is only true when it represents the other, turns back there, and dissolves there. As Nietzsche says, "Dionysos speaks the language of Apollo, but Apollo, finally, the language of Dionysos" (p. 131). For Nietzsche, tragic myth "never finds an adequate objective correlative in the spoken word" (p. 103). What Nietzsche seems to suggest is that there is end beyond which apollonian objectification cannot go. This limit is consciousness and conscious dialogue. Even in Greek tragedy it is the action, "the structure of the scenes and the concrete images," rather than the speech of the characters that better expresses tragic truth. There is a point at which apollonian objectification also becomes *méconnaissance* for Nietzsche, but unlike Lacan, he does not fundamentally apprehend the apollonian-imaginary axis as *méconaissance*, because he does not conceive the symbolic, dionysiac as structured like language. And therefore his conception of the dialogue between the two is actually less tragic, alienated, or complex, less open to misapprehension than Lacan's.

Nietzsche thinks that images, music, and actions do express the myth. Language remains associated in his mind with consciousness, and therefore myth and dream are nonverbal and themselves imaginary. Unlike Lacan, he cannot think of the nonverbal as structured like language, although his very descriptions come close to suggesting that addition or substitution which Lacan proposes. Thus, his theory remains basically caught in objectification (although these must be destroyed); he cannot like Lacan say that creating a dialectic and speech and not objectification is what is essential.[3] Nietzsche is only able to see that creating the dialectic between the symbolic and the imaginary, the unspeakable and speakable, is important. Within the pain and contradiction of the myth, there *is* recognition and not only *méconnaissance*.

Nietzsche's vision of Dionysus is Lacan's vision of "the other." The chorus of satyrs call on the Father, evoke and name him. Behind the Father, for Nietzsche, stands the primordial womb of the Mother. This happens in a dream because Apollo is the dream God. He dreams and sees the break between culture and nature, art (language, symbols) and sexuality. His very dream is that break and gap, for it gives birth to form (structure), myths, characters and their actions. For Nietzsche, consciousness, which breaks this primordial unity of man and nature, must also seek to reapprehend it in tragic truth, the one place where it is still accessible to us. For Lacan this is a reapprehension that is in a sense ultimately not possible, for our consciousness is synonymous with the symbolic, the structure of language, and that structure signifies the death of the nonsymbolic, of nature. We begin in a determination that is already apollonian, already metanatural. The Will that lies behind Apollo is, for Lacan, something that cannot ever be evoked because it is prehuman.

Language for Lacan is always doubly negative: a presence made of an absence and the symbolic forever lacking the real (p. 65). Death, the sepulchre, is the first symbol in every awareness. In a sense, all that we retain of nature in consciousness is the awareness of its death, the knowledge that it has been put aside, murdered, lost. The symbol is always "the murder of the thing." The beginning of human life, its affirmation, is a negation of nature that is absolute. Negation is a "desperate affirmation of life" in which we see the death instinct in its "purest form" (p. 104). Before speech, there is death. From death our "existence takes on all the meaning it has" (p. 105).

For Nietzsche the link between man and nature is also death, for it is the reality of death that we above all experience in tragic myth. Yet in Lacan and Nietzsche this death comes as if from opposite directions. In Nietzsche it comes from nature and is in nature. In Lacan it comes from man and creates therefore a bar or barrier between ourselves and nature, of which henceforth nothing can be known. A tragic art modeled on Lacan could go to the seam of nature and culture, but never beyond it. In Nietzsche, what is beyond that seam can be evoked and mirrored though it can never actually be seen as it is. The break between man and nature is absolute in Lacan. In Nietzsche there is a difference, but there is no absolute disjunction. Nietzsche does not consider that that which is structured (the symbolic) according to the laws of language (or the imagination) may not be able to apprehend the different structure or the unstructured nature of the real. Thus, although we may guess that behind our symbols and myths lies an encounter with our own sexuality and behind that the encounter with nature's, we can never guess what these latter two encounters may in fact be. In Nietzsche we can always hear in tragedy the voice of the pretragic: it is better to die, better never to have been born. The tragic triumphs over death by death; the pretragic accedes to death and returns to nature. In the pretragic, nature triumphs; in tragedy, man. Tragedy proper celebrates the advent of a new kind of spontaneous, intuitive no in man. From the point of view of the pretragic this new no to death, the acceptance of unpleasure, seems meaningless, functionless, and irrational. But it is in this new unreason, this overturning of nature's reason, that tragedy proper begins its life.

For Nietzche, man and nature's mutual, though contradictory, dependence on art is tragic (p. 95). Man cannot maintain the vitality of his culture without returning to its source in nature through the medium of tragic myth. He saw his own era, dominated by bourgeois drama and opera, as largely deficient in this contact. Only Luther's chorales, Goethe's and Schiller's classical drama, Kant's and Schopenhauer's critiques of the human mind, the art of Dürer, and the music of Wagner could be listed as exceptions to that death of tragedy which occurred already in the time of Socrates and Euripides. For Nietzsche the life and historical development of post-Sophoclean tragedy has been almost pure aberration. Nietzsche measures and evaluates the profundity of Western history and of his own era by its lack of a sense of the tragic. Socrates and Euripides between them killed off tragedy; it was never reborn.

Socrates made consciousness a new elemental force, a daimon, and forgot Dionysus. His intellect spelled the death of the tragic spirit. For Nietzsche there is an unresolvable antagonism, an "eternal conflict," between reason and tragedy, between "the theoretical and the tragic world view" (p. 104). Socrates' substitution of the instinct of nature with a consciousness claiming to be instinct is a turning point in Western civilization—and one which Nietzsche seeks to reverse. He attacks the noble moment of Socrates' death in the *Apology* as nothing but a denial and misunderstanding of tragic truth. Socrates refused to accept death as a tragic reality. Instead he questioned it, dissolving it into ironic possibilities of something or nothing, until its terror vanished. For Nietzsche, Socrates' dissolution of death into possibility and theory, his openness toward it, and his accepting, tentative, questioning exploration of the significance of this boundary, are an outrage, a lie, a sign of the absolute folly, idiocy, and arrogance of reason.

Euripides' tragedies already bear all the signs of this intellectual denial and devaluation of Dionysus. They are imbalanced in favor of the apollonian representation and images and dissociated from the myth. In them the dialogic and dialectic win out over action. In *The Bacchae*, Dionysus is only barely tolerated, like a nightmare that one hopes will soon be over and past. The truth of Sophocles and Aeschylus is merely the obscure for Euripides, which he "corrects" by elimination. The intellect can only comprehend and believe in the daimon of Socrates. For Nietzsche any change in tragic structure or content can be nothing but forgery and mystification.

Nietzsche was, no doubt, right in making a sharp distinction between the ironic Socratic spirit and the tragic spirit. The tragic hero is not an ironist because he does not stop at the question or bring matters toward a question; he aims for conclusions. He is not interested, as the ironist is, in detachment, objectivity, impartiality, abstraction, or a negative freedom from contradictions. He feels compelled to immerse himself in contradictions; he is not only fatally attracted to them, but committed to their resolution. The ironist is a spectator; the tragic hero an actor. Even when the tragic hero is more and more both an actor and an ironic spectator of himself, as in the theater of Shakespeare, his absolute need is still to act in the very midst of the most ironic, unsolvable, and uninterpretable contradictions. Macbeth does not share Oedipus' ignorance.

> If it were done when 'tis done, then 'twere well
> It were done quickly; if the assassination
> Could trammel up the consequence, and catch,
> With his surcease, success, that but this blow
> Might be the be-all and the end-all here,
> But here, upon this bank and shoal of time,
> We'd jump the life to come.
> [1.7.1–7]

Macbeth knows whom he is about to murder and is aware of the ironic contradictions, effects, and conditions—psychological, moral, social, religious—into which he is about to plunge himself, but plunge, nonetheless, he must.

For this reason, the tragic hero also cannot listen to the voice of caution and deterrence that we hear everywhere in tragedy. Jocasta's voice in *Oedipus Rex* ("I beg you—do not hunt this out—I beg you") signals the inhibition of tragedy by fear, the threat of annihilation, and the value of self-preservation.[4] Avoidance is a call to danger which arrests action. It is, as Kenneth Burke has argued, a form of the prenegative.[5] The value of avoidance, however, is what the tragic hero invalidates and nullifies. Tragedy has no tolerance for the prenegative. Tragedy does not evade; it negates.

Oedipus Rex makes ironically and consummately clear that the perfection of the philosophy of avoidance means never having been born. Oedipus should never have been born or he should have perished as an infant as his father intended him to. Living means accepting a most dangerous lot. The only freedom that we have in this inexorable fate is a negative one: the freedom not to be. Man's right not to be signals the birth of his subjectivity. Jocasta takes advantage of this freedom and kills herself. Oedipus endures to extend the boundaries of endurance: the value of self-preservation is affirmed not by avoidance but in the face of the worst. Life is accepted under completely new conditions of pain and radical unpleasure.

Only when man discovers his right not to be can he truly claim that he chooses to be, that he chooses his lot rather than letting it choose him. Man begins, whether in the manner of an Oedipus or an Antigone, to make triumphant use of his merely negative freedom. He turns the possibility of self-negation into a power and a weapon.

Irony witholds judgment; it can remain in suspension. Tragedy seeks judgment; it seeks to live and act out contradictions. It will not avoid them. The nonironic, psychological imperative that drives tragedy toward conclusiveness and finality has in some respect a greater affinity to doubt than to irony, for doubt's telos is certitude. Doubt can be more tragic than irony because it seeks to penetrate the object which the ironist says has no reality. In tragedy, as in doubt, there is a war of conquest and all is destroyed because the essence that the tragic hero is after, his selfhood, lies behind his actions, is anterior to his acts. The tragic hero's destiny, however, to find himself by action is ineluctable. It cannot be avoided or overcome because the tragic hero's existential impatience is not assuaged, as the ironist's is, by appearances or symbols.

The hero makes patent and radiant in a tragic manner the ironic nature of both the subjective and objective conditions. But the tragic hero is exactly the one who refuses the ironic posture that would best match these conditions. The tragic hero makes, one could almost say, war upon the ironic posture. He seems to know what Kierkegaard's analysis of Socrates revealed: that irony is merely negatively free, that it knows only negative conclusions, that it is not ontological, and that it is a standpoint that has no being.[6] The tragic hero seems to know that the ironic man becomes alienated from actuality and from himself, that his own being is not actual. He seems to know, in other words, that the ironist's logicality is an evasion of the psychological and the affective.

One sign of the ironist's rationality is that he is never angry. The tragic hero, by contrast, has a notorious capacity for anger. "Anger has always been your greatest sin!" Oedipus is reminded in Oedipus at Colonus.[7] Anger is the tragic hero's protest against and nonacceptance of the given conditions of life and death. It is a stubborn refusal to coordinate the sense of intuitive awakened life with the rhythm of the merely natural or primitive yes or no, with pleasure, or with what can preserve it or reestablish it. The hero's anger, the sign of his unpleasure, is also a positive evaluation of his own consciousness and developing inwardness.

Just as the ironist courts the danger of unreality, so tragedy itself can also begin to sound too detached, too analytical, or too deinvolved whenever it becomes too ironic. This, for example, is the case with Jacobean tragedy, as Sewall has noted, where we are often struck by a sense that action is being recorded rather than lived and where the heroes themselves cannot rid themselves of their deep sense of unreality.

My soul, like to a ship in a black storm,
Is driven, I know not whither.
[The White Devil 5.6]

Sewall, therefore, calls irony the tragic frontier: it is the alternative to which the dramatist turns "when the values that sustain tragedy begin to disintegrate."[8] Within tragedy, however, moments of absolute ironic detachment abound. Macbeth's "Tomorrow, and tomorrow, and tomorrow" is one example, par excellence. It is Macbeth's recognition of the absence of feeling for death or life. The very basis of selfhood, the pleasure-pain polarity itself has been extinguished; but Macbeth does not accept this and it is against this state that he wars at the end, the very state that he recovers in his final action: his humanity in his fear of death and his human condition in the need to once again conquer this fear.

Thus, although it is important to distinguish between ironic and tragic rationality, one wonders whether there is any point in calling, as Nietzsche does, the obvious development of consciousness in tragedy mere inauthenticity, and further whether there is any point in demanding that consciousness be ever turned toward the recognition of nature. In the light of Lacan, one wonders whether this latter demand is even possible. One wonders whether Nietzsche is not right insofar as he stresses the inalienable inherence of tragedy in the pleasure-pain polarity, its fundamental, strange ambiguity and turnings of what can be pleasure and what pain, but one also wonders whether this testing of pleasure and pain comes not unavoidably to seek a ground in the passive-active, subject-object polarities of consciousness. One wonders, obviously, whether there is any point in ignoring tragic intellection, which is neither merely rational nor ironic, and which knows pain and pleasure, life and death in itself, in its actions (the passive-active polarity) and in its intellection (the subject-object polarity).

Nietzsche failed somehow to perceive or refused to grant significance to the fact that intellection is always present in tragedy to an extraordinary degree. Every tragic hero seems to be caught, as is Oedipus, in a vast and terrifying puzzle which does not yield to reason, but the hero almost always goes through the excruciating motions of trying to make it yield to reason.

> Then let them anatomize Regan, see what breeds about her heart. Is there any cause in nature that makes these hard hearts?
>
> [*King Lear* 3.6.80–81]

Reason cannot reach, unseal, expose, or express the affective experience, but it is the constant presence of extraordinary and powerful intellection and reasoning that helps to make this evident.

"To be or not to be," Hamlet's immortal speech—the Renaissance *locus classicus* for the question of suicide—initiates its secularization by tragic intellection. It makes suicide human, opening it up as a possibility: " 'tis a consummation devoutly to be wish'd." There is nothing in life itself to arrest suicide, only the "dread" of an afterlife. Life even encourages ideas of self-annihilation. Hamlet's fatal words reawaken the pre-tragic impulse in a conscious and therefore more terrifying form.

Tragic theater is about the power of action and acting. And *Hamlet* is the drama in which Shakespeare seems to play with the impairment of action, with what seems like external passivity, to point to the bliss and pain of an inner consuming action. Tragedy is action, not character, said Aristotle in his *Poetics*: "Without action there could be no tragedy, whereas a tragedy without characterization is possible."[9] First of all, Shakespeare gives the lie to Aristotle by making the distinction purely academic: if a character cannot act, there is no action, for action and character are inexorably one. Second, Shakespeare makes the action internal: Hamlet's torn reflections on the varieties of acting, the possibility of acting on others or on oneself, of murder or suicide. What engages his reflection is not the obvious possibility of murder, in which he is encouraged, but the mystery of a forbidden suicide. Suicide may be more significant in so "rank" a world, and suicide is not passive, but violent and active, an action of taking "arms" against oneself. If living necessarily involves acting against others, it is also a possibility to act against oneself. Is not suicide the terrible internal perception of the activity of nothing as it makes one nought? Is it not a form of self-annihilation in which negation rushes back to its primal, pretragic form? From his first appearance to his last, Hamlet's ambivalence is one with his obsession with suicide, because suicide is the essence of action. In *Hamlet,* plot or action becomes autonomous from fate as it moves back toward its genesis in character.

Hegel and Lukács

Hegel's and Lukács' thoughts on tragedy recognize the inwardness of tragedy, the phenomenon of internalization which exhibited itself here earlier than in any other genre. For Hegel, the genealogy of the tragic theater is one with that of consciousness and its negativity. The conflicts, contradictions, and collisions of tragedy are the issue of the mind's incessant and restless activity of negation. Here it is negation and the will of man for himself, for his authentic self, and not only, as in Nietzsche, the will's need for illusion, art, which impel change. In Hegel it is man's ever-partial development that comes into conflict with the totality of Absolute Mind. Man's development by negation entails the development of the object-subject polarity, and hence the presence of this polarity in tragedy is more clearly articulated in Hegel's theory as the fundamental source of pain. But for Hegel, unfortunately, the aim of tragedy is ultimately to establish the dominance of Absolute Mind. The pain of nonidentity, the conflict of the subject-object polarity, should finally dissolve in a recognition of and a reconciliation with Absolute

Mind. In the most ideal and beautiful kind of tragedy, such as *Oedipus at Colonus*, Absolute Mind is apprehended in its positive character as affirmation and eternal justice. In the less ideal kind of tragedy, Absolute Mind is also apprehended, but its destructive, divisive, negating force is foregrounded and appears dominant.

Thus Hegel's view of tragedy, as his view of absolute reality, culminates in the nontragic, in affirmation and identity, in a reconciliation with "eternal justice." As such it is the fundamental opposite to Nietzsche's view, where the final "reconcilation" can only be with what can by contrast be called "eternal injustice," the injustice of the ineluctable, contradictory unity of life and death. Nietzsche's synthesis of Dionysus and Apollo is never an identity. His Will remains in essence a contradictory, divisive, tragic totality, and opposed to Hegel's nontragic, reconciled totality of Absolute Consciousness. In Nietzsche there can be no reconciliation in Hegel's sense of the word. There is only the simultaneity of life and death. The ultimate affirmation can only be an affirmation of the simultaneity and coexistence of affirmation and negation, the equally powerful and confounded pull both of yes and no, of Dionysus and Apollo, of nature and art. In Hegel, negation though ever-present and nonarrestable is finally in the service of affirmation, of perfect, ultimately noncontradictory identity.

In Hegel, tragedy is a phenomenon of consciousness, of reason, of the ultimate reasonability of reality. For Nietzsche, tragedy is a phenomenon of the unconscious, of nature. Although their visions of ultimate reality differ, both thinkers claim and demand that tragedy make available the ultimate vision of reality. For both tragedy is a metaphor capable of attaining completion, capable of substituting one whole by another. In Nietzsche the ultimate metaphor that tragedy translates is affectively experienced as bliss, as pleasure *and* pain. In Hegel the affective experience is pleasure, a rational, and ultimately, nontragic oneness.

By contrast, in Lacan a tragic metaphor could never even come into being. Given Lacan's theory of the symbolic as structured like language and therefore lacking the real, tragedy can only be a metonymic translation, always painful, because always beginning with and in a partial substitution. For Lacan, therefore, tragedy would be the genre that would stay closest to the human truth, to the fact that we begin by substituting a part for the whole, language, an illusory whole, for the real whole. Tragedy would be the record of the fact that we begin with absence, death, partial substitution, and in the lack of any kind of total, real being, whether natural or spiritual. Thus, in a vision of tragedy derived from Lacan, reconciliation becomes in fact impossible. Affectively, tragedy for Lacan would lead us neither to Nietzsche's bliss or Hegel's pleasure. It could only lead us to the seam of our human nature where we encounter our lack of access to being and our bewilderment at being able to express this truth only in language.

For what has Lear's final cry to do either with reconciliation or bliss?

And my poor fool is hanged! No, no, no life!
Why should a dog, a horse, a rat, have life
And thou no breath at all? Thou'lt come no more,
Never, never, never, never, never!
                        [5.3.305–308]

His cry is a lament against privation, the deprivation of the "breath" that is synonymous with the existence of life in any form. It is an effort to record, verbally and factually, that something is not, or is no more, or is no longer. It is an effort to comprehend nonexistence, the meaning of "no life," the irreversible and absolute absence of "breath." For the distinction between absence and presence is merely a relative one, but the category of existence-nonexistence is absolute and one must leap to grasp it. Lear states the incomprehensible and, therefore, meaningless truth in the form of a question precisely because it has not yet been understood and because a question opens up the possibility of denial. Still, existence-nonexistence has only one dimension here. It is a bitterly meaningless logical notation. But "no more" means that life had existed previous to its nonexistence; it is a mnemonically end emotionally charged statement. The distinction between "no" and "no more" involves a leap to a new and more painful dimension. In that second dimension of unending loss, of the nonrecurrence of desired recurrence ("ever, ever, ever, ever, ever"), the pain of an infinite "never" can only be arrested, can only be dealt with by outright denial, the strongest form of negation: "look, her lips,/Look there, look there." If there is solace for Lear, it can only occur in denial, in the linguistic possibility given to us by language to deny what nature has done to us. If Lear's final utterance signifies that he is on the brink of bliss, this is not the substantial Nietzschean bliss of nature, but the insubstantial, untrue bliss of language, that ever most partial off all partial substitutions. Tragic pain does not expand into a vision of the Will or Spirit; it can only contract and expand into language. Linguistic denial, rather than being a reconciliation, is a reversal that measures by its very intensity the impossibility of our affective reconciliation with the natural irreversible. It is an absolute sign of nonreconciliation, for the effort to be "reconciled" in speech with the truth of the self's desire also means to break the self. The price of self-solace and self-expression in denial is madness.

Lear begins in total ignorance of what negation in any of its modes or intensities signifies. All he cares for is affirmation. Lear's idea of negation is the common-sense one that negation is equivalent to the absence of something or to absence in general, or to nothing, in the sense of an unreal thing, or in the sense of a nonentity. "Nothing will come of nothing," replies Lear to Cordelia's refusal—a refusal which issues out of her profound sense of boundaries and out of her sense of her own separateness. Cordelia refuses him; she does not deny him. But Lear treats her refusal like a denial and thoughtlessly denies and banishes her. He knows nothing about boundaries or that boundaries are the conditions of communication, or that "not" is one of these boundaries, and yet we see him in the very beginning in the act of dividing his kingdom and of setting up new boundaries that he himself, however, hopes freely to cross and to ignore. He learns soon in dismay (as in this scene with Kent in the stocks) what refusal means or how little it can mean when there is a constant exterior negative with which one collides:

> Kent. It is both he and she,
>   Your son and daughter.
> Lear. No.
> Kent. Yes.
> Lear. No, I say.
> Kent. I say yea.
> Lear. No, no, they would not.
> Kent. Yes, they have.
> Lear. By Jupiter, I swear no.
> Kent. By Juno, I swear ay.
> Lear. They durst not do't, they could not,
>   would not do't.
>
>   [2.3.14–23]

Lear suffers the impotence of his own refusals and denials, the increasingly harsh denials of Goneril and Regan, and the steadily increasing pain of his perception of Cordelia's absence. He learns to know death as the separation from what one loves. He discovers more and more as he is drawn into the merely negative ethical world of commands and countercommands, how love is outside of this world altogether; it is, in a sense, the nothing that meets with its own opposite, a powerful something.

Lear's careless words, "Nothing will come of nothing"—*ex nihilo nihil*—have behind them a long history; they echo one of the major intellectual debates in Europe about the origin of creation. The Eleatic school believed that nothing comes of nothing and their doctrine came to predominance at the end of the Greek period, but the predominant Judaeo-Christian belief came to be that God created the world of nothing. The contradiction between the pagan *ex nihilo nihil* and the Judaeo-Christian notion of creation out of nothing was solved in two primary ways. One way was to turn *ex nihilo* into a material cause where matter, however, signifies something like God's superessence. Scotus, for example, said God is both yes and no; He is in a sense nothing because He is everything. Thus the nothing out of which the world was created is the superessence of God. Others, like Anselm and Aquinas, did not want to identify nothing once again with something. *Ex nihilo*, Anselm said, means without cause and the (to us) incomprehensible. Aquinas said that the *ex* refers not to the material but the order. God needs no matter to create. *Ex nihilo* means *non ex aliquo*, i.e., the notion of creation from something is denied. Aquinas asked what the preposition *ex* negated, and by this question he turned the problem of nothing into the problem of negation.[10] The structure of *Lear* manages to do the same. It dramatizes the processes of negation in consciousness. But it also turns Lear into a symbol of the destructive powers of "naughting": "O ruined piece of nature! This great world/Shall so wear out to naught" (4.6.137–38).

All the modalities of linguistic negation are acquired in the second year of life and they seem to be acquired in a certain sequence: nonexistence, rejection, denial. The first syntactic appearance of "no" or "no more" signifies the semantic category of nonexistence. Here nonexistence refers to what had existed previously. This "no" is a "negation of recurrence." It connotes a distinction between relative rather than absolute absence-presence. A child will say there is "no apple" or "no more apple" to indicate nonpresence and the expectation of existence or the recognition of previous existence.[11] Its delight at this phase in the play of hide and seek with itself and its favorite objects, and its delight in looking at itself in the mirror, are manifestations of its elementary knowledge of "no" as nonexistence.

The second modality of negation is rejection-acceptance. Here the syntactic "no" and "don't" signal the contrast between external and internal. There appear to be two forms of rejection. One form develops together with the sentence-subject "I" and the verbs "want" or "need." The child is able to express rejection of something it doesn't want to do or to have. It is able to mark its desires concerning events and objects, to register its inner states in relation to outer ones. But the development of this "I"-form of semantic rejection is preceded by the knowledge of rejection as expressing the negation of the child's "own desire or wish to have or to do something." Thus the child knows itself first as the receiver of this negation and then as its agent. After gaining a certain competence in both structures, the child is able to express rejection involving someone else as an actor-agent, approaching "the adult form of the negative imperative," "where the sentence–subject is the unexpressed 'you' " (Bloom pp. 197–98). Thus rejection is the awakening of the negative commandment, of desire, of both the "I" and the "You." We have movement from a subject-object world to a far more dramatic intersubjective world.

The strongest mode of negation is denial. It develops last in the child because it is semantically most complex and entails a symbolic referent. It requires the child "to hold in mind two propositions at once" (p. 219). Syntactically, therefore, it is at first the least complex, and structurally the least productive form of negation. To signal its semantic intent, the child will use the simplest negative form ("no apple") and only the context can make clear that here the utterance means that this is not an apple at all, but something else. Nonetheless, it is in this "no, but," this simple denial and substitution, that the child's abilities to transform and to create are born.

For Piaget, by this operation the child's thinking becomes dynamic. For as long as a child "centers on the static aspects of a situation, he is unlikely to appreciate transformations. If he does not represent transformations, he is unlikely to reverse his thought. By decentering he becomes aware of the transformations, which thus lead to reversibility in his thought."[12] For Piaget these three aspects of thought—centration-decentration, static-dynamic, irreversibility-reversibility—are interdependent. Reversibility is the child's mental capacity to undo, nullify, cancel, or invert a mental operation. It signals the child's ability to add and subtract, and it is coterminous with the child's ability to make more complex surface sentences which involve deletion.

Lear has to relearn and endure negation in its most primitive and elemental forms in order to comprehend the significance of himself as a man who exists and has spoken. He learns the distinctions between a careless, superficial denial and one made in desperation in the face of irreversible separation. He is drawn, as it were, into the deep structure of his own negation and forced to face its mystery. Ultimately he can no longer find himself except in the continuity of the life and power of negation. The obscurity of the definition of man is one with the obscurity of his ability to negate. Man negates others as well as himself, what he has said as well as what cannot yet be said, driven by an illegible sense that he is yet other than what has been stated. Negation is at the brink where death becomes indistinguishable from life.

Lukács' theory of tragedy, like Hegel's, stresses the development of consciousness. But Lukács puts the stress not on general consciousness, but on the individual, existential consciousness.

> Everything human is possible only for an abstract absolute idea of man. The tragic is a becoming-real of its [the idea's] concrete essence. Tragedy answers the most critical question of Platonism: the question whether individual things can also have essences firmly and surely. Tragedy's answer turns the question around: only that which is established as individual by having been driven to its limits is equal to its idea, is truly existent. The all-inclusive, colorless and formless general is too powerless in its universality and too empty in its unity to become truly existent.[13]

Tragedy awakens the individual soul and its longing for selfhood. It is an ego-forming and ego-creating genre, where "the self stresses its selfhood with a power that excludes and annihilates all else." The self, however, acquires reality only when it acquires boundaries:

> The experience of the boundary is the awakening to consciousness, to self-consciousness of the soul: it [the soul] is, because it is bounded; it is only because and in so far as it is bounded.
>
> (p. 231)

Lukács contrasts the mystic's and the tragic hero's experiences of selfhood. The former experiences the essence of self-loss; he destroys boundaries and, hence, form. The tragic hero experiences the essence of self; he creates boundaries, and he creates himself as he creates his boundaries (pp. 237–8). Tragedy is the "definite and the defining," the fixed, the certain, the single-minded (p. 220). Tragedy is a sudden determination that simply happens, like a miracle. And this miracle is the consequence of boundaries. "The wisdom of the tragic miracle is the wisdom of boundaries" (p. 230). Death, therefore, "the boundary as such," says Lukács, is for tragedy "an ever immanent reality tied up inextricably with all of its actions" (p. 231). "Boundary" here signifies limitation and failure—the exclusion of possibilities—as well as fulfillment, the self's recognition of what belongs truly to itself and only to it. However, this graspable essence of selfhood that one must add to Lukács becomes more elusive as the self discovers itself to be purely relational—to be but this boundary set by saying yes and no, perhaps, until neither can be said.

Tragedy is the affective experience of separation and the simultaneous experience of the presence of all the modalities of negation—nonexistence, rejection, denial—because to define itself the subject has to negate. The object, however, from which the pain of detachment occurs, changes. The most significant experience of separation for the Greeks was that between man and the cosmos. Greek tragedy is, therefore, essentially ontological. Their notion of subjectivity was shaped by their perception of the cosmos—divine, everlasting, indestructible, unshakable, and incorruptible. God was not outside the world but a predicate of the world. Thus, Greek cosmology was a natural theology. The hero suffers dread because he discovers his disrelationship from the cosmos. He suffers ontic insecurity.

When the Greek hero discovered his separateness from his divine cosmos, he simultaneously lost his immortality and his mental omnipotence. He created a symbol of what resisted and opposed him, calling it fate or *ananke*. Fate, as Kierkegaard saw, is the negative concept that gave a boundary to Greek culture, that limited and defined Greek experience.[14] Fate, the Greek hero feels, is his lot and yet he does not associate it with his most essential self. It is and is not his most authentic self. It is the negative exterior to our essence that has, nonetheless, made us what we are.

In classical tragedy, as Kierkegaard said, plot dominates over character, as ontology does over psychology.[15] This, however, is not to deny the fact that Greek tragedy is profoundly psychological and absolutely centered, as all tragedy is, upon man and his selfhood. Rather, it means that the inside is made clear by the outside: the irrational is the lot, which we cannot explain, but which explains us and our lack of wisdom, foresight, and self-knowledge. If we continue to respond to classical tragedy more immediately and spontaneously than to any other form of tragedy, it is, undoubtedly, first because we still recognize and feel this ontic insecurity, this ultimately precarious, tangential situation of ourselves in the world, and second, because we may still suspect that only in the fact of such an ultimate and real ontic insecurity lies the true explanation for our anxiety and desperation. In other words, some part of us still believes that our irrational anxiety is like fear, which has a real objective correlative.

Greek tragedy issued out of the most fundamental questions: Is it better to be or not to be? How secure is it to be? These questions, as every question does, opened up the possibilities of the most dreadful negative replies. It is just as well, or better, not to be; even worse, we seem to live under conditions where there is, paradoxically, a constant pressure on us not to be. The pressure of nonbeing never leaves tragedy. The tragic theater takes away all that is positive: all security, all certainty, all knowledge, and all relationships. It exposes us to terror, violence, despair, madnness, nihilism, misinterpretation, error, disrelationships, nonbeing. And yet, tragedy is not nihilistic because against the negative that it reveals and gives birth to it posits the power of human negation, man's search for himself.

Pascal noted in the *Pensées* that there are three modes of existence and that each is a wager: to believe, to doubt, or to deny. Tragedy denies. The tragic hero lives by denial and refusal and in order to deny and to refuse. To believe is always to affirm something. The tragic hero believes in nothing but himself. He acts; he discovers; he creates. He creates the cosmology of negation and discovers himself in his negativity.

Shakespearean tragedy seeks the boundaries between men or within man. Its focus is upon intersubjectivity or intrasubjectivity. It knows that the decalogue, the "perfection" and "fulfillment" of the negative, as Kenneth Burke so aptly calls it, is only an external way of establishing moral limits.[16] It seeks to define what establishes limits, boundary, and form internally, "amorally." It is a theater of psychic limitations. Lady Macbeth and Macbeth break the fifth commandment, but no God or justice is necessary to undo them; the interiority of man is sufficient. Their act delivers them over to a series of involuntary, unconscious processes: to sleeplessness, hallucination, guilt, and madness.

> What man dare, I dare.
> Approach thou like the rugged Russian bear,
> The armed rhinoceros, or the Hyrcan tiger.
> Take any shape but that and my firm nerves
> Shall never tremble. Or be alive again,
> And dare me to the desert with thy sword.
> If trembling I inhabit then, protest me
> The baby of a girl. Hence, horrible shadow!
> Unreal mockery, hence!
>   Why, so. Being gone,
> I am a man again.
>
>   [3.4.99–108]

Macbeth could tolerate anything better than his uncontrollable, unreal, ungraspable internal hallucinations. This, however, unmans him.

Greek tragedy never knew madness—"the torture of the mind to lie/In restless ecstasy" [3.2.21–22]—in the way Shakespearean tragedy knows it, because madness is the consequence finally of the confusion of inner psychic levels. Madness belongs to the theater that rests primarily upon denial, that witnesses things "more strange" than murder [3.4.82]. Macbeth begins at the point where the powers of language and of reality have already been confused. "Fair is foul, and foul is fair" means nothing but contradiction and confusion, the capacity of language to devalue the structure of the real. The witches, the ghost, the apparitions, and finally the moving Birnam Wood are but the most obvious signs of a shattered and confused boundary between consciousness and the unconscious, between the word and the image. Lady Macbeth succumbs quickly to the punishment for transgression: madness and death. Macbeth, more reflective, more sensitive to his guilt, and morally more imaginative, resists these more obvious, inner, instinctual dangers. His wariness, ambivalence, and guilt, however, are not a boundary. Evil is an unbounded real. Nothing, we realize, will stop Macbeth. He runs into the unbounded; he crosses the merely imaginary barriers between humanity and inhumanity with ease, even imperceptibly. Suddenly he is dehumanized. This is the astonishing, tragic event.

Macbeth's heroism avails him nothing against the strange and inevitable advance of inner meaninglessness and lack of feeling, a state in which Macbeth discovers that nothingness defines his own being. "The horror," Rosalie Colie wrote,

is no more, and no less, than Macbeth's awareness that his active, violent life was not lived, that he has been crushed out of "being" by the pressures of the moral void. He has become the embodiment of his paradox, that nothing is but what is not: the most terrible thing about that whole tragedy is that he knows it absolutely.[17]

When all feeling is arrested, there is nothing.

> . . . It is a tale
> Told by an idiot, full of sound and fury,
> Signifying nothing.
> [5.5.26–28]

Then words like "man" and "doing" on the basis of which Macbeth organized his reality turn to mere sound, to nothing, to nonsense. Then man has lost the basis on which he constituted himself. He becomes unreal, lost to himself, unguided by pleasure and pain because these too have lost their definiteness and direction.

Rejection is the hero's reaction to what is, a struggle with exterior reality, an experience of negating and being negated. Rejection is the hero's desire and the creation of his intellect and reality-ego. Denial is the hero's reaction, on a yet deeper level, to what has developed in himself under the pressures of rejection. Denial is the hero alone and separated, reflecting and acting upon his own essence. Denial is, in *Oedipus Rex* for example, the moment of his self-punishment, the moment of his extraordinary statement simultaneously of guilt and autonomy. By his self-punishment, Oedipus overcomes the inner instinctual danger and indirectly affirms his power of negation, the only kind of affirmation that tragedy ever allows. Negation infuses the hero's action and his thought with something purely subjective, something absolutely novel and unique, something not found in the objective world. And that is why his actions appear so astonishing, like a transformation or creation. Denial is, compared to the idea of an objective fate, a more subjective and human way of making sense of reality and, compared to death (Jocasta's response), a more objective way of making sense of oneself. Oedipus' self-punishment is cruel, but it is a sign of autonomy, a self-determining, self-limiting act; it is also the sign of a real ability to distinguish between the objective and the subjective. It is the symbol of Sophocles' knowledge of the definition of the human.

The myth behind Greek theater is one of gods and heroes. Against the heroic myth, the Greek theater stresses the psychological and human. The myth behind Shakespearean theater is Christianity, particularly as an ethical model, an ideal of interrelationship and love as exemplified in the New Testament by Jesus. The pretragic of avoidance here is centuries of sermons and devotional admonitions which this "brave new world" of men everywhere breaks, betrays, and outrages. The cosmos of intersubjectivity is full of deceit, mistrust, and treachery: the father may not trust his son, or the king his subjects, or the lover the beloved. Instead of obeying the great tribal "thou shalt nots," men live to watch each other die. They live under conditions where there is constant pressure on them not to be, not from fate, but from others.

The myth behind the modern theater is that of man's symbolically creative autonomy. Against this myth the tragic theater stresses the bankruptcy of art and language and of man's self-consciousness and will. The characters in Beckett and Pinter, for example, have only an indistinct memory of the pleasures and pains of that dialogue which was so central in Shakespeare. They are so close to death and silence that only will-lessness and empty time appear to keep them from crossing the boundary. Volition even in evil had a grandeur, a telos, a demonic setting all its own, the hell of the past or the repressed. It signified lovelessness and automation, but it had a destructive energy or, at least, as in Ibsen, the memory of a destruction. Nolition, "the inability to wish or want anything," is by contrast powerlessness. It is a disease of the will: one cannot do what one wants to. "In the stage between thought and expression an inhibition, a contrary impulse, or a cross impulse can make the action impossible."[18] Without language and will man is a nonentity, an example of negation in empty, actionless purity. Man can no longer say "no" to either life or death. Negation has lost its function and direction, both its tragic and pretragic energy and power. The three great polarities of life—subject/object, active/passive, pleasure/pain—are extinguished. In this state, man is incapable of knowing or asserting that he is tragic, and in that indefinable feeling, if in anything, consists his tragedy.

Notes

1. THE GENEALOGY OF NEGATION

1. For a historical discussion of these issues, see Gertrud Kahl-Furthmann, *Das Problem des Nicht: Kritisch-historische und systematische Untersuchungen*, 1934; rpt. in *Monographien zur Philosophischen Forschung*, Bd. 56 (Meisenheim am Glan: Anton Hain, 1968).
2. Sigmund Freud, "Negation," in *General Psychological Theory: Papers on Metapsychology*, ed. Philip Rieff (New York: Collier Books, 1970), pp. 214–15.
3. For a history of dialecticism and a discussion of various dialectical models and their transformations, see Alwin Diemer, *Elementarkurs Philosophie: Dialektik* (Düsseldorf and Vienna: Econ, 1976).
4. Quoted in Evelyn Underhill, *Mysticism: A Study in the Nature and Development of Man's Spiritual Consciousness* (New York: Dutton, 1961), p. 127.
5. Quoted in Underhill, *Mysticism*, pp. 389–90.
6. *The Poems of St. John of the Cross*, trans. Roy Campbell (New York: Grosset & Dunlap, 1967), p. 13.
7. *Ibid.*, p. 49.
8. *Plato's Symposium*, trans. Benjamin Jowett (New York: Liberal Arts Press, 1956), p. 52.
9. Sigmund Freud, *On Dreams*, trans. James Strachey (New York: Norton, 1952), p. 65.
10. John Milton, *Paradise Regained, the Minor Poems and Samson Agonistes*, ed. Merritt Y. Hughes (New York: Odyssey Press, 1937). Future references are to this edition.
11. *Shakespeare: The Complete Works*, ed. G. B. Harrison (New York: Harcourt, Brace, 1952). Future references are to this edition.
12. Friedrich Nietzsche, *The Genealogy of Morals* in *The Birth of Tragedy* and *The Genealogy of Morals*, trans. Francis Golffing (New York: Doubleday, 1956), pp. 177–78.
13. The translation in this instance is from *The New American Bible* (New York: P. J. Kenedy, 1970). At all other times I am referring to the King James version.
14. Cyril Tourneur, *The Revenger's Tragedy* in John Webster and Cyril Tourneur *Four Plays* (New York: Hill & Wang, 1960), p. 307. Future references are to this edition.
15. Rosalie L. Colie, *Paradoxia Epidemica: The Renaissance Tradition of Paradox* (Princeton, N.J.: Princeton University Press, 1966), p. 518. Future references are to this edition.
16. Francis Bacon, *The New Organon and Related Writings*, ed. Fulton H. Anderson (New York: Bobbs-Merrill, 1960), p. 51. Future references are to this edition.
17. Quoted in Maurice Cranston, "Bacon, Francis," *The Encyclopedia of Philosophy*, 1972 ed., 1:235.
18. *Ibid.*, p. 237.
19. *Selected Essays of Montaigne*, ed. Walter Kaiser (Boston: Houghton Mifflin, 1964), p. 171. Future references are to this edition.
20. Jacques Derrida, "Structure, Sign, and Play in the Discourse of the Human Sciences,"

262   1. THE GENEALOGY OF NEGATION

in *The Structuralist Controversy: The Languages of Criticism and the Sciences of Man*, ed. Richard Macksey and Eugenio Donato (Baltimore, Maryland: Johns Hopkins Press, 1972), p. 250.

21. René Descartes, *Meditations*, trans. John Veitch, in *The Rationalists* (New York: Doubleday, 1960), pp. 116–17. Future references to the *Meditations* and the *Discourse on Method* are to this edition.

22. Quoted in Colie, *Paradoxia Epidemica*, p. 219.

23. *Ibid.*, p. 400.

24. *Pascal's Pensées*, trans. Martin Turnell (New York: Harper & Row, 1962), p. 76, (130–441). Future references are to this edition. The first number refers to the order of the Lafuma edition, the second to that of the Brunschvicq edition.

25. Jean Racine, *Phèdre*, trans. Margaret Rawlings (New York: Dutton, 1962), p. 40. Future references are to this edition.

26. Immanuel Kant, *Critique of Judgment*, trans. J. H. Bernard (New York: Hafner, 1968), pp. 83, 91. Future references are to this edition.

27. *Goethe's Faust*, trans. Barker Fairley (Toronto: University of Toronto Press, 1972), p. 10. Future references are to this edition unless otherwise indicated.

28. My translation here modifies that of Walter Kaufmann, *Goethe's Faust* (New York: Doubleday, 1963), pp. 469–70.

29. G. W. F. Hegel, *The Phenomenology of Mind*, trans. J. B. Baillie (New York: Harper & Row, 1967), p. 76. Future references are to this edition.

30. *Symposium*, pp. 40–41, 43.

31. Jacques Lacan, *Écrits: A Selection*, trans. Alan Sheridan (New York: W. W. Norton, 1977), p. 132.

32. *The Complete Poetical Works of Keats*, ed. Horace E. Scudder (Cambridge Edition, Houghton Mifflin, 1899), p. 39.

33. Chateaubriand, *René* in *Atala/René*, trans. Irving Putter (Berkeley: University of California Press, 1952), p. 95. Future references are to this edition.

34. Wordsworth, *The Prelude or Growth of a Poet's Mind* (Oxford: Oxford University Press, 1970), 2:176–80.

35. Johann Wolfgang von Goethe, *The Sufferings of Young Werther*, trans. Bayard Quincy Morgan (New York: Frederick Ungar, 1968), p. 120. Future references are to this edition.

36. Octavio Paz, *Claude Lévi-Strauss: An Introduction*, trans. J. S. Bernstein and Maxine Bernstein (New York: Dell, 1970), p. 131.

37. G. W. F. Hegel, *The Philosophy of Fine Art*, trans. F. P. B. Osmaston (New York: Hacker, 1975), p. 122.

2. THE NOVEL AND THE SELF'S NEGATIVITY

1. Jane Austen, *Emma*, ed. Stephen M. Parrish (New York: W. W. Norton, 1972), p. 1. Future references are to this edition.

2. Sigmund Freud, "Negation," in *General Psychological Theory: Papers on Metapsychology*, ed. Philip Rieff (New York: Collier Books, 1970), p. 214. For an application of Freud's principle, see Maire Kurrik, "Robinson Jeffers's Negations: The Dialectics of 'Not' in 'The Bloody Sire,' " *Psychocultural Review* 1(2) (Spring 1977): 195–201.

3. Samuel Johnson, *The History of Rasselas, Prince of Abissinia*, ed. D. J. Enright (Middlesex, England: Penguin Books, 1976), p. 147.

4. Henri Louis Bergson, *Creative Evolution* (New York: Holt, 1937), p. 291.

5. Gaston Bachelard, *The Philosophy of No: A Philosophy of the New Scientific Mind*, trans. G. C. Waterston (New York: Orion Press, 1968), p. 30. Future references are to this edition.

6. Georg Lukács, *The Theory of the Novel*, trans. Anna Bostock (Cambridge, Mass.: M. I. T. Press, 1971), p. 93. Future references are to this edition. For another discussion of *The Theory*, see Maire Kurrik, "The Novel's Subjectivity: Georg Lukács's *Theory of the Novel*," *Salmagundi* 28 (Winter 1975): 104–24.

7. *Kierkegaard's Concluding Unscientific Postscript*, trans. David F. Swenson and Walter Lowrie (Princeton, N. J.: Princeton University Press, 1971), p. 78.

8. George Eliot, *Middlemarch: A Study of Provincial Life*, ed. W. J. Harvey (Middlesex, England: Penguin Books, 1966), pp. 25–26. Future references are to this edition.

9. Quoted in Darrel Mansell, Jr., "George Eliot's Conception of 'Form,' " in *George Eliot: A Collection of Critical Essays*, ed. George R. Creeger (Englewood Cliffs, N. J.: Prentice-Hall, 1970), p. 76.

10. Leo Tolstoy, *Anna Karenina*, the Maude translation, ed. George Gibian (New York: Norton, 1970), p. 431. Future references are to this edition.

11. Quoted in Charles I. Glicksberg, *The Literature of Nihilism* (Lewisburg, Pa.: Bucknell University Press, 1975), p. 30.

12. Søren Kierkegaard, *The Sickness Unto Death*, in *Fear and Trembling* and *The Sickness Unto Death*, trans. Walter Lowrie (Princeton, N. J.: Princeton University Press, 1968), p. 146.

13. *Kierkegaard's The Concept of Dread*, trans. Walter Lowrie (Princeton, N. J.: Princeton University Press, 1969), p. 65.

14. *Ibid.*, p. 62.

15. *Ibid.*, p. 43.

16. Friedrich Nietzsche, *The Birth of Tragedy* in *The Birth of Tragedy* and *The Genealogy of Morals*, trans. Francis Golffing (New York: Doubleday, 1956), p. 88.

17. *The George Eliot Letters*, ed. Gordon S. Haight (New Haven: Yale University Press, 1954–1956), 4:301.

18. Fyodor Dostoevsky, *The Brothers Karamazov*, the Constance Garnett translation, revised by Ralph E. Matlaw, ed. Ralph E. Matlaw (New York: Norton, 1976), p. 590. Future references are to this edition.

19. Quoted in Edward Engelberg, *The Unknown Distance: From Consciousness to Conscience, Goethe to Camus* (Cambridge, Mass.: Harvard University Press, 1972), p. 89.

20. Jacques Lacan, *Écrits: A Selection*, trans. Alan Sheridan (New York: Norton, 1977), p. 269 and passim.

21. Henry James, *The Future of the Novel: Essays on the Art of Fiction*, ed. Leon Edel (New York: Vintage Books, 1956), pp. 76, 79.

22. F. R. Leavis, *The Great Tradition* (London: Chatto & Windus, 1960), pp. 19–20.

23. David Cecil, *Early Victorian Novelists: Essays in Revaluation* (London: Constable, 1934), pp. 27, 43, 49, 58.

24. Victor Shklovsky, "Art as Technique," in *Russian Formalist Criticism: Four Essays*, ed. Lee T. Lemon and Marion J. Reis (Lincoln, Nebr.: University of Nebraska Press, 1965), p. 13.

25. Charles Dickens, *Our Mutual Friend*, ed. Stephen Gill (Middlesex, England: Penguin Books, 1971), pp. 267–68. Future references are to this edition.

26. For a further discussion of this issue, see Maire Jaanus Kurrik, *Georg Trakl* (New York: Columbia University Press, 1974).

27. Sigmund Freud, "Repression," in *General Psychological Theory*, p. 106.
28. Freud, "Negation," pp. 214–15.
29. Sigmund Freud, "Instincts and Their Vicissitudes," in *General Psychological Theory*, p. 97. Future references to this essay as cited in the text are to this edition.
30. Freud, "Repression," pp. 110–11.
31. Charles Dickens, *Great Expectations* (New York: New American Library, 1963), p. 521. Future references are to this edition.
32. Freud, "Repression," p. 107.
33. *Ibid.*, p. 105.
34. Sigmund Freud, "The Economic Problem in Masochism," in *General Psychological Theory*, p. 193.
35. Freud, "Repression," p. 114.
36. Freud, "The Economic Problem in Masochism," p. 200.
37. Freud, "Repression," p. 108.
38. Freud, "The Economic Problem in Masochism," p. 201.
39. Daniel Defoe, *Moll Flanders* (New York: New American Library, 1964), p. 73.
40. Sigmund Freud, *Beyond the Pleasure Principle*, trans. James Strachey (New York: Bantam Books, 1959), p. 92.
41. Lewis Carroll, *Alice in Wonderland*, ed. Donald J. Gray (New York: Norton, 1971), p. 12. Future references are to this edition.
42. Kenneth Burke, *Language as Symbolic Action: Essays on Life, Literature, and Method* (Berkeley: University of California Press, 1968), p. 420 and passim.
43. Lacan, *Écrits*, p. 86.
44. Gustave Flaubert, *Madame Bovary*, ed. and trans. Paul de Man (New York: Norton, 1965), p. 309.
45. Quoted in Tony Tanner, *City of Words: American Fiction 1950–1970* (New York: Harper & Row, 1971), p. 33.

3. MODERNISM: DELETION VERSUS NEGATION

1. For a discussion of transformational rules, see Adrian Akmajian and Frank Heny, *An Introduction to the Principles of Transformational Syntax* (Cambridge, Mass.: M. I. T. Press, 1975). For an interesting parallel between generative grammar and music, see Leonard Bernstein, *The Unanswered Question: Six Talks at Harvard* (Cambridge, Mass.: Harvard University Press, 1976).
2. Michel Foucault, *Language, Counter-Memory, Practice: Selected Essays and Interviews*, trans. Donald F. Bouchard and Sherry Simon, ed. Donald F. Bouchard (Ithaca, N.Y.: Cornell University Press, 1977), pp. 50–51. For another discussion of negative and positive dialectics in relation to the novel, see Maire Kurrik, "Mati Unt's *Via Regia*: Form and Praxis," *Journal of Baltic Studies*, 8(3) (Fall 1977): 214–22.
3. See Roland Barthes' comparison of bliss and pleasure, which I use freely, in *The Pleasure of the Text*, trans. Richard Miller (New York: Hill & Wang, 1975), pp. 19–23 and passim.
4. Octavio Paz, *Alternating Current*, trans. Helen R. Lane (New York: Viking Press, 1973), p. 129.
5. Quoted in Martin Jay, *The Dialectical Imagination: A History of the Frankfurt School and the Institute of Social Research, 1923–1950* (Boston: Little, Brown, 1973), p. 172.

6. Theodor W. Adorno, *Negative Dialectics*, trans. E. B. Ashton (New York: Seabury Press, 1973), p. 186. Future references are to this edition.

7. Samuel Beckett, *Three Novels: Molly, Malone Dies, The Unnamable* (New York: Grove Press, 1965), p. 291. Future references are to this edition.

8. Samuel Beckett and Georges Duthuit, "Three Dialogues," *Transition Forty-nine*, No. 5 (1949); rpt. in *Samuel Beckett: A Collection of Critical Essays*, ed. Martin Esslin (Englewood Cliffs, N. J.: Prentice-Hall, 1965), pp. 19, 21.

9. *Ibid.*, p. 18.

10. H. Ginsburg and S. Opper, *Piaget's Theory of Intellectual Development* (Englewood Cliffs, N. J.: Prentice-Hall, 1969), pp. 151–52.

11. Alain Robbe-Grillet, *For a New Novel: Essays on Fiction*, trans. Richard Howard (New York: Grove Press, 1965), pp. 161–62. Future references are to this edition.

4. NEGATION AND THE TRAGIC

1. Sigmund Freud, *Beyond the Pleasure Principle*, trans. James Strachey (New York: Bantam Books, 1959), pp. 67–71 and passim.

2. Quoted in Friedrich Nietzsche, *The Birth of Tragedy* in *The Birth of Tragedy* and *The Genealogy of Morals*, trans. Francis Golffing (New York: Doubleday, 1956), p. 29.

3. Jacques Lacan, *Écrits: A Selection*, trans. Alan Sheridan (New York: Norton, 1977), p. 88.

4. Sophocles, *Oedipus The King*, trans. David Grene in *Greek Tragedies*, ed. David Grene and Richmond Lattimore (Chicago: Phoenix Books, 1964), 1:157.

5. Kenneth Burke, *Language as Symbolic Action: Essays on Life, Literature, and Method* (Berkeley: University of California Press, 1968), pp. 422–24.

6. Søren Kierkegaard, *The Concept of Irony*, trans. Lee M. Capel (Bloomington, Ind.: Indiana University Press, 1971), p. 276 and passim.

7. Sophocles, *Oedipus at Colonus*, trans. Robert Fitzgerald in *Greek Tragedies*, ed. David Grene and Richmond Lattimore (Chicago: Phoenix Books, 1964), 3:151.

8. Richard B. Sewall, *The Vision of Tragedy* (New Haven, Conn.: Yale University Press, 1970), p. 82.

9. Aristotle, *On Poetry and Style*, trans. G. M. A. Grube (New York: Bobbs-Merrill, 1958), p. 14.

10. For a more complete discussion of the long debate, see Gertrud Kahl-Furthmann, *Das Problem des Nicht: Kritisch-historische und systematische Untersuchungen* (Meisenheim am Glan: Anton Hain, 1968), pp. 266–81 and passim.

11. Here I follow Lois Bloom's definitions in *Language Development: Form and Function in Emerging Grammars* (Cambridge, Mass.: M. I. T. Press, 1970), pp. 170–220. Future references in the text are to this edition.

12. H. Ginsburg and S. Opper, *Piaget's Theory of Intellectual Development* (Englewood Cliffs, N. J.: Prentice-Hall, 1969), pp. 151–52.

13. Georg Lukács, *Die Seele und die Formen: Essays* (Neuwied and Berlin: Hermann Luchterhand, 1971), p. 232. This and future translations in the text are mine and based on this edition.

14. *Kierkegaard's The Concept of Dread*, trans. Walter Lowrie (Princeton, N.J.: Princeton University Press, 1969), p. 87.

15. Søren Kierkegaard, "The Ancient Tragical Motif as Reflected in the Modern,"

Either/Or, trans. David F. Swenson and Lillian Marvin Swenson (New York: Anchor Books, 1959), 1:141.

16. Burke, p. 422.
17. Rosalie L. Colie, *Paradoxia Epidemica: The Renaissance Tradition of Paradox* (Princeton, N.J.: Princeton University Press, 1966), p. 237.
18. E. Bleuler, *The Theory of Schizophrenic Negativism*, trans. William A. White (1912; rpt. New York: Johnson Reprint, 1970), p. 4.

INDEX

274   INDEX